# THE BLACK MYSTERY

# THE BLACK MYSTERY

## Coalmining
## in South-West Wales

# Ronald Rees

*For Diana*

*with love and gratitude*

First impression: 2008

© Ronald Rees and Y Lolfa Cyf., 2008

The author and publishers wish to thank David Grenville Thomas,
chairman of Strongbow Exploration Inc., Vancouver, Canada,
formerly of Morriston, for the financial support for the publication
of this book.

Cover design: Y Lolfa

ISBN: 9 780 86243 9 675

Printed on acid-free and partly recycled paper
and published and bound in Wales by
Y Lolfa Cyf., Talybont, Ceredigion SY24 5AP
e-mail ylolfa@ylolfa.com
website www.ylolfa.com
tel 01970 832 304
fax 832 782

# CONTENTS

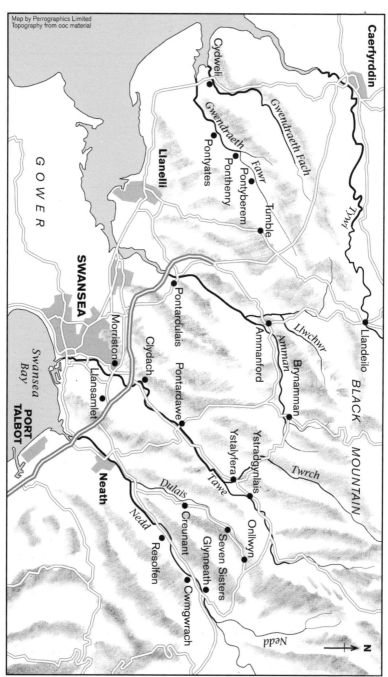

Caerfyrddin

Cydweli

Llanelli

Gwendraeth Fawr

Gwendraeth Fach

Pontyates

Pontyberem

Ponthenry

Tumble

Tywi

GOWER

SWANSEA

Pontardulais

Llwchwr

Ammanford

Amman

Brynamman

Llandeilo

BLACK MOUNTAIN

Morriston

Clydach

Pontardawe

Twrch

Swansea
Bay

Llansamlet

Ystalyfera

Ystradgynlais

PORT
TALBOT

Neath

Dulais

Tawe

Onllwyn

Nedd

Creunant

Seven Sisters

Resolfen

Glynneath

Cwmgwrach

Nedd

N

*The Western Coalfield*

# FOREWORD

A S A GRAMMAR-SCHOOL BOY in south Wales, just after the Second World War, I lived in a bipartite world: the coastal town, which was my home, and the valley that lay behind it. The town and the school I saw as avenues to a larger world, the valley as a tunnel leading back into the narrower world of Wales. The perception was reinforced at school by the differences between the 'valley boys' and us, sophisticates of the town. Countrified in manner, their speech heavily accented, and, frequently and unforgivably in those days, Welsh-speaking, the valley boys embodied most of the traits that the school hoped to eradicate. Every morning they arrived by slow train, fugitives from the dark hinterland of coalmining and upland farming, to be taught and polished by the Anglo-Welsh luminaries of the town. The villages they came from, Cwmgwrach, Resolfen, Creunant, Coelbren, Onllwyn, Banwen, were shadowy places, seldom visited then because few families had cars and, in any case, they held no interest for us. It was the worst time to be Welsh and working-class. The prejudices of the school were redeemed to some extent by the quality of the instruction it offered, but my own I can only regret.

Only after leaving the school did I get to know something of the world that lay behind the town. One summer I worked as a bus conductor, and for several weeks I was assigned to the Dulais Valley route. The Dulais is a tributary of the Nedd valley. My driver was an astute man, who warned me that Creunant, a few miles up the Dulais, and our first stop, was a tipping point. An old village, only a half dozen miles from Neath, Creunant was just within the restraining influence of the town. But beyond Creunant, he warned, we were more or less on our own in territory where the bus inspectors feared to go, or at least chose not to. The issue was tickets. The local miners, who travelled from house to pit on the scheduled valley bus, were reluctant to take them, or, more to the point, reluctant to pay the bus company. The last run of the evening picked up miners coming off the afternoon shift and a session at the pub, where they would have settled the dust with a few pints. By long practice, they stood or sat in the bus with a few coins in their hands, usually about half or two thirds of the official fare, and, when approached, they handed over the money with a firm, 'No ticket, bach,' or, 'Put this in your pocket.' It was my first experience of labour's contempt for capital. On Saturday nights, when the drinking had been steady and the bus was full, I lined my pockets. The bus company, of course, knew of the deception but, presumably on grounds that it was better to lose a few pounds than antagonize an entire valley, decided it was an issue better to avoid than engage.

In those post-school, college summers, I also got to know a miner, Dai Jones. We worked together on a small council gang that repaired burst water pipes. Dai, who was then about sixty, had spent most of his working life as a collier and had come out of the mines because of the dust. His lungs were coated with it and each heavy exertion was accompanied by a whistling exhalation not unlike the sound of air escaping from a balloon. Dai and I were both labourers and our job was to dig down to the burst pipe, usually no more that a couple of feet below the surface of the pavement, and clear a space large enough for the pipe-fitter to work in. We usually worked turn and turn about; one of us would dig the hole and the other would keep the surface of the pavement as rubble free as possible and watch for unwary pedestrians. My pick and shovel were standard council issue – a blunt pick and a heavy shovel – but Dai's were his own. His pick was sharper than mine and his shovel was small-bladed, sharp-edged, and shiny. They had come up from the mine with him. Our holes, too, were as different as our tools. Mine were just large enough for the fitter to work in and, because they would be filled in as soon as he had finished, they had ragged edges and rough bottoms. We were digging for the most part in rubble, not clay. Dai's holes, on the other hand, were immaculate: neat squares with sides as smooth and upright, and bottoms as flat, as he could possibly make them. Impatient pipe-fitters could wait. Dai's explanation, when I felt I knew him well enough to ask, was simply that he liked to keep things tidy. But there was more to it than this; he was, as we would say now, making a statement, although he probably would have denied it. He might have lost his stall in the mine and, with it, his status in the community, but he was still a craftsman with his own tools and his own standards, and no overman or fitter was going to find fault with his workplace. In short, he was still a collier.

This book was written at the suggestion of Morriston-born Gren Thomas who is today one of the most successful prospectors and private mine developers in Canada. As a young man he worked as a miner in Morriston and Clydach and by attending first night school and then Cardiff University he graduated as a mining engineer. Emigration to Canada in the 1960s released the entrepreneur in him. He now has mining interests in Europe as well as Canada, most recently in the about to be re-opened Pentreclwydau mine at Cwmgwrach near Glynneath. Although written at the suggestion of an expert, the book is designed for general readers and it should be approached as an exploration. Knowing relatively little about coalmining, I began with a few elementary questions: how was coal formed, how found, and how and under what conditions was it first wrested from the deep earth? Colliers both early and late spoke of mining as the black mystery. And as an industry that dominated large parts of south Wales for more than a century, what kind of landscape and society did it create? The emphasis throughout is on the general features of mining and the phases in its development, from its mediaeval beginnings until its virtual end in the last years of the last century. In spite of my allusion to the war between labour and capital, readers will find little here on the politics and economics of the mining industry. They are not my field and they have been covered fully in other places. A further limitation is geographic. The inquiry is restricted to the region west of and including the Nedd, or the Neath valley. The high eastern valleys have no need for another exponent, and they were in any case less well known to me than places immediately north and west. Except in cases where English or anglicized place names are so entrenched that change would have seemed pedantic, I have reverted to the original Welsh. Thus the Nedd and the Tawe valleys, but Neath and Swansea rather than Castell Nedd and Abertawe.

Like all writers of histories, I am indebted to a number of librarians and archivists in south Wales, particularly those at Swansea University and at the Miners' Library on the Hendrefoelan campus at Swansea. But my largest single debt is to Mary Doon of the St Andrews Community College, New Brunswick, who, during those periods when I was not in Wales, made sure that I was the recipient of a seemingly endless stream of books and articles. My intellectual debts are to the writers and historians of south Wales, most particularly to Paul Reynolds for his careful reading of the manuscript, to Professor Ieuan Gwynedd Jones for his gentle and peerless commentaries on Welsh life and Welsh communities, and to the remarkable B. L. Coombes, the *Neath Guardian*'s former 'Valley Miner Author', for his reflective books and articles. Readers who wish to know what it was like to be a collier in south Wales in the middle years of the twentieth century need look no farther than Coombes' *These Poor Hands* and *Miners Day*. My other large debt is to the writers of MA and PhD theses. Kept in the store rooms of university libraries, theses are seldom seen by general readers, but for writers they are a rich and indispensable source of ideas and information.

# 'A FUEL OF LAST RESORT'

IN EARLY APRIL 1837, the thirty-eight-year-old, Canadian-born manager of the Forest copper works at Morriston, near Swansea, came upon the fossilized remains of two trees in the headwaters of the Tawe valley. The trees were exposed on the side of a narrow, wooded ravine, Cwm Llech, cut by a tributary stream. They were preserved in the upright, growth position, their roots anchored in a bed of hard clay and their trunks penetrating the horizontal strata above. The trunks, smooth and segmented, were clearly not those of native trees. William Edmond Logan, a self-taught geologist, who would become the founding director of the Geological Survey of Canada, left no account of that day but his discovery was of such moment that an associate, the eminent botanist Lewis Weston Dillwyn, made a record of it in his diary, 3 April 1837: 'Four large Sigillariae [tree ferns], rising vertically through strata of shale and sandstone, as if they had grown on the spot, were this day discovered by my friend, W E Logan Esq., in Cwm Llech, near the head of the Swansea valley.' In its annual report the following June, the Swansea Philosophical and Literary Society, of which Logan and Dillwyn were founder-members, added a little more detail. The report noted that there were indications of so many other trunks in the vicinity that '...it is not extravagant to imagine that, were the sides of the dell cleared away, a whole primeval forest of those gigantic Segillaria [sic], standing as they grew, would be exhibited to the wondering eyes of the beholder.' When growing, the Cwm Llech sigillariae would have been ninety to a hundred feet tall, their trunks forking near the top to form two short-necked, monster-like heads, each crowned by a large spray of grass-like leaves. The remains of the two fossilized trunks were excavated by Henry De la Beche, who, as director of the British Geological Survey, was then conducting a survey of the mineral basin of south Wales. After freeing the trees from the rock face, he took them to Swansea and placed them, in their upright position, on the front lawn of the newly-built Royal Institution of South Wales, a reincarnation of the Philosophical and Literary Society. No longer protected by enclosing sediments, the 'Logan trees' have weathered and worn, but they are still in the position in which De la Beche placed them.

In his time-off from the copper works, William Logan applied himself to the task – formidable even for an experienced geologist – of identifying and mapping the coal seams in the western half of the coalfield, between the Nedd Valley and Cydweli. The arrow-like Nedd Valley, its direction guided by a series of folds and faults aligned on a north-east/south-west (Caledonoid) axis, is the topographical divide between the two halves of the South Wales coalfield. East of the Nedd, and separated from it by a high, almost impenetrable plateau

*Drawing of fossilized tree ferns found by W. E. Logan at Cwm Llech in the upper Tawe valley, 1837.*

*'Logan's Tree',*
*Swansea Museum.*

*Base of fossilized tree fern,*
*Swansea Museum.*

of Pennant sandstone, are the narrow, enclosed valleys of the Afan and the Rhonddas. West of the Nedd, the Pennant moorland is lower and less intimidating and has been more thoroughly dissected by the rivers that flow through it: the Nedd itself, the Tawe and the Llwchwr. Beyond the Llwchwr, the Pennant moors shade into the gentler lands of Carmarthenshire and Pembrokeshire to the west, while to the south they are replaced by the softer shales of the coastal lowlands. North of the Pennant moors, in the shales along the northern edge of the coalfield, the Amman and the headwaters and tributaries of the Tawe and the Nedd have cut a broad lateral trough, overhung by a high brow of resistant sandstone.

A scholar by nature, Logan was interested in the origin as well as the disposition of the coal seams and, by examining outcrops, descending pits, and talking to miners and mineral surveyors, he learned that beneath each seam of coal was a bed of compacted clay, variously described by the miners as *dan*-stone or *carreg gwaelod*, under or bottom stone, penetrated by the fossilized remains of fibrous roots. He would also have been told of the 'farewell' beds of Carboniferous limestone, which cradle the coal measures, beneath which there was no prospect of finding coal. Logan's immediate attention, however, was on the underclays and fossilized root systems beneath each coal seam. The association was so unfailing that a south Welsh miner, Logan declared, would as soon live in a house without a foundation as work a seam without an underclay. Other observers in other coalfields had also noted the conjunction of coal seams and clays and, like Logan, had surmised that the fossilized fibres were the roots of plants that had once grown in the clays and, on dying, had been converted into coal. Logan's trees, which at Cwm Llech appeared to be rooted in a bed of shale or clay, were the evidence he needed to confirm the supposition. On subsequent excursions to coalfields in Nova Scotia and Pennsylvania, Logan noted the same relationship of coals and clays and, on the strength of the observation, he wrote a paper, which he submitted to the Geological Society of London, on the *in situ* theory of the formation of coal. 'Diluvialists', who argued that the seams were the remains of floating masses of vegetation that had become anchored in shallow seas or lakes, or of trees felled by age and storms and marshalled into great rafts by primeval floods, demurred, but the *in situ* theory accorded with so many of the known facts that it proved impossible to dismiss. Writing after the 1838 meeting of the British Association for the Advancement of Science, at which Logan's paper had been presented, De la Beche was able to report that the '… whole kit of Geologicals… are now coming around to the [idea of the] growth of coal in place.'

As well as accounting for the origins of coal, the *in situ* theory also explained the great sedimentary sequences of limestone, shale and sandstone in which coal seams are usually found. In the south Wales coal measures there are roughly a hundred seams, divided into Upper, Lower and Pennant Series, interbedded with 12–13,000 feet of sediments. The seams, ranging in thickness from a few inches to eighteen feet, but thicker when local earth movement has doubled a seam back over itself, make up less than 2 percent of the whole. While the diluvial theories called for successive catastrophic storms and floods, the *in situ* theory required only periods of cyclical growth and decay in swamps, estuaries, and shallow lakes of stagnant, oxygen-poor water. Without oxygen to penetrate and rot the plant cells, the plants only partly decayed, leaving behind energy-rich, black carbon that would eventually become coal. These cycles of growth and death in phenomenally lush primal jungles were followed by subsidence and the deposition of layers of sand and mud.

The problem presented by the presence of fossilized tropical plants in temperate Cwm Llech, growing moreover in underclays which had the same composition as muds found in tropical swamps today, was solved in 1915 by the German geologist and climatologist, Alfred Wegener. His theory of continental drift is now a commonplace, but in its day it was revolutionary. The break-up of an original single continent and the drifting apart of the pieces accounts not only for the differences between past and present climates, but also for the current configuration of the land masses and the disposition and character of many of the rocks that constitute them. The islands that now constitute the British Isles were, in the late Carboniferous period, roughly 290 million years ago, close to the equator and nuzzled up against then tropical Greenland

and Newfoundland. Through movements in the crust, the great, pear-shaped trough or syncline, some ninety miles long, in which the coal measures of south Wales accumulated 290-360 million years ago, has been folded, cracked and torn. The broad eastern section of the basin survived more or less intact, but from the Nedd valley westward, where the basin narrows, the folds and 'leaps' in the ground, as early geologists described the faults, are far more severe. Parts of the basin are missing and parts have been invaded by the sea.

Movements of the crust also help to explain variations in the nature of coal. Opinions are divided over the precise physical and chemical causes of the variations but, despite anomalies, there is general agreement that the greater the pressure from folding, faulting and the weight of overlying sediments, the harder the coal. The assertion that anthracites, the hardest of the coals, came from a different vegetable source than the softer coals, has little support. Accumulations of vegetation that stay more or less on the surface form solid masses of peat, but, when buried, the moisture and the gaseous and volatile matter are squeezed out to form first brown, then black coal. In the case of the dense, hard anthracites, the deepest and most severely compressed of the coals in the lower coal measures, the carbon content may be as high as 97 per cent. In the less disturbed eastern half of the South Wales coalfield, the coals are of the soft to semi-hard bituminous variety, but in the west and north-west, where the disturbances were greater, a belt of anthracite extends in an arc from the head of the Afan Valley, across the valleys of the upper Nedd, the Dulais, the upper Tawe, the Llwchwr and the Gwendraeth, to Pembrokeshire, where the contortions below ground are belied by the gentle relief of the surface. South of and, stratigraphically speaking, above the coals of the anthracite belt, in the vicinity of Swansea, are the fine steam coals of the Pennant series and, in a discontinuous belt between Neath and Llanelli, where the pressures were not as great, the more volatile coals of the upper coal measures. Looking east from Pembrokeshire, George Owen, the Elizabethan chronicler, who may have been the first writer to recognize that the same rocks (in this case coal and limestone) succeed each other in regular order through a large stretch of country, observed: 'The further Est the vaynes runne the softer groweth both the coal and lymestone, and the easier to be digged.'

By breaking the continuity of the strata, severe faults, which in south-west Wales usually run at right angles to the folds, are the bane of the modern miner and mining engineer, but Edward Martin of Morriston, an accomplished mineral surveyor and engineer, saw a silver lining. In a paper presented to the Royal Society in 1806 he noted: 'Contrary to what is generally supposed, a very obvious advantage arises from these slips [faults]. By throwing the strata of coal up and down in various ways they are spread over the face of the coalfield and the slips throw more and more of them up so near the surface of the ground as to be within our reach than could otherwise possibly be got were the strata to keep the same dip without any interruption or break.' To take one example, at Neath the six feet thick Greenway seam was more than a hundred feet deep, but at Neath Abbey, about a mile away, a fault had thrown it to within twenty feet of the surface.

As a carbon concentrate, coal has at least twice the calorific value of dry wood and, as a relatively common mineral[1], it was available at or near the surface in many parts of England, Wales and Scotland. Yet as a fuel it did not threaten the dominance of wood until comparatively modern times. Archaeological evidence from south Wales points to its use in Bronze Age cremations and indicates that the Romans – in Caerleon, Ely, Gelligaer and Llantwit Major – used it as a household fuel. Etymological evidence suggests an even greater antiquity: the roots of coal, *glo* (in Welsh, Cornish and Armoric) are Celtic, not Latin. Yet except in Pembrokeshire, where the coals were virtually smoke-free anthracites, coal was vilified. Until the introduction of chimneys, in the sixteenth century, fires were placed in the centre of the room and the smoke was allowed to escape through an opening in the roof or through louvres and the unglazed panels of high windows. The typical room lay open to the rafters and, even with wood as a fuel, it could still be unpleasantly smoky. 'Fful sooty was hir bour and eke hir halle,' was Chaucer's pronouncement on the apartments of the widow among his Canterbury pilgrims. But though smoky, wood, almost invariably, was preferred to coal. When appealing in Elizabethan times for permission to cut wood for Ludlow on crown land in the Welsh marches, Sir Henry Sydney's justification for the application was that neighbouring woodlands were so reduced they were compelled to burn 'that noxious mineral pit-coal.'

Recorded complaints about coal-burning date from the thirteenth century. In 1257, Queen Eleanor was driven from Nottingham castle by smoke and fume rising from coal fires in the city below. In 1283, many Londoners complained about the fume from sea coal, a soft, bituminous coal imported from Tyneside, then being used in the suburbs to burn lime. With conditions no better in 1306, Edward I issued an injunction against the lime burners, but threats of 'great fines and ransoms' had no effect. Lime burners and others continued to burn sea coal, prompting Queen Elizabeth, two centuries later, to prohibit its use during the sitting of Parliament, '… lest the health of the knights of the shire should suffer during their residence in the metropolis.' By the seventeenth century, however, the battle against coal had been lost. Clearing for agriculture, and the demands for fuel from a growing population in a climate that, with the onset of the Little Ice Age, was becoming steadily colder, meant that wood alone could no longer heat towns and cities. Yet the animus against coal remained. In his *Annals* (1632), Stow recorded that, 'The nice dames of London would not come into any house or roome where sea coles were burnt, nor willingly eat of the meat that was… roasted with sea cole fire.' The most virulent attack in pre-modern times came from John Evelyn, in his 1661 essay *Fumifugium*: 'And what is all this, but that Hellish and dismal Cloude of Seacole… that her [London's] inhabitants breathe nothing but impure and thick Mist accompanied with a feluginous and filthy vapour.' Outdoors, coal-smoke obscured the sun and corroded stones and iron bars, while indoors, critics contended, it penetrated every opening and rotted wall hangings and tapestries that had to be replaced by wainscoting.

South Welsh coal was neither as volatile nor as 'feluginous' as Newcastle sea coal, but it was seldom the fuel of choice. In his richly detailed history of the Nedd valley, D Rhys Phillips remarked that, although most of the grand houses in the valley burned some coal, not one of the bards for the great families made a single flattering reference to a coal fire. While wood remained plentiful, and there were no brick chimneys to channel the smoke from open-hearth fires, the rich burned seasoned logs or charcoal, and the poor, provided they had rights of collection, dead-falls. True poverty in Glamorgan, D Rhys Phillips noted, was a holiday without mead and a feast without a log fire: '*Gwyl heb fedd a gwledd heb foncyn.*' In places where wood was scarce, and where they had no rights of collection, the poor burned peat or turf, supplemented in some places by furze or gorse. Peat, cut on common land, appears to have been the chief household fuel of Swansea. It was also widely used in Pembrokeshire, particularly in and around the Preseli Hills. George Owen described peat as a kind of black rotten earth found on moors where standing water annoys the ground, but he found Preseli peat, when dried and well-seasoned, 'singularly good' and little inferior to coal. Improperly seasoned peat, however, and peat that came from less favoured places, made a great deal of ash and gave off a 'loathsome smell.'

In his engaging history of Pembrokeshire (1603), George Owen distinguished between two types of coal: *Glo caled*, hard or stone coal, and *Glo rhwm*, ring coal or running coal. A cousin of Newcastle's sea coal, running coal, when hot, '... melteth and runneth as waxe and groweth into one clodde and is noysome for smoke and loathsome for the smell.' *Glo caled*, on the other hand, the anthracite of Carmarthenshire and Pembrokeshire, 'burneth apart and clyngeth not together.' It made 'a ready fiere, and very good and sweete to rost and boyle meate.' It was also 'voyde of smoake' and, no small consideration even in times when servants were legion, 'doth not require man's labour to cleve wood and feede the fiere continually.' Once kindled, it gave 'greater heate than light,' and such fume as it produced was inoffensive. The smoke from ring coal, however, as he pointed out in a petition to Queen Elizabeth in 1589, was 'loathsome for the smell' and 'annoyeth all thynges near it, as fyne lynen [and] mens hands that warm themselves by it.' Stone coal, by contrast, was so pure that 'fyne camericke or lawne' could be dried by it 'without any staine or blemishe.' Welsh anthracite was the finest in Britain and, the anthracite fields in Stirling and Lanark being much smaller, the only major source. Much of it, too, shone with a pleasing, oil-like lustre: the Pembrokeshire miner's 'peacock' coal.

In Pembrokeshire, the advantages of anthracite were so patent that householders living near coal workings, or near waters on which coal could be carried easily and cheaply, used it in their kitchens and halls. By Leland's day, it was the standard household fuel: 'Commonly the people make fire… as they do also about Carmarthen, though there be plenty wood.' For the parlour, however, seasoned wood and charcoal were still preferred. Low in bitumen, *glo caled*'s flame was less tenacious than that of other, more volatile coals and it was easily put out by the bellows. The generally fine texture of Pembrokeshire anthracite, which was sometimes no more than powder, also made it unsuitable as a fuel for open hearths. And even when in sizeable lumps, it needed help from dried branches and binding or soft bituminous 'house' coal – imported by sea from Swansea or Neath – to sustain an open-hearth fire. Had the British adopted the enclosed stoves of Germany or Scandinavia, for which anthracite was admirably suited, the history of anthracite production would have been far different. Instead, as the puzzled American historian J U Nef noted, the British rejected stoves on the same grounds (which he clearly found perverse) that for so long they rejected central heating: that after leaving a warm room, cool outside air would be doubly chilling. Yet even allowing for the limited uses of anthracite, Pembrokeshire and western Carmarthenshire were probably the first counties in Britain to appreciate the value of coal as domestic fuel.

In Pembrokeshire, too, much use was made of culm, a fine powder or natural slack produced by the severe folding and faulting of the coal measures. In time, the term would be applied to all small or refuse coal but initially it designated the small of the hard coals of Pembrokeshire. In the far south-west, great lateral pressures, causing one side of a slip or fault to slide over the other, ground and crushed the coal, which, being generally weaker than the surrounding rocks, often disintegrated into a fine soft powder. Culm was mined in the pinched, pear-shaped, western end of the coal basin between Milford Haven and St Bride's Bay, and most collieries produced far more of it than coal. A coal fire topped with a layer of culm could burn untended for many hours. Walter Davies, the nineteenth century agricultural historian, quoted a Mr Fenton, who observed, in 1796, that '[such a fire] does not require that constant pabulum which other fires do; as, made up in the morning, it is known to endure a whole day, without renovation; and, besides, like the vestal fire, is never extinguished; for at bed-time it is plaistered over with what is called a *stumming* of the same, on which it feeds, and being only stirred in the morning, is, in a moment, equal to any exigency that may arise; so that the business of the kitchen, the parlour, the study, or the counting-house, may go on at any hour without the smallest impediment or delay, which all other fuel is liable to occasion.' Mixed into balls with clay, culm also made a good household fuel, known as *pele* (from the Latin *pila* for ball), that burned far more readily than raw culm. Covered or stummed at night with a shovelful of balls and with one or two air holes poked in the top, a kitchen fire could, as Fenton observed, be kept alight indefinitely. In houses with flagstone floors and weeping stone walls, a near-permanent fire was a great asset. To make a load of culm balls, small, powdery coal was spread on the ground and then covered with a layer of clay. The clay was lightly watered, mixed in with a shovel and, for good measure, trampled by a horse – if one was available.

Culm balls could also be used decoratively. The Welsh geologist F J North quoted an observation made in 1830: 'The good housewives not unfrequently display their taste by the fanciful way in which they place these balls edgewise in the grate and, under the active influence of that passion for whitewashing (which extending from the church to the belfry to the pig-sty, adds very materially to the picturesque nature of Welsh scenery), they are not unfrequently, together with the bars of the grate, whitewashed also... The appearance presented by a fire of this description, with various articles of linen hung up to dry... is not a little singular to any one accustomed to the 'bleezing ingles', and 'black diamonds' of the North of England.' The writer might also have added that the Welsh whitewashed not only the walls of buildings and pig-sties, but also the stone walling at the base of hedges. The passion for whitewash was undoubtedly aesthetic, but whitewash, as the historian B H Malkin noted, was also regarded as the very best preventative against infection and impure air.

In spite of the general reluctance to burn coal, by the end of the sixteenth century, the need for more farmland, and the demands of the building, shipbuilding and iron-making industries, had so reduced the amount of woodland that in the large towns even the rich had to turn to coal for fuel. Between the early sixteenth century and the middle of the seventeenth, the population of Britain more than doubled. When George Owen examined old Pembrokeshire records in 1603, he discovered that what then were great cornfields had once been forests and that the county 'groaneth with the general complaint of other countries of the decreasing of wood.' In his *Annals* (1632) Stow remarked on the increasing dependence on coal: 'Not only in the City of London, all haven towns, and in very many ports within the land, the inhabitants in general are constrained to make their fiers of sea coale or pit coale even in the chambers of honourable personages.'

Yet the adoption of coal for domestic heating was not just a matter of scarcity or cost. Wood burns well in large, open hearths, but fireplaces which had been designed for wood were seldom well suited to the burning of coal. To burn well, coal must be contained in a compact mass and provided with a draught. And whereas wood smoke tends to drift upward, even when unchannelled, coal smoke, being denser and heavier, hangs in the air. Before coal could become a universal or even a desirable household fuel, the hearth had to be removed from the middle of the room to a side wall, provided with a grate to contain the coal and encourage combustion, and covered with a hooded chimney with a tapered flue to draw the smoke upward. By the seventeenth century, large manor houses were using enough coal to have a clause, written into their mineral leases, for the free provision of coal from any coal works on the estate. By the eighteenth century, coal had also won over the middle classes. Thanks to grates, chimneys and narrow flues, soft, easily ignitable house coal, or bituminous coal with its languid flames had taken over as the household fuel, its hegemony so complete by the end of the century that a colliery available for lease at the mouth of the Nedd could advertise its 'Veins of Excellent Sweet Binding Coal.'

While wood remained plentiful, coal was the fuel of choice only for trades that required a constant fire and a fuel that could burn slowly at relatively low temperatures. In his *Chorographia* (1649), William Gray cited only two, blacksmithing and lime-burning: 'Coals in former times was onely used by smiths, and for burning of lime.' At the Pembrokeshire mines 'riddlers' separated the coals by size and price: in descending order of value, they were 'fire' coal, the largest blocks; 'smith' coal, and 'lime' coal. At each pit, according to George Owen, there were two riddlers, who first took out the large lumps, the fire coal, and then riddled the remainder, to separate the small coals for the smiths and the dust, or culm, for the lime burners. For the forge, a fuel that not only burned slowly but could also be watered and blown was prized. Forge iron had to be re-heated repeatedly, and the forge blown each time. When watered, soft or running coal cakes and becomes even more durable and, under the bellows, it does not, unlike charcoal, blow away in a shower of sparks or, unlike hard coal, go out. John Leland noted the difference when he visited Carmarthenshire in 1536-39: 'There be ii [two] manner of coals. Ring coals for the smiths be blowed and watered. Stone coals be sometimes watered but never blown, for blowing extinguisheth them.' Writing of Pembrokeshire anthracite, seventy years later, George Owen also noted that 'stone coal serveth also for smiths to work though not so well as the other kind called the running coal, for that when it first kindleth it melteth and runneth as wax and groweth into one clod.' In south Wales, ring or running coal was also known as smiths' coal.

Lime-burning also called for a slow and long-lasting fire. In the early kilns, layers of limestone were interleaved with layers of oak and brushwood, and the pyre lighted from below. The warm piles attracted vagrants who, sleeping near the mouths of the kilns, were sometimes suffocated in their sleep by escaping fumes. By the thirteenth century, coal and culm had begun to replace brushwood and oak and, so that they could be fed from the top and raked from the bottom, the kilns were often set into banks. Poor quality coal and even dust could be used but the ideal was a nutty slack, a mixture of small coal and culm, at a ratio of 2:1: that is ten inches or so of limestone to five inches of coal.

The chief use for lime was, by mixing it with sand, to make mortar and plaster for building. An ample supply of lime was critical to the castle-building programmes of the twelfth and thirteenth centuries. In a 1282 record of costs for the construction of the castle at Aberystwyth there is a reference to the purchase of limestone from Tenby and five hundred cartloads of coal from David the coal dealer. But there were also peaceable uses. Slaked lime was the chief ingredient of whitewash and, when spread on fields, lime not only reduced soil acidity but broke up clayey soils by encouraging the compacted soil particles to form discrete clumps or floccules. Among the chief users of Pembrokeshire culm were the lime burners of Somerset, Devon and Cornwall, who, from limekilns at the ports, supplied farmers inland. The West Country had very little coal. As the methods of improved English agriculture gained ground in Wales, the local demand for lime increased. George Owen declared that liming, which had greatly increased in his day, had improved '… the hue and face of the ground' by destroying the 'ffurse, fearne, heathe and other like shrobbes.' In Carmarthenshire, lime was used so liberally that it was known as the 'prevalent manure.' To make lime for use on his Gnoll estate, Sir Humphrey Mackworth shipped limestone from Oxwich on the Gower peninsula to Baglan, near Neath.

Coal's slow-burning qualities and, in the case of anthracite, freedom from smoke and smell, in time won over other trades which required substantial amounts of fuel. Dye making, salt making and brewing, all of which involved the heating or boiling of liquids, became major consumers of coal. To produce a pan full of saleable salt, eight pans of sea water had to be boiled dry. For the delicate malting process in brewing, the fuel had to have a low arsenic content and be free of any unpleasant odour. In the final stage, the germinating barley was spread out on the perforated floor of the kiln and heated from below. Even wood could impart a bitter taste to the beer, and the more demanding palates insisted that it be replaced by straw. In Pembrokeshire, as George Owen pointed out, the preferred fuel was heather or ling. Cut in summer, and formed into ricks, it was the 'cheefest and sweetest fuell for drieing of Mault,' surpassing both wood and straw. As substitutes for ling or straw, all coals but anthracite were ruled out. 'The small pieces of stone coal,' wrote Defoe, 'are stiled Culm, which is very useful in drying Malt, and is the cheapest and best Firing in the World for Hot-houses and Garden stoves, burning long with a bright red colour, and very little Flame or Smoak; affording at the same time a strong and equal Heat.' In the brewing trades, fuel was also needed for distilling spirits of vinegar and for refining cider and other beverages.

Although there was a steady demand from local householders and lime burners, the chief markets for the clean, hard and semi-hard coals of south-west Wales were distant: in the West country, the Channel Islands, Ireland and France. By 1580 there was a well established trade with Normandy and Brittany. In the shipping season, between spring and autumn, small craft, seldom carrying more than a hundred tons, sailed to Somerset and Devon and around the Cornish peninsula to Falmouth, Exeter and Plymouth. A Begelly company owned two small sailing vessels, a sloop carrying about twenty tons that supplied culm and coal to the local market around Carmarthen Bay, and a brig of about one hundred tons that carried coal to the south of England, frequently returning with cargoes of limestone, bricks or timber. Other vessels sailed up the Severn and the Wye to Gloucester, Worcester, Monmouth and Hereford. There were occasional shipments of anthracite to London in the 1750s but, as at least one Pembrokeshire native discovered, the distance – around the Cornish peninsula and through the English Channel – was too great and the costs prohibitive. 'This cole, for the rare properties thereof, was carried out of this countrey, to the citie of London, to the lord treasurer Burley [Sir William Cecil, Lord Burleigh], by a gentleman of experience, to showe how farre the same excelled that of Newcastel, wherewith the citie of Londin is servid; and I thinke, if the passage were not soe tedious, there would be greate use made of it.'

Swansea, Neath, Llanelli, Milford Haven and Tenby were the leading coal ports and, by the seventeenth century, coal was the principal export from both Glamorgan and Pembrokeshire. In the sixteenth century, Swansea claimed to be the third largest coal port in England and Wales after Newcastle and Sunderland. Neath, in 1562, for a terse Elizabethan recorder, was simply 'a pill within a baye for small boats where there is a myne and a Trade of coals.' A century or so later, he could have added boxed batches of salmon and laver bread that were stowed in hatches on the coal vessels. Defoe, in the 1720s, described Swansea as 'a very considerable town for trade, with a very good harbour. Here is also a very good trade for coals, and culm, which they export to all the ports of Somerset, Devon, and Cornwall, and also to Ireland itself, so that sometimes may be seen a hundred sail of ships at a time loading coals here.'

At both Neath and Swansea there was much debate at customs over definitions of coal and culm. Coal destined for foreign parts, including Ireland, was taxed at the port of exportation. As the less valuable of the two, culm qualified for a lower rate of duty, so in mixtures of large and small coal, exporters pressed for assessment as culm. The large coal was picked out at the collieries and the rest sold as culm. When customs officials suggested that the coals be riddled or sieved before shipping, the producers objected that the soft bituminous coals of the southern belt would be further broken, and thus devalued, by the procedure. The hard coals of Pembrokeshire, however, could be riddled without fracturing, so in the far west the controversy never arose. Chiefly as a result of its trade in coals and culm, Milford by the eighteenth century had become the 'largest, richest, and... most flourishing town of South Wales except Carmarthen.' Of Tenby, only slightly less important, Guy Miege could write in 1727 that 'its inhabitants are principally traders in sea-coal.' Llanelli, Defoe described in the 1720s as a 'tolerably good town' whose 'inhabitants are principally traders in sea-coal.' As the farthest west of the ports, and a purveyor of prized anthracite and culm, Milford had the most far-ranging sea trade of any coal port. It was the chief port for exports to Ireland, but small quantities of Milford coal also found their way to Flanders, Holland, Norway, the east coast of England, France, Spain, Portugal and even the West Indies. On the Continent, Pembrokeshire anthracite was especially valued for its use in hothouses, a demand that probably explains why it was wanted only in small quantities. The largest recorded single shipment of coal in the seventeenth century, 448 tons, was from Milford to Rotterdam in 1681. By 1700 coal was the chief item of export from Pembrokeshire, and there was not always enough to meet the demand. John Allen, who owned collieries in the Cresselly District, wrote in April 1748: 'I can't think there will be enough [coal] in all Milford to supply the trade… several of my most constant customers likewise are enquiring for a little coal, as they are most apprehensive of the scarceness of it.'

By the middle of the seventeenth century, coal had become Britain's main industrial and domestic fuel. But the modest needs of lime burners, brewers, dye makers and householders, although increasing year by year, could hardly have occasioned exponential growth. At the end of the seventeenth century, the combined populations of Glamorgan, Carmarthenshire and Pembrokeshire living within 10-15 miles of a coal works, was only about 100,000. Only consumers with larger appetites than householders and small industrialists could have changed the pattern of coal production. The development that tipped the scales was the adoption of coal by the metalworking industries. Coal could be used for heating and working iron and other metals, but for smelting, the process which drew the metal from the raw ore, early attempts to substitute coal for charcoal had failed. The smelting industries used vast quantities of wood. 'If only,' wrote Fuller in the middle of the seventeenth century, 'this coal could be so charked as to make iron melt out of the stone, as it maketh in smiths' forges to be wrought in the bars.' Not until the end of the seventeenth century did barriers to smelting with coal begin to come down. Copper was the first to yield. By the end of the sixteenth century, Ulriche Frosse, a peerless German copper smelter, had discovered a means of heating and melting Cornish copper ores with a mixture of charcoal and coal. He came to Neath in 1584 and, at Aberdulais, a few miles upriver from the town, he calcined (heated) and smelted Cornish ores using local coals mixed with charcoal. By the middle of the seventeenth century, charcoal had been dispensed with, and from Neath copper smelting spread east to Cwmafan and Taibach, and west as far as Penclawdd and Llanelli. By the beginning of the nineteenth century, an arc of coastal smelters, with a heavy concentration in the lower Tawe valley, produced 90 per cent of Britain's copper and much of the world's.

Coal of the right quality and the right price was the magnet. On a tour of Wales in 1774, H P Wyndham noted that the 'plenty' of coals in and around Swansea and 'the convenience of exportation [have] induced the copper companies to prefer this spot to all others.' Outcropping on the sides of the Tawe Valley, it was the cheapest coal in Britain: one-third of the price of Flintshire coal and one-half the price of Lancashire coal, according to the copper master Robert Morris. To make a ton of copper metal at the beginning of the nineteenth century required thirty tons of coal and about twelve of ore. Aside from logistical considerations, the free-burning, non-binding semi-anthracites of the Pennant series made little ash and, when mixed with about one third of softer bituminous coals, they formed a layer of clinker that rested comfortably on the bars of the furnaces. When used alone, free-burning coals tended to slip through the furnace bars. Neath, Swansea and Llanelli coals proved irresistible to Cornish ores and, as they could also be used to heat the 'fire' or steam engines that pumped water out of the Cornish copper and tin mines, the ore boats carried them as return cargoes. Once an overseas trade in copper ore had developed, on their outward voyages Swansea ore barques rounded Cape Horn to deliver coal to smelters near the Chilean ore mines. Copper smelters at home and abroad consumed enormous quantities of coal. When Edward Donovan visited Taibach in 1804, he commented on the 'amazing quantity' of coal consumed. He found the Inn crowded with captains and mates of ore vessels, and the country behind seamed with wagon roads, tram roads and canals that funnelled coal from the collieries to the smelters on the coast.

For the coal industry of Britain, however, the more critical breakthrough was the application of coal to the smelting of iron. At the beginning of the industrial revolution, iron was essentially a forest product; twelve cords of wood – approximately two thousand square feet – converted into charcoal, were required to produce a one ton bar of iron. By 1680, Britain was importing more than half its iron from forest-rich Sweden. Alarmed by the scarcity of wood and its rising cost, iron smelters in Britain were deeply frustrated by the abundance of its logical substitute, coal, and their inability – when coal and ore occupied the same furnace – to prevent the sulphur, tar, and gases in the coal from tainting and making brittle the metal. The obvious solution was to remove the tars and the gases from the coal by 'charking' or baking it, in much the same way that wood was baked to make charcoal, but not until 1709 did Abraham Darby design an oven in which this was possible. The product, coke, allied to improvements in the smelting furnaces, revolutionized the making of iron.

A few years after Darby's invention, Thomas Newcomen patented his steam or 'fire' engine and by doing so initiated a chain of mutual dependencies that were the cornerstone of the industrial revolution. Coal-fed steam engines, made of iron, drove the bellows that heated the coke that melted the ore in the smelting furnaces. Darby's Coalbrookdale Works cast the first iron cylinders (they had previously been made from brass) for the Newcomen engine. Profligate of fuel, the Newcomen engine could be used only where coal was abundant and cheap, namely at the coalmines or the Cornish copper mines where coal was a return cargo. In 1769, James Watt patented a separate fuel-saving condenser and, backed by the irrepressible Birmingham industrialist Matthew Boulton, he built an engine that was four times more fuel-efficient than Newcomen's. Watt's engine, like Newcomen's, was also used to pump water out of coalmines but its efficient use of fuel gave it mobility, allowing it to migrate from the coalmines to the foundries and the factories. Between them, Boulton and Watt had produced the workhorse of the industrial revolution and, in the process, confirmed coal's position as the fuel of the industrial age. Britain's coal industry, through mounting domestic and small-industrial needs, was already sizeable by the end of the eighteenth century but it would expand tenfold by 1830, and double again by 1854. By the middle of the nineteenth century coal, unquestionably, was king.

# EARLY WORKINGS

---

COAL IS SO HEAVY and so difficult to handle that, until the building of canals and railways, there was little choice about where it might be worked. Coal for local use had to be dug more or less on the spot because moving it by pack horse or cart along rutted or mud-filled tracks and roads could double the price every few miles, more if the haulage happened to be over turnpike roads where there were tolls to pay. Because little was known about the depth and disposition of the coal seams, and because there was only muscle power to work them, they also had to be on or very close to the surface. If the coal was intended for distant markets, a further condition was that the seams be on, or near, navigable water. In south Wales, the only places where mining for export was at all practicable were the coastal hinterlands of Neath, Swansea, the Burry estuary, Tenby and Milford Haven, all places where sea waters had invaded the coal measures and faulting had thrown seams close to the surface.

By the end of the eleventh century, most of the land in south Wales was held by Norman lords, who had acquired it by conquest. Each lordship was a separate unit of government with its own customs and laws. Mineral rights were claimed by the lord and all appeals by the Crown to a principle of Norman law that held that subjects derived their title not only to land, but also to minerals, from the monarch were ignored. In England and Wales, custom became law in 1566, when the Court of the Exchequer, in a dispute between the Queen and the Earl of Northumberland, ruled that the right to mine all minerals, except the precious ones of silver and gold, rested with the landowner. As outright owner of the minerals, the landlord could either mine them himself or, more commonly, grant others permission to mine, usually for a fee or a portion of the yield. In the earliest reference to coalmining in south Wales, Owen ab Alaythur, in 1250, conceded to the monks of Margam Abbey the right in perpetuity to mine all the stone coal, '*totum*

---

*carbonem lapideum*' on his lands, which included much of the basin of the Nedd. Ab Alaythur's grant also allowed the movement, without 'any charge or exaction or demand' of carts, wains or other vehicles that the monks found convenient to transport the coal. The rent was token, or peppercorn: one mark and half a *crannog* (bushel) of wheat, paid annually on Christmas Eve. In 1306, William de Breos, Lord of Gower, allowed the burgesses of Swansea, then a garrison town, to take coal for their own use from Gelliwastad, a district probably just north and east of the town. There were also workings at Clyne and, from the fourteenth century, at Llansamlet in the Lordship of Kilvey, east of the Tawe.

Unlike the more valued minerals, coal was part of the perquisites of the manor and, in the Middle Ages, use of it was subject to the same regulations as governed the use of turf, peat or wood. In some cases, usage might have been subject to stint, or labour services, but as the least regarded of the fuels, tenants, in general, were allowed to take it at will from the commons and waste lands. When coal was dug for sale, however, the landlord might exert rights of ownership by demanding rent and/or a portion of the yield. George Owen noted at the beginning of the seventeenth century that in Pembrokeshire, 'the lorde of the land hath eyther rent or the third barrel after all charges of the work deducted.' These demands might be waived if the coal became 'knotty' or difficult to work for 'real gain' or profit. The tenant's right to take coal by custom of the manor persisted long after the collapse of the manorial system. On his own land, but not on the commons and wastes, the tenant's rights were absolute. A decision given at the Baron's Court of Gwauncaegurwen in 1610 held that all sea-coal and stone coal under the lands of a customary tenant 'belongs and appertains to the tenant and not to the lord. He can dig, cut, sell and convert into their respective uses all such coal-mines or veins without the lord's license.'

Because in south Wales outcrops were legion, and coal distant from navigable water of little value, landlords in general were slow to exert their rights. The coal seams, as a nineteenth century mineral surveyor put it, were 'so intersected by the operations of nature [precipices and deep dingles] and art [road works and quarries],' that none lay undiscovered for very long. In 1747, Gabriel Powell, steward to the Duke of Beaufort, was called upon to adjudicate a claim by tenants in the fee of Trewyddfa that they had a right to dig coal, both on their own land and the commons and wastes, without lease or permission from landlord. Powell insisted, correctly, that on the commons and wastes they had no such right, pointing out that, because coals at a distance from navigation had no value, the tenants were 'indulged' in working a little coal for their own use. This they did by making small holes in the sides of hills. 'Had they not talk't of setting up a Right' to dig they might, Powell added, have been allowed to do so in perpetuity.

Conditions varied from estate to estate. On the Ynyscedwyn estate in the upper Tawe Valley in the 1750s, in exchange for the right to dig coal, tenants were bound by covenant to supply household coal to the owners of the estate as well as coal to the mills, kiln and forge on the Gurnos. Some, too, were obliged to take limestone to the kiln and deliver coal to the poor. The particular demands varied from lease to lease but each lease named the recipients and stipulated the number of horse-loads of coal to be carried annually. The Ynyscedwyn tenants were also bound to keep their landlord's collieries in good working order: i.e. well-propped, well-supported and well-drained. The landlord, James Gough Aubrey, sent anthracite coal nuts on packhorses to Neath for export, one of his tenants having to keep five good horses for the purpose. Another had to carry twenty horse-loads of coal annually from Ynyscedwyn to Mackworth's yard near the Neath bridge, a distance of ten miles.

Many of the tenant farmers were also part-time colliers and coal carriers. On his death in 1624, David Morgan, a farmer near Penclawdd, bequeathed, in addition to his animals, plough irons, harrows and yokes, 'coals and pits of coals' in a field just below the farm. In the mining areas of Begelly and St Issell's, Pembrokeshire, farmers dug coal and carted it from the landlord's coal works to the shore. Mining and farming, however, were not always compatible, however much they might seem to complement each other. Farming was chiefly a summer occupation, and mining, when gases or 'damps' were not as prevalent, a winter one. Coal sales, too, were at their quietest in the summer. But, as in New England and New Brunswick, where lumbering was the alternative to farming, farming probably got short shrift. Returns from mining coal were better and quicker, to the detriment, in the mining parishes, of husbandry.

Carting, too, disturbed rural life. Carts loaded with coal, culm or lime tore up the roads and, because carting was less demanding than the steady work of farming, it allowed for frequent tippling that sometimes led to sottish behaviour. Apart from the harm done to husbandry, small scale mining, which left a rash of abandoned workings, also ruined farmland. The antidote, according to Charles Hassall, a canal enthusiast, was to replace rough roads and carts with barges. Navigation – which he estimated would be only about one fifth of the cost of carting – would spare the roads and release carters for farm work so that land which, as he put it, 'now lies in the most disgraceful state of sterility' could be cultivated and improved. By 1806, a decade after Hassall's pronouncement, there were still no canals connecting the mines and the quays, and the coal districts were even more unsightly – defaced, as one observer remarked, by spoil banks in almost every field and common.

By the beginning of the sixteenth century there were coal works throughout the western half of the coalfield, with the heaviest concentrations around the ports. On his journey west, circa 1536, John Leland commented on workings at Neath, on a moor half a mile above the town. To collect the coal, boats and 'shipelettes' from the Severn came up the river as far as the town bridge, then a timber structure built a little lower on the water than the town itself. On his way through Llanelli, he noted that the townsmen dug coal for their own use and that there were workings at Cydweli on both sides of the Gwendraeth Fawr. He contrasted the bituminous, or 'ring coal' of the Llanelli district, that could be blown and watered and was suitable for the forge, with the hard, stone coal of the Gwendraeth Valley, a mere six miles distant. Coal for export was shipped from the Burry estuary. Small vessels sailed up rivers and pills to places where they could safely ground in sand or mud at slack tide and take on coal from wagons, barrows or pack horses. In Pembrokeshire, he remarked on workings at Kilgetty and Tenby, on the southern flanks of the Pembrokeshire coal belt. At Tenby, coal was worked under ideal conditions: '... on a hill-top [that made drainage easy] near the sea, not far from the town.' By the end of sixteenth century, a narrow coal belt, served by the long inlet of Milford Haven and its tributary valleys, crossed the county from east to west between Talbenny and Begelly. Few parts of the British coast offered so many harbours and shipping places suitable for maritime trade.

The earliest workings were mere scrapings or scourings of the surface where the coal seams outcropped along the southern edges of the basin, or where they were exposed by river erosion on the sides of valleys. Along weathered outcrops, the coal was so soft that it was only a little more difficult to dig than turf and, in Pembrokeshire, many regarded it as a kind of surface deposit that would in time be used up. Early documents refer to 'taking' and 'digging' the coal rather than mining it. In Pembrokeshire, the practice was known as 'smutting'. So apprehensive were the householders of Pembrokeshire about exhausting the supply that they welcomed the imposition of additional tariffs on exports to Ireland and the continent. Higher tariffs would increase the price and, if fortune were on their side, reduce the outflow that they feared would '… in tyme… wholly weare out the Coale and soe leave the Countrie destitute of fuell.'

The preferred areas for digging or smutting were in drift-free country which had no glacial layering or overburden. Any surface covering was scraped away and the coal dug along the seam and, for a short way, down its dip. With no support for the roof, it was a form of quarrying. When surface diggings proved no longer worthwhile, a vertical shaft was dug to a seam thought, from the position and dip of the outcrop, to be near the surface. From the base of the shallow shaft, the miners dug horizontally until there was too much danger of a cave-in, producing a hollowed-out, beehive or bell-shaped pit from which the coal was carried in willow baskets up ladders or hauled up by windlass, as in an old-fashioned domestic well. Once all the safe coal had been taken, the pit was abandoned and a new one started a few yards away. Waste rock and rubbish from the new pit was simply dumped into the nearest old one.

Surface scourings and bell pits could only have satisfied local, or at best regional, demand and, as Gabriel Powell and others have indicated, the hinterlands were probably riddled with them. Occasionally, pits were dug so close to the public roads that they were a hazard to travellers. In the Begelly area of Pembrokeshire, the dangers of driving a carriage or cart along the Narberth to Tenby road were known in 1581, but there was no official alarm until 1676, when the clerk to the privy council wrote to the mayor and corporation of Tenby, pointing out that people returning from markets in the town were '... in hazard of their lives by reason of dangerous passages in the dark among the coal pits.' From the surface diggings, the coal was hauled away in carts and panniers and some of it sold from door to door:

Pegi'r Glo

*Yng nghrog y bo, mewn ty heb do*
*Yr hen widdanes Pegi'r glo;*
*Du ei gwyneb, byr ei becwn,*
*Glo yw dannedd hon debycwn;*
*Yng nghrog y bo Pegi'r Glo,*
*Sy'n hala ofn ar blant y fro!* [2]

In Carmarthenshire the practice of small diggings and local or regional marketing continued well into the nineteenth century. One of Ann Lewis's earliest childhood memories was of waking to the thudding noise made by her father as he dug coal beneath the house. She was brought up on a farm between Tumble and Pontyberem, in the Gwendraeth Valley. Coal lay all around and, once or twice a week, around 1850, her father rose at 4.30 am to dig coal from a roadside outcrop. Ann, who was then 10, arrived at 6.30 with a donkey, properly panniered, onto which she and her father loaded a hundredweight or more of coal. She then set off for Carmarthen, to meet, along with other donkey-driving exporters and small colliery entrepreneurs, the Bristol boat at the Carmarthen Quay. On the way, in response to requests from roadside cottagers, she might have sold a few lumps of coal for a penny or two.

To supply an extensive export market, larger workings were necessary. Where, as in west Glamorgan, the land was elevated and

*Mouth of an old drift or level above Cadoxton in the lower Nedd valley. NMW.*

dissected by deep valleys, coal workers had two choices if they were to do more than scrape the surface. They could either follow an exposed seam by digging away the topsoil and tunnelling into the side of a slope or valley, or they could sink a shaft to meet a seam that they knew to be not far from the surface. The tunnels were called drifts, subdivided into levels if they were more or less horizontal, and slants if sloping, but the terminology was imprecise. In places where the seams were thick and near the surface, the roof was supported by pillars of uncut coal, and the roadways and headings leading to the working areas, drained by gravity wherever possible. A report to the Royal Society in 1697 pointed out that, in Llanelli, the 'coal works were not pits sunk like draw wells, but great inroads made into the side of the hill, so that three or four horsemen might ride in abreast. The top is supported with pillars [of uncut coal] left at a certain distance, and they make their by-lanes... as the vein requires.' The advantage of tunnelling was that the coal could be dug without delay, but there were disadvantages. If the seam angled downward, the cut coal had to be hauled uphill, 'to the rise,' and any water that made its way into the slant ran downhill into the workings. Although drifts were cheaper to develop, over time, there grew a preference for shafts because they could be sunk in positions where coal could be worked to the rise and the coal delivered to the bottom of the shaft by gravity.

The first shafts or pits were shallow and they were sunk only in places where previous workings or the angle or dip of the outcrops indicated that seams should be found at no great depth. In 'ould tyme', according to George Owen, a shaft of four fathoms, twenty-four feet, was 'counted a great laboure.' Investors were guided, as a contemporary of Owen remarked, 'by the judgement of those that are skilful in choosing the ground for that purpose.' Their success rate depended largely on the amount of mining already conducted in the district, because every successful strike added to the data available on the depth, quality, and disposition of the seams. But even in extensively exploited districts, the miners sank many useless shafts.

To locate seams very close to the surface, Pembrokeshire miners drove a pointed bar, with a slightly hooked indentation near the point, to a depth of ten or eleven feet. If the bar passed through coal or culm some of it might lodge in the indentation. Deeper probes involved drilling or digging. In the early eighteenth century, drilling, or boring, was a percussive/rotative process in which wrought iron rods, attached to a chisel, were bounced on a beam supported on a wooden tripod. The rods, from four to nine feet long and fitted with screw-on ends, were suspended from a large timber tripod by block, pulley and rope. The process of drilling, or 'pouncing', is graphically described by P F, the anonymous author of the *Compleat Collier*, 1708: 'We have two labourers at a time, at the handle… and they chop or pounce with their hands, up and down to cut the stone or mineral, going round, which of course grinds either of them small, so that finding your rod to have cut down four or six inches, they lift up the rod, either all at once, as there is conveniency for its lift; or by joynts fixing the key which is to keep the rod from dropping down into the hole.' The chisel was given a quarter turn after each bounce and sharpened at the end of each sequence. Samples of rock were collected in a device known as a wimble. Pouncing was slow, exhausting work, and in hard rock the cut was no more than a few feet per day. In Pembrokeshire, women as well as men did the pouncing, three women at one end of the beam balancing two men at the other. Less exhausting and more efficient than pouncing was a system employed by Sir Herbert Mackworth in the 1780s. An auger, turned by a horse, could penetrate fifty fathoms of rock in ten months, but gentlemen of fortune, noted the diarist who reported its use, could not be persuaded to adventure with the machine. In 1804, James Ryan, an Irishman, invented a drill similar to an auger but which brought up cores of the rock passed through instead of loose samples. Although demonstrating the principle on which modern boring is based, this device, too, failed to satisfy the trade.

The success of any boring operation depended on the skill of the borer in keeping the rods or drill vertical and on the correct interpretation of the samples which were brought up. Many miners were sceptical of the efficacy of boring, arguing that while useful for revealing the presence or absence of coal, the evidence provided by the wimble or an auger was not enough to determine the thickness and quality of a seam. 'I have known,' wrote George Sinclair, the seventeenth century Scottish mineralogist and mathematician, 'a Coal boared, which the Boarer... hath judged four foot in thickness, yet... hath not proven one.' For determining the quality, thickness and declivity of a seam, the evidence from digging, or sinking, was much more conclusive. It was also argued that, in deep bores, the time and effort required to raise the rods and sharpen the chisel offset any monetary savings from using fewer labourers.

By 1700, in Pembrokeshire as in most coalfields, shafts of 120 feet were common. These were shallow by later standards, and mere pinpricks in the surface compared with contemporary salt and copper mines in Poland and Bohemia, but Guy Miege, in *The New State of England*, 1691, found it '... a great Depth for workmen to go and rake a Livelyhood.'[3] Once the seam was reached, the miners worked outward in as many directions as possible: 'The coal being found,' George Owen reported, 'The workmen follow the vein every way until it end or be letted by water or rock [ie. a fault].' Even without water or faults, there were limits on how far miners could push their workings away from the bottom or 'eye' of the shaft. With distance from the eye, ventilation became a problem and there were economic and practical limits on how far coal could be hauled. Hauling was so costly that it was often cheaper to sink another shaft than haul over long subterranean roads.

Once shafts were sunk, and levels and slants had reached far into hill and valley sides, the immediate problem for the miner was how to prevent the roof from falling in. In south Wales the standard practice, which prevailed until well into the nineteenth century, was to use the coal itself as a support. Between each stall or work area, was a pillar, usually several yards wide. As George Owen put it, 'They work sundry holes, one for every digger… each man working by candle light and sitting while he worketh.' The advantage of the system was that, unless abused, it was relatively safe and cheap, saving the cost of pit props in a region where wood was becoming scarce. Lord Mansel's coal steward complained about the cost of pit props, made from straight-grained softwoods from the Baltic and America, as early as 1717. Local hardwood, which was knotty, heavy and difficult to work, was of limited use. The disadvantages of the pillar and stall system were that it wasted coal because as much as half could be left in the ground, and if, to reduce waste, an owner encouraged the cutting back of the pillars, then he could endanger the miners and his mine.

In Pembrokeshire, the hewers or cutters, sitting or kneeling, worked at the coal face with short-shafted picks, hammers, sledges and wedges, all designed for working in confined spaces. To cut the coal, the hewer kneeled or lay on his side, pushing the waste rock and coal behind him. The waste was dumped by bearer boys in worked-out spaces nearby and the useable coal was then carried or hauled in willow baskets, or dragged on crude sleds shod with runners of oak or ash, to the base of the shaft or the entrance to the drift. Commonly, the bearer boys hauled the baskets of coal in relays of twenty or thirty yards. From the pits, coal was carried to the surface, either up ladders or hauled up in baskets by a windlass that might also have been used to lift water and let workers up and down. In Pembrokeshire, according to George Owen, ladders were preferred: 'In former time they used not engines for lifting up of the coals out of the pit, but made their entrance slope, so as the people carried the coals upon their backs along stairs, which they called landways.'

Makeshift practices prevailed and the low yields were adequate for

*Windlass at the Hook Colliery, Pembrokeshire, 1906.*

the needs of small local and export markets. But by the end of the seventeenth century, the quantum increase in industrial and domestic demands for coal called for both new methods and capital investment in amounts that groups of miners or small merchants could not raise. 'At Newcastle and in Wales,' according to an anonymous petitioner to Queen Elizabeth, 'the coalworks are so greatly overwrought that they are grown so deep and drowned with water, as not to be recovered without extreme charges.' In south Wales, the costs, or extreme charges, were first met in Neath. There, as elsewhere, coal working was haphazard. In 1612, the Earl of Pembroke had granted to the burgesses of Neath title to lands on which they had held rights of common pasturage since the fourteenth century. It was known that there was coal beneath the commons, so, to safeguard his financial interest, the Earl, in exchange for the surrender of title, demanded a fee of sixpence for each wey of coal extracted and a further sixpence for every wey exported. A wey was a variable measure of volume, not weight, and in early seventeenth century Neath it was the equivalent of five and a half tons.

The coal was dug at will by the burgesses themselves and at first most of it was for their own domestic use. In 1666, the Pembrokes, realising that they had granted away a valuable asset for a token return, tried to recover title to the commons. The burgesses, however, held firm, insisting that certain coal workings within the borough would be held by them 'forever'. Their workings, which were close together, were either quarryings or shallow pits on or near the outcrops. Unlike the miners of the Forest of Dean, whose Miners' Court laid down that no miner should sink a pit within one hundred yards of another, the burgesses of Neath made no effort to coordinate their diggings. Inevitably, as headings were driven from the base of the shafts, neighbour met neighbour and, just as inevitably, property being the issue, disputes and even lawsuits followed. There had been similar difficulties at Llanelli. In 1609 Robert Reeves alleged that Walter Vaughan's miners were harassing his workmen by discharging water from their mine into his, and in 1613 John Griffith was charged with trespass upon the pits of a rival, William Vaughan, and burning straw or 'some ill-favoured stuff' to smoke out Vaughan's colliers.

To bring order to the near-chaos at Neath, in 1637 the burgesses leased their mining rights to Edward Evans, on condition that he sell coal to the burgesses for two pence per wey and pay a duty of one shilling (twelve pence) for each wey exported or 'sold to Sea'. The burgesses' decision may well have brought a measure of order to mining in the Neath district because, in 1654, the steward of the Lordship of Cadoxton, near Neath, paid two seamen who owned compasses to 'dial', or conduct an underground survey, of a mine leased to Lewis Griffith. Dialling, *geometrie souterrain*, was a seventeenth century French practice. The sailors measured the length and direction of the roadways and headings and, one assumes, the depth of the seams. In Neath itself, the Evans family prospered and within sixty years it managed to lay the foundations of a large estate, the Gnoll, overlooking the town. On Edward Evans' death, the lease passed to his heirs, and ultimately to Mary Evans, who in 1686 married Sir Humphrey Mackworth, a charismatic lawyer from the English Midlands. Although not practising at the time of his marriage, Mackworth was a distinguished barrister, who had been knighted at twenty-seven for legal services to Charles II and chosen, a year later, to present an address of welcome to the new monarch. His reasons for leaving the Bar were never disclosed but his many critics and enemies contended that marriage to Mary Evans was the first calculated step on the path to industrial autocracy in Glamorgan. Mackworth made no secret of his ambition, declaring that his objective had been to 'outdo all the works in the kingdom.' For his Whig detractors he was the 'Church-Tory Knight of the Gnoll,' and for a local lampoonist he was an opportunist with 'the art to make the Lady part with a good old ancient estate.' In 1697, Mackworth leased the Neath Commons in his own right for thirty-one years.

However undisguised his ambition, Mackworth was an avowed moralist who subjected himself to daily, or at least frequent, bouts of soul-searching. William Waller, the manager of Mackworth's copper and lead mines in Cardiganshire, saw in him not the covetous or grasping nature assigned to him by his rivals but 'a frank disposition for public good.' As well as savouring his own gains, Waller continued, 'he took delight in the advantages he brought to others, especially the poor miners and labourers.' He was one of four laymen who, in 1699, founded the Society for the Promotion of Christian Knowledge, and his admirers claim that the idea of circulating schools, attributed to Griffith Jones of Llanddowror, may have been implanted by Mackworth. To justify his industrial ambitions, Mackworth took the Burkeian position, that for evil to triumph it was only necessary that good men do nothing. He wrote in his private diary, 27 September 1696, that it was not enough to simply eschew evil. 'We must also do good,' and, if he were to do good, then 'it would not be convenient to hide his talent in a napkin.' If God had seen fit to award him a coal work against the wishes of his adversaries then he ought to apply himself in such a way that his children, the poor, and the whole town and country about Neath, benefited. Mackworth was as good as his word. During the next thirty years, he rescued coalmining from the doldrums in which it had languished for the previous thirty. Coal works, he declared, had been lost 'for want of Air... and could not be recovered for want of Artists in that Country.'

Although Mackworth may have exaggerated the run-down state of the mines in order to cast the most favourable light upon his own achievements, there had not been, in the years before his accession, any increase in the production of coal, and the export trade was in a state of collapse. Trade was so slack that mounds of coal on the Neath wharf had been allowed to moulder. The town's pits were shallow and neither they nor the drifts had been driven, in the historian D Rhys Phillips's phrase, far 'beyond the sight of daylight,' i.e. the bottom of the shaft or the mouth of the drift. In 'fiery' or 'gassy' mines, where it was dangerous to use candles, roads or headings leading from the bottom of the shaft to the coalface could not be driven 'in advance of the fresh air.' In most cases, this meant not moving beyond the limits of natural lighting. Large mirrors were sometimes used to reflect light from the 'eye', or base of the shaft, but the maximum working distance from the eye, as in Neath's Greenway pit, was usually not more than forty yards. Instead of isolated shafts serving long underground roadways, the early eighteenth predilection was for short roadways served by a close pattern of shafts that might be contained in a single, small field.

Mackworth's interest in coal seems to have begun with his decision, in 1695, to build a copper works on the Cryddan brook, about half a mile south of Neath. A copper works is a great maw, and to supply it with coal as well as meet the demands of West Country customers and the burgesses of Neath, he realised that he would have to invest heavily in his mines. He also recognized that mining that ventured beyond self-draining drifts, and surface or near-surface workings, was a craft, and that for solutions to the problems of drainage, haulage, timbering and ventilation he would have to look to the coalfields and colliers of England. In coalmining, as in other industries, invention had been mothered by necessity: the need to mine deeper seams and mine them more extensively. Around Neath, where the coal had been dug from seams either near to the surface or exposed on the sides of slopes, there had been no such pressures. To study the most up-to-date developments, he promptly visited the Midlands and the north-east of England to view, as he put it, 'all the mines and Workhouses' of Shropshire, Derbyshire, Yorkshire and Northumberland.

In almost all mines of any depth, the two greatest problems were a shortage of air and a surfeit of water. Of the two, water – for the mine-owner at least – was by far the greater and more pervasive problem. 'But for it,' as the author of the *Compleat Collier* famously remarked, 'a colliery might be called a goldmine to the purpose,' and, the corollary of this, that whoever invented a strong and adequate engine for de-watering mines would have such encouragement as would keep his coach-and-six. Mines and drifts were ready receptacles for the rainfall, roughly one third of the total that seeps into the ground. The belt of water-bearing strata can begin at or near the surface and extend to depths of three hundred to six hundred feet. Pits in the water-bearing zone were reservoirs from which removal had to be continuous to prevent flooding. There are no figures extant for the amounts of water that might have been lifted, but, in the 1960s, the authors of the *Lower Swansea Valley Project* learned that for several years the Swansea Vale Works pumped 2.8 million gallons weekly from the old Six Pit, without any discernible lowering of the water table. In other words, the rate of replenishment was equal to the rate of extraction. Water that collected in pits or drifts had either to be drained by gravity or lifted out, and accomplishing the latter – if the number of patents is a reliable index – was one of the great engineering problems of the industrial age. Gravity drainage was usually cheaper than lifting, so it was used wherever possible. In drifts where the seam sloped upward, water simply drained out of the entrance, but where the slope or dip was downward, only by digging a separate adit or tunnel on the side of the slope below the outcrop and the entrance to the mine could gravity drainage work. In the early pits, the usual practice was to sink a shaft near the outcrop and then work back up the dip slope of the seam. All water in the underground headings would run downhill to gather in a hollow or sump at the base of the shaft and from there could be raised to the surface. Working down the dip slope, on the other hand, would result in water accumulating at the coal face.

By 1700 there were various lifting mechanisms, most operating on the principle of buckets attached to a continuous chain driven by a water-wheel or a 'water engine'. At Neath, Mackworth's solution was the whim gin, a mechanism which he had seen in Shropshire and Northumberland. The gin consisted of a drum and a rope-roll connected to a vertical axis or stern-pole. From the stern-pole projected horizontal levers or bars to which one or two horses could be yoked. The rope, which was coiled around the drum, connected to pulleys mounted over the mouth of the pit and then descended to the bottom of the shaft. In short, it was a geared system not unlike that of a bicycle and more effective than its predecessor, the cog and rung gin, that sat directly above the shaft. By walking around the drum, the horses drew up buckets filled with water, or baskets laden with coal. To lower the baskets or buckets, the horse walked around in the reverse direction. As well as lifting water and coal, the gin was also used to raise and lower colliers. The usual practice was to insert a foot into a loop at the end of the rope and, holding the rope in one hand, use the other to prevent collisions with the sides of the shaft. Sometimes a pick shaft thrust through the strands of the rope served as a primitive stile on which a collier could stand or sit. Boys either sat astride the knees of the men or clung onto the rope and twined their legs around it.

Before Mackworth's introduction of the whim gin, water from the Neath mines was hauled up in barrels by four men operating a windlass. His 'new method of coffering out Water from his Shafts and Sinking pits,' as William Waller remarked, 'thereby prevent[ed] the Charges [costs] of Water Engines.' By 1710, however, Mackworth's shafts had

*Gin Pit, Neath. 'Mackworth's Works at Neath', watercolour by the Hon. John Byng, c. 1787, NMW.*

reached depths which obliged him 'to carry up Levels and place Engines to drain the Water, without which he cannot take Advantage of his Works.' Once pits exceeded depths of a hundred feet, water had to be raised in stages. To drain the Swansea Four Foot Vein at Bynea, near Llanelli, c.1750, the owners used a number of shafts, of diminishing depth, connected by drainage tunnels. The deepest workings were two hundred feet below the surface. The first horse or water engine raised the water to the level of the second pit, discharging it into a communicating drift or passage that took it to the shaft. From the second pit it was raised to the level of the third pit, and from the third to the point of discharge at the surface.

Waller's reference to Mackworth's new method of coffering out his shafts is thought to refer to the practice of 'tubbing', yet another Mackworth introduction. When passing through wet or water-laden strata, shaft sinkers could, by lining the shafts with wooden staves shaped like those used in the sides of a barrel, prevent water from pouring into the shaft. Fir, which swelled when wet, was the preferred wood, and hemp caulking driven into the joints the preferred seal. Mackworth's genius, however, did not extend to the invention that would eventually solve the problem of shaft and mine drainage. Steam engines had been available to mine owners since Newcomen's patent, in 1712, of his 'Miner's Friend'. When installed at the Griff Colliery, Warwick, between 1715-17, it 'did discharge as much water as did before 50 horses.' In south Wales, the first known use of steam was at Penclawdd, in 1734, in a pit known as the 'Fire Engine Pit'. There are no records naming the owner of the pit but the Mackworths had mining interests in the Penclawdd-Llwchwr district and would certainly have known of the introduction. In 1719-20, Kingsmill Mackworth pressed upon his father, Sir Humphrey Mackworth, the advantages of a fire engine over 'windmills and horses', but apparently without success. After his father's death, Herbert Mackworth, who had no reservations about steam engines, wrote to his agent, Pleydell Courteen, that, 'A fire engine will be necessary here at last.' By 1740, there is evidence that one was operating. There is also evidence that, by 1800, there were more than a thousand steam engines operating in British coalmines.

The other perennial problem in mining was how to provide air for the miners in currents that were also strong enough to disperse suffocating and explosive gases. Coalmining is particularly dangerous in that to the problem of air circulation, which is common to all mining, must be added the continual threat of gases or 'damps'. *Dampf*, the German word for vapour or fog, was introduced to Britain by German miners who were invited to open copper and lead mines. The mediaeval writer Agricola (Georg Bauer) referred to damps as the breath of noxious demons that could fell miners by either the foulness or explosive qualities of their breath. By the seventeenth century, however, natural science had established a connection with coal. When exposed to air, coal, through the slow oxidation of the carbon trapped within it, produces 'chokedamp', a mixture of carbon dioxide and nitrogen, which snuffs out candles and, in high concentrations, can suffocate miners. Heavier than air, it collects in low-lying pockets, and in the early days of mining it was considered the most dangerous gas. But as mines became deeper and workings, to justify the costs of sinking, more extensive and more difficult to ventilate, it was overtaken on the danger scale by 'firedamp', carburetted hydrogen or methane gas. Firedamp could occur in shallow pits, and would sometimes be seen escaping from the surface, but, as a rule, fissures in coal seams and associated rocks near the surface were more likely to be filled with either water or chokedamp. By snuffing out candles, chokedamp normally gave the collier some warning, but firedamp could 'blow up the pit' without the colliers even suspecting it was there.

Methane is the product of chemical and bacteriological processes completed several hundred million years ago. As vegetation decayed and as coal seams were formed the gas was trapped underground and not released until colliers burrowed or tunnelled into the crust of earth. Most coalmines are, in effect, methane or firedamp factories. Firedamp is odourless, lighter than air and, unlike the heavier chokedamp, it collects in pockets and fissures near the roof. In Dulais Valley mines, in the late nineteenth and the twentieth century, it was known as the barber, *barbwr* in Welsh, because, when ignited, it flashed across the roof and singed the hair of the colliers. Telltale signs of its presence were a blue cap or 'ghost' above a candle flame that had become slightly enlarged. Firedamp burns readily in air, and explosively in particular proportions. In dry air charged with coal dust it is even more lethal, a minute quantity (2 percent) being enough to trigger a violent explosion. The explosion itself could maim or kill, but more often the greater killer was the insidious 'afterdamp', lethal doses of carbon monoxide, produced by the incomplete combustion of methane and coal dust, that followed in its wake.

Experience showed that, the more volatile the coal, the greater the danger from damps. Pembrokeshire mines were not free of damps, but firedamp, significantly, is not listed in George Owen's catalogue of disasters that could befall Pembrokeshire miners: falling of the earth, starvation from stopping the way forward, and sudden irruptions of standing waters in old works. One of the earliest methods of dealing with firedamp, cited in a seventeenth century document, was to deposit a bushel of lime in the pit and to renew the lime when saturated. Lime readily absorbs gases, and any methane in contact with it would be converted into carbon dioxide and water. A more common and more effective, if more dangerous method, which may have been employed first at a Flintshire colliery in the seventeenth century, was to fire or explode the gas. If only small quantities were suspected, it was ignited by a lighted candle fixed to a long pole. In gassy mines this was done every morning by the 'fireman' before the men entered the pit. Clothed in wet rags, he crawled along the floor, holding aloft his pole with its lighted candle at the end. As the flame ran along the roof he lay flat until it passed over him. When dangerous amounts of firedamp were suspected, the fireman made a hole in the floor of the pit below where gas was thought to have concentrated. He then set a candle on a board, to which he had attached a string, and lighted it in an area known to be free from gas. Holding the end of the string, he crawled into the hole, pulled a piece of board over it for protection, and then slowly reeled in the lighted candle until the firedamp exploded. To avoid risk to the fireman, the colliers at Lumley, in Durham, according to an account given to the Royal Society in 1678, tested for gas by throwing lighted coals down the shaft before going down themselves. They are said to have made the discovery when, befuddled and playful at the surface, they began tossing lighted coals around the head of the shaft. Some fell down the shaft and made the firedamp 'discharge with a great noise.'

The role of coal dust in firedamp explosions was suspected as early as 1697 but not verified until two centuries later. In a remarkably discerning report on the state of mines in and around Neath, Anthony Thomas, agent for the Baglan mines, noted that, where the coal was 'good & hard', there was no difficulty, nor danger, in working it. The only problem was want of light, there not being enough air for the candles. In other places, the candles burned and flared so fiercely that fires were frequent. ''Tis thought by all that 'tis want of air that is the cause, and yet in other pits... where air was wanting their candles would not burn but go out... so that 'tis not merely want of air but some latent quality in the coal. For where the damp is, there the coal was much alter'd from a bright hard coal to a darker, softer mellower & smaller coal.' And then the remarkable conclusion that predated by almost two centuries the conclusions now held by mining experts: 'There's nothing burns it seems but the air without it be the dust of coal.'

The obvious solution to the problem of damps was to eliminate flames and provide enough ventilation to dissipate the gas and, to some extent, coal dust. But until the invention of a safety lamp, in 1815, nothing could be done to make flames safer. In 1696, Anthony Thomas recounted how colliers at Baglan, when troubled by firedamp, had enclosed their candles in a 'lanthorn', stopping the crevices with clay and wrapping the lantern in an old garment, leaving only one horn light free to the air. The man holding it had been assigned to look for danger, but in spite of his vigilance, 'on an instant' the Lanthorn 'burst open and flew to pieces in [his] armes.' It engulfed the 'street' in flames and 'miserably sing'd & scalded all the bare places of him that held the lanthorn & of two more that were in the same place.'

In his *Natural History of Staffordshire*, Robert Plot concluded that all damps are caused by lack of motion and, the corollary to this, that all remedies 'may plainly be reduced to motion, which I take to be the catholic remedy of all damps.' At Neath, Mackworth, drawing on his experience in Staffordshire, introduced a two-shaft system, so that by natural convection cool, pure air from the surface could descend to the main coal levels, and warm, exhausted air from the mine escape through an upcast shaft. Vent pits, or ventilation shafts, could also be sunk to improve the circulation in drifts. In a Neath document, dated 1707, there is a reference to an 'Air Shaft for the Coalery' that resulted in an improvement in 'Circulating the Air'. Down-cast and up-cast shafts worked most efficiently in winter, when differences between surface and mine temperatures were most pronounced. George Owen noted that, 'Hot weather is the worst by reason of sudden damps that happen, which oftentimes causes the workmen to swoon, and will not suffer the candles to burn, but the flame, waxing blue of colour, will of themselves go out.' In summer, downcast and upcast shafts were most effective in the early morning, before the heat of the day equalized surface and subsurface temperatures. In Lord Mansel's mines at Llansamlet, ventilation was so poor that the men were obliged to work from 3am to 11am 'for conveniency of air.' When Robert Morris obtained a half interest in Herbert Mackworth's Trewyddfa colliery in 1728, Mackworth insisted that the new partner, before taking any profits, sink another shaft, '... as without it we can't work in warm weather for want of air.' To encourage up-draught, a furnace was often built at the base of the up-cast shaft and sometimes a chimney at the top. At a colliery near Gwauncaegurwen, which had a ventilating furnace, workmen travelling on the rope through the shaft were sometimes singed and set alight by flames as firedamp passed over the furnace.

Mackworth's Shropshire miners were particularly adept at 'carrying the air'. Using wooden panels or brattices, they created 'windways' that channelled fresh air into places that unaided convection would not have taken it. In places that were particularly inaccessible, they might also have used an arrangement of bellows and hollow wooden pipes – the invention is attributed to Derbyshire miners – by which fresh air could be forced in and stale air drawn out. More effective ventilation through the use of vent shafts and windways meant that roadways in Mackworth's mines could be extended and the working area increased.

To speed up haulage over the longer roadways and reduce mounting costs, Mackworth built tramways or wagon-ways: wooden rails two inches high and two feet apart, resting on oak sleepers, that he had seen used in Shropshire and Newcastle. Until the introduction of tramways, the average distance from the shaft to the coal face was about sixty yards, and the longest about two hundred. The wagons, which had wooden wheels fitted with iron rims, were pushed by hand to the mouth of the drift, and from there to jetties on the riverbank and smelters on the Cryddan brook, a distance of about three quarters of a mile. At the riverbank, the coal was loaded into empty ore boats that delivered it to the 'fire' or steam engines that drained the Cornish copper mines.

As well as speeding up the movement of coal, the wagon-ways also spared roads which otherwise would have been torn up by the constant passage of wagons and carts. Nine years after Humphrey Mackworth's death, Herbert Mackworth, whose enthusiasm for coalmining surpassed even his father's, appears to have pioneered the use of horses underground. In 1736, the manager of a Neath colliery wrote to Pleydell Courteen: 'There is a scheme formed and actually begun to be executed that will be of very great use in Greenway... that is to wagon the coal with horses underground and it is agreed by Nash and all the rest that it will be very easily done... The consequence of this work will be to secure us from the plague and expense of employing 14 or 15 Wagoners, and having cutters enough, we may have as much coal constantly out of both pits as they can wind out of them, and at two-thirds of the expense we are at now in getting less than two-thirds of the coals.' All depended, according to the manager, on finding a way of getting the horses in and out of the pit. The letter to Courteen is the earliest known reference to horse haulage and precedes by four years the first record of a similar use in England.

Once out of the mines, Humphrey Mackworth's trams were drawn either by horses or, on days when there was a favourable tail wind, powered by small sails fixed to the wagons. William Waller, the manager of Mackworth's copper and lead mines in Cardiganshire, marvelled at his ingenuity: '... new Sailing Wagons for cheap carriage... of Coal to the Waterside whereby one Horse does the work of ten at all times,

and when any wind is stirring, which is seldom wanting near the Sea…
one Man and a small Sail does the Work of twenty.' Mackworth was
a phenomenon and his enterprise and ingenuity inspired panegyrics in
both prose and verse:

> *Thy famed inventions, Mackworth, most adorn*
> *The Miners Art, and make the best return.*
> *Thy speedy sails, and useful engines show*
> *A Genius Richer than the mines below.*
>
> (Thomas Yalden, 1710)

Later in the century, John Byng was moved to equally fulsome praise:
'Sir Humphrey Mackworth must be one of the most extraordinary and
enterprising geniuses in this kingdom; ever employ'd and in the greatest
works; he, here, surveys beneath and around him, the wonderful
works of his own indefatigableness: colliers digging, – copper works
smoking, – a domain of parkish ground, cultivated from barreness to
rich fertility… and about three hundred men in daily pay.'

To solve the problem of labour, or 'want of Artists', for his mines,
Mackworth was forced to import workers. He recognized that
coalmining was skilled work, and that men capable of cutting the coal,
timbering, wagoning and coursing the air would not be available locally.
His objective was a workforce that would be able, to some extent,
to double between the mines and the copper works so that, in slack
periods, no men would be kept 'at dead Wages'. For each heading in
his mines he needed seven workmen: three cutters at the coal face, who
would also do the timbering, and four wagoners. Wagoners, according
to Mackworth, were as valuable as cutters, and, although they were
paid less, he regarded the loss of one as serious as the loss of a hewer.
In any mine, the windings and turnings and changes in level were so
idiosyncratic that the skill that was needed to keep a wagon on the
rails in one pit was not transferable to another. The work also was
so laborious that few men, Mackworth remarked, would undertake it.
Each wagon contained almost a ton of coal. For the work of ventilation,
drainage and cutting Mackworth employed experienced Shropshire

miners and housed them in a row of cottages on *Cae Mera*, a field or open area then on the edge of the town. With names such as Mort, Hill, Emmanuel and Mainwaring, they came to be known as Gŵyr y Mera[4] and their wives as the now celebrated Merched y Mera, who, speaking in a distinctive English/Welsh patois, sold pegs, trinkets and household goods in the town and the valley. They were strong, prominent women by whom their husbands were customarily identified: thus *Twm gŵr Jemima* (Tom, Jemima's husband), to take one example.

Shropshire miners, however, were in demand all over Britain and, therefore, difficult to get, and local labourers were reluctant to undertake work that they perceived as unusually difficult and dangerous. Those who were induced into the mines were bound by serf-like conditions. In 1659 and 1665, Herbert Evans, Humphrey Mackworth's predecessor as lessee of the Neath mines, used housing to bind colliers to his pits. Two ninety-nine year leases for houses on New Street and High Street in Neath bound not only the lessees, Hywel Leyson and a seaman named Edward Caldwell, to his mines, but also their heirs, executors and assigns, should they become colliers. Conditions in Scotland were even

*Coalmine and Mera cottages, Neath. The mine workings are in the left foreground and the Mera cottages on the near right edge of the Corporation Field (now Victoria Gardens) in the middle ground. Neath Antiquarian Society.*

*Nell Downey, Queen of the Mera. Mrs Downey (nee Mort), dressed here in Welsh flannel, had a shop in the Mera. Although her hand is on a book, she could neither read nor write. Neath Antiquarian Society.*

more draconian; children, at baptism, were bound to work as colliers for the Laird. With labourers for mining at a premium, Mackworth resorted to convicts. In 1700 he appealed to judges on the Norfolk circuit to offer prisoners five years of bonded work in his mines in exchange for the remission of their sentences. Seventeen accepted the offer and ten of them came to Neath by ship via London; Mackworth's request that gaolers accompany them to Neath had been refused. Two of the bonded men promptly broke their bond and deserted, causing such great consternation in the town that, when asked by the Secretary of State if he would consider taking convicted pirates as well as convicts, Mackworth demurred. Without the authority of an Act he feared incurring the censure of Parliament, and, with or without Parliamentary approval, he judged that 'the Gentry and Commonalty of Wales would be alarmed and dis-satisfied at it.' In 1786, the idea of using convict labour arose again, a writer to the Home Department considering a gloomy, cavernous mine the best punishment, 'likely to Bring the mind of man to sincere reflection.'

The importing of felons and the practice of bonding his labourers, which protected them from impressment or military service, were pretexts for attacks by Mackworth's many rivals and enemies. Incensed by his success, they sought every opening to engineer his downfall. By 1704, Mackworth's mines, largely through the improvements made by his Shropshire miners, had become so efficient that there was enough coal not only for his copper works but for buyers in the West Country. He began exporting the surplus, unavoidably cutting into the trade of neighbouring colliery owners. The most vindictive of his rivals were the Mansels, his competitors in the coal export trade and one of the most powerful political families in Glamorgan. The principals were Sir Edward Mansel of Margam, his son Thomas, and nephew Thomas Mansel of Briton Ferry. Associated with them was Thomas Popkin, a landowner and business partner. Thomas Mansel, the son, was the Member of Parliament for Glamorgan, while Sir Edward Mansel and Thomas Popkin were county JPs. Thomas Mansel of Briton Ferry owned property in Neath and was both a burgess and an alderman of the town. All were moderate Tories or Whigs, who supported the current wars with France and Spain, while Mackworth, a high Tory, opposed them. Their attacks on Mackworth ranged from the petty to the potentially ruinous.

Abusing his entitlement to coal on demand from town land leased to Mackworth, Thomas Mansel sent agents, servants and friends to Mackworth's yards every other day. As a burgess, Mansel was entitled to a domestic supply of coal at a token price. Mackworth accused him of making 'extravagant fires' in order to consume and waste his coal and obstruct his export trade. He locked the gates of the coal yard, only to have agents of the Justices break the locks, knock down an adjoining stone wall, and take the coal by force. More serious were the Mansels' attacks on his business integrity. In 1704/5 they sent agents to Bridgewater and other West country ports, to raise doubts about the quality of the coal arriving from Neath, and to spread rumours that Mackworth's coal works were about to close. Neath's export trade was chiefly with the West Country and the towns of the Severn Valley. To divert coal boats away from Neath, these same agents also threatened with the Press Gang seamen who came to Neath to load coal at Mackworth's bank. There was, in fact, little or no danger because the coal trade was now so important that statutes enacted in 1672 and 1695 exempted from impressment virtually all men engaged in loading coal or serving in coal ships. Vessels of one hundred tons were allowed two able seamen and vessels of fifty tons one. Royal Navy officers, attempting to impress exempted seamen, were fined ten pounds for each offence – payable to the offended master – and declared unfit for service in His Majesty's ships of war. John Williams, master of the *Two Sisters* of Bridgewater, testified, however, that he felt so intimidated by the Mansels' agents – the statute notwithstanding – that he sailed to Swansea to pick up coal.

Mansel agents also set the excise men on Mackworth. At the beginning of the eighteenth century, scarcely a coal boat returned from Ireland or abroad without brandy or Irish 'sope', 'shagg', 'stuff' or candles concealed under false bulkheads or stowed amongst non dutiable material. A raid on the Gnoll, however, backfired; the excise men found nothing and the instigators found themselves facing charges. Caught in the middle of the Mackworth-Mansel disputes was the unfortunate William Noy, Collector of Customs at Neath, who had married Ioane, the daughter of Thomas Mansel. On his broken tombstone, as well as on that of his wife, in Neath's St Thomas churchyard, historian D Rhys Phillips was able to discern the names of his enemies as well as scraps of rhyming verse which tell that, in his role as Queen's Collector, William Noy had taken little joy.

There was also a sustained attack on the character and behaviour of Mackworth's coal workers. Some were bonded felons and others, who must have seemed almost as threatening, were 'strangers in the country,' some of whom were 'above two hundred miles from home.' In a deposition got up by Mansel agents and signed by the 'principal inhabitants of Neath,' they were described as 'disorderly livers' who spent days in drinking and debauchery, and impregnating and then deserting the young women of the town. With England at war with France, bonding (to avoid recruitment) was a contentious issue and one that the Mansels used to their advantage. In May 1705, Edward Mansel and Thomas Popkin, both justices of the peace, issued a warrant for the impressment of a number of Mackworth's miners and copper workers, ignoring the fact that most were bound and, in some cases, long-time servants. About a dozen were rounded up, among them virtually irreplaceable wagoners, causing the rest, about eighty men, to flee 'in great Terror' to the hills. At the *Black Boy* in Swansea, William Blewer, one of Mackworth's bonded or covenanted Shropshire colliers, was tricked into accepting the Queen's shilling by a sergeant of the Company of Captain Bussy Mansel. Mackworth insisted on his discharge, whereupon, the Mansels concealed him in an ale house in Greek Street, Soho. To free him required a writ of *Habeus Corpus*. Mackworth also succeeded in getting the earlier impressment order quashed at the Cardiff Great Sessions, but his troubles were not over. The following month, the Neath Justices ordered that all workmen employed by Mackworth who 'came from other Parishes or Places' be removed from the parish. When Mackworth contested the order at the Neath Quarter Sessions, the proceedings were so violent that most of the available attorneys refused to take Mackworth's fee, and those who had accepted returned it on grounds that the Court was so bent against them that, were they to retain it, they must expect never to practise again.

Mackworth's coal works came to a standstill and, in what presumably they hoped would be a *coup de grace*, that August the Justices successfully indicted him for public nuisance. His tramway, which crossed the Neath-Cardiff road on town common land, had been built in 1698, eight years earlier, without permission from the burgesses. The indictment was presented by the powerful Gabriel Powell ('a Creature of the Mansels', according to a Mackworth supporter), and approved by a Grand Jury on which sat Thomas Popkin. The ground crossed by the wagon-way, formerly a deep pool of water and mud that Mackworth had filled with slag from his copper works, served not only his wagons but the coach from Neath to Cardiff. Attorneys and freeholders in the court cried out, 'in one Voice', that it was the best part of the road between Neath and Cardiff, but to no purpose. With a legal decision in their favour, Mansels' agents, among them two notorious 'wicked fellows', John Morgan and Philip Williams, descended on the tramway, tearing up the wooden sleepers and cutting through the rails with pick axes, hatchets, saws, iron bars and shovels. There were seven separate attacks. Mackworth's men retaliated, first by dragging the wagons across the road and, when the Mansels' agents dug a hole to prevent this, they loaded the coal into baskets on the backs of horses When a seaman, Thomas Williams, who was incensed by the vindictiveness of the Mansels, tried to prevent the breakage by standing on the rails he, too, was indicted for malicious and unneighbourly behaviour.

But in spite of fearsome rivalries and the failure of his company (the Company of Mine Adventurers), the indomitable Mackworth survived. Thomas Mansel died in 1706 and with his death the local animus subsided. On his own death, in 1727, Mackworth was able to bequeath his coal works to his son Herbert, who integrated the family's mining and manufacturing enterprises and expanded the export trade. Thanks to Sir Humphrey Mackworth, Neath, from being a pill within a bay where there was a mine and a trade of coals, had become a substantial town that today regards itself as the cradle of Welsh industry.

Mackworth, who was never slow to congratulate himself, prepared this testimonial: 'These Coal-Works and Work-Houses employ a great number of men, women and children, to whom several thousand pounds are paid every year, which circulates in the neighbourhood, and other trades are thereby increased, the market much improved, and the rents better paid.'

West of Neath, in the Swansea and Llanelli districts, events took a similar turn. Progress in mining depended on a few men with energy, imagination and capital. Swansea's coal trade dated from at least the fourteenth century but primitive methods of transport and restricted markets had limited its growth. John Burroughs, steward from 1705-35 of the Mansels' Briton Ferry estate, pointed the way forward. The Mansels' home, Margam Abbey, lay on the east side of the River Neath but the estate extended west as far as the Tawe. Recognizing the limitations of small workings, and an export trade that required Mansel mines in the lower Tawe Valley to ship coal by packhorse to Neath or to jetties at Foxhole, on the right bank of the river opposite Swansea, Burroughs declared: 'That of which I have most hopes is of ye sea trade which will never be opened without a copper works.' By this he meant that a smelter on the Briton Ferry estate would not only consume large quantities of coal but, as at Neath, coal would also be a return cargo for the Cornish ore boats.

Burroughs' assessment was endorsed by Robert Morris, the managing partner of the Forest copper works near Morriston. In 1727, Morris took control of a copper works at Landore, in the parish of Llangyfelach. Under the original owner, John Lane, the works had been held to ransom by Thomas Popkin, from whom he leased land to build his works and from whom, by restrictive covenant, he was bound to buy coal. Popkin took advantage of his monopoly by supplying, at high prices and in inadequate amounts at irregular intervals, 'muck and dirty coal'. Lane, who lost heavily in the South Sea Bubble, became bankrupt, whereupon Popkin, Morris observed drily, 'lock'd up the copperworks.' It was eventually unlocked by Robert Morris and his partners but not without Popkin insisting on the terms of the original covenant. Morris's first task was to get rid of Popkin and his 'shifts' and 'tricks', and obtain a dependable supply of coal at a fair price. If only, he once sighed, 'Old Popkin would but die, or be good humoured.' So difficult were his negotiations with miners and grasping landowners over prices, mineral rights, and rights of way, that he offered this advice to estate owners with coal reserves: 'I would have all who have money to spare adventure in mining, especially on their own estates. First get honest miners, if there are such to be had. Ask them how much money will suffice for a trial [shaft], and then resolve to spend no more unless some very extraordinary encouragement should happen. I never knew an honest miner out of his own country, and they are very scarce in their own.'

To thwart Popkin and secure a steady supply of coal for his works, in 1728 Morris took a lease of Herbert Mackworth's Craig Trewyddfa mine at Treboeth. In spite of surrendering 'half profits' to Mackworth, it was a profitable move, Morris attributing the subsequent well-being of his works to the new colliery. Like both Humphrey and Herbert Mackworth, coal may have been Morris's first love. There are intimations of this in a letter to his partner, Thomas Lockwood: 'The candles burn well in our new Coal works. You will be pleased to forgive me leading you underground and if you lose by it you shall put me underground without candles.' Eventually, he moved the Forest works to a new site below the mine. The new site was a mere half mile from the old. He was still not free, however, of Popkin's shifts and tricks. The Trewyddfa mine worked the same vein as Popkin's Penvilia mine, 700 yards away, and colliers 'Learned in the Black Mistery' assured him that Popkin had been working clandestinely '[under]our Limits; and there is all ye Probability of it that can appear on ye surface. It will cost 100 to prove it.'

In 1746, Morris greatly extended his coal interests by taking a lease from the Duke of Beaufort that allowed him to work coal virtually anywhere on the western side of the Tawe between Landore and Morriston. He followed this by opening up the Five Foot vein around Craig Trewyddfa, partly to supply his Forest works and partly to increase his exports of coal. His collieries were not far from the sea and he was keen to find a market for coals that might not be suitable for his furnaces. Above Swansea, the coal measure rocks dip less steeply, and in the Morriston-Llansamlet area, the dip, at less than five degrees, is almost negligible. Coal seams exposed on the sides of the valley could be mined with comparative ease and pits sunk with confidence. By 1760, Morris had begun to work the deeper and richer Six Foot vein below the valley floor. Access to the coal might have been relatively easy, but collieries on Craig Trewyddfa were notorious for their drainage problems. At his Clyndu colliery (c 1754), just outside Morriston, Morris drove a level, eight feet high and nearly five wide, eleven hundred yards under the mountain. There was so much water that boats three feet wide and twenty long, with a capacity of two wagons or four tons, could, in a narrow channel, float up the heading to a point where the laden wagons could be tipped into them. It was, so it has been claimed, the first navigational level or underground canal ever built. Boats emerged from the level into what was described as a sort of basin and from it entered a canal that led to the Forest works. Coal not destined for the works served what had become a thriving export trade from Swansea. At first, it was conveyed to the shipping wharves in panniers on horseback, but Morris found the practice so 'dilatory' that he replaced the pack-horses with wagons and rough tracks with purpose-built roads. Wagons may have been more efficient than pack-horses but no sooner had they trundled down the Swansea streets than the inhabitants, 'one and all', complained that the rumbling noise and tremors produced by the 'cumbrous machines' threatened to sour the beer in their cellars.

By the last decade of the eighteenth century, the Tawe Valley's drifts and pits were beginning to attract tourists. The largest of the pits was the Pentre pit that John Morris, Robert Morris's son, and Anthony Lockwood had sublet from Gruffydd Price in 1788. Price had started mining deeper seams in 1768 because the shallow measures were, in his words, 'nearly exhausted'. In 1791 E D Clarke hired an open chaise at Swansea and drove to the mine. He recorded his observations in his *Tour*, published in 1793: 'The entrance is vaulted, and perfectly level and continues so for about one hundred yards, when our guides made us turn off to the right, to a sort of staircase, which they call the horse road. By this we descended to a depth of eighty fathoms, and came to a spacious area, where the miners were sending up the coal in baskets through a shaft, to the vaulted level we had just quitted. It is there put into carts, with friction wheels, and drawn by oxen to the mouth of the mine.

'It is pleasing to see the ease and quickness with which these amazing works are carried on. If a stranger beholds the dark passage by which the horses descend, who bring the coal from the place where it is dug to the shaft, he would be astonished, and unable to conceive how these animals can be taught to practise without stumbling, and with facility, what he with care and attention would find it difficult to perform. Proceeding onward we came to some miners who were engaged in blowing up part of the rock with gunpowder, in order to make the communication from one part of the mine to another. Still further onward, about half a mile from the entrance, we came to the cutters, as they are called, a troop of miserable black devils, working away their very lives amidst sulphur, smoke and darkness.'

By 1791, John Morris was clearly learned in the Black Mistery.

*Coal wharf, or 'staithe', in the lower Tawe Valley. Watercolour by Julius Caesar Ibbetson, 1792. NLW.*

E D Clarke's reference to 'friction wheels' was to cast iron tram rails that Morris had Abraham Darby of Coalbrookdale make from wooden models about 4 feet long and 5 inches wide. Clarke described how they work: 'The wheels [of the trams] are placed on the iron bars, which they receive in a groove, and these bars being continually parallel to each other, they serve both as a guide to the cart and by lessening the friction, greatly diminish the weight of the load.' The carts were drawn by horses and, when empty, '… the driver lays in along in them, seizing the beast by the tail, which serves him as a rein to guide the animal round the different turnings and windings in the passage.' Morris and Lockwood had also learned how to combine drifts and deep mines. According to T Bryn Richard, a Tawe Valley miner and historian, the entrance to the Pentre pit was via the Cwm Level. The 'sort of staircase' to which Clarke was led by the guide was a connecting road from the Five Foot seam worked by the Cwm Level to the deeper Six Foot seam worked by the Pentre mine, 120 feet below.

To drain the Pentre pit, Morris and Lockwood knew that not only could they not rely on whimsies but that they would need a more powerful steam engine than the one used by Gruffydd Price. Price had installed a steam, or 'atmospheric', engine, probably of the Savery/ Newcomen type, in 1768. After taking over the colliery in 1788, Morris and Lockwood quickly exhausted the accessible coal and, to carry on, they were forced to mine deeper. The existing Newcomen engine, however, was strained to its limits and would have to be replaced. The alternative was a new engine, patented by Matthew Boulton and James Watt in 1769, that was more powerful than the Newcomen engine and, by condensing the steam in a separate cold chamber, much less demanding of coal. But for colliery owners, who could heat the boiler with the soft, broken and unsaleable coal that accumulated at the pithead, lower coal consumption was no great incentive. More power, however, was another matter, but Lockwood and Morris were not convinced that the Boulton-Watt engine had been adequately tested. Morris's diary entry for June 1775 reads: 'Since I have been at home I have been considering Landore [Pentre] Colliery. From several circumstances I think another fire engine necessary, having power to spare useful.'

Twelve days later, 17 June, he was '... more satisfied about another engine [but] think Bolton's [sic] not sufficiently tried.'

Three years later, however, attitudes had changed. In response to a letter from Lockwood late in 1778, Matthew Boulton wrote an engaging reply: 'At my return from Cornwall, I found myself favoured with your letter of the 19th inst, and although we have undertaken to erect as many engines as will fully occupy us throughout the year 1779, yet so favourable an opportunity of introducing our Engine into Wales under the auspices of a gentleman whose superior knowledge raises him above prejudices and whose example will vanquish it in others – are sufficient motives to induce us to give it preference to some others more profitable to us.' He continued by explaining that, because Morris-Lockwood coal was known to be of high value, they would take in payment a sum equal to the value of the amount of coal saved by using their engine as against common fire engines. 'In many collieries the proprietors value their engine coals at nothing consequently we are obliged to deviate in such cases from our rule of taking 1/3 of the value saved, because 1/3 of 0 is 0 and our time is too valuable to work at that price even if it be interlarded with honour.' Although beguiling, the terms offered were the standard terms for any purchaser of their products. The remaining correspondence is largely technical, the two engineers needing to know the amount of water to be drawn from a depth of 360 feet in winter and for how many hours in twenty-four the pump might be expected to work. Because Lockwood and Morris expected to raise coal as well as water, Boulton estimated that the engine, Brobdignagian by modern standards, would require 'a power of 1600 pounds through an 8 feet stroke, and that the whole power required will consequently be about 20,000 pounds which, at the above load... will require a cylinder of 52 inches in diameter.' To work at six strokes per minute it would also require a boiler seventeen feet in diameter that would consume sixty-four bushels of coal in twenty-four hours. Boulton recommended that the engine be of a size sufficient to drain the water in twelve hours in the wettest season, and he wondered if a double engine might suit their purposes better. A double engine, however, was more difficult to operate and maintain, and if this should be their choice they might consider sending a man to Cornwall in one of the returning ore boats to observe one in operation. Boulton, a salesman as well as engineer, could not resist a parting flourish. Because their engines were watertight and constantly polished by a grease piston, the cylinders were not as subject to erosion as those of common engines, and they also worked quietly.

The correspondence continued until the end of August 1786 and, although the concluding letters have not survived, it did lead to business. After he left the copper firm, John Morris, who like his father seems to have been in thrall to coal, installed a Boulton & Watt pumping engine to drain the extensive workings at Landore. The *Swansea Guide* for 1801 noted, 'A new stupendous engine installed by Mr Morris at Landore which cost upward of 5000 pounds to complete giving 1000 gallons per stroke at 12 per minute or 72,000 gallons an hour.' A later guide, published in 1813, described Boulton & Watt's celebrated steam engine as 'the largest in the kingdom'. When the Duke of Beaufort visited Swansea in 1846, after the engine had been out of commission long enough for the lower workings of several collieries to be 'drowned out', he expressed his intention of restoring 'this celebrated specimen of Boulton and Watt ingenuity.'

The other leading capitalist in the Tawe Valley, and a contemporary of Robert Morris, was Chauncey Townsend (1708-1770), a London alderman and linen merchant, who made a fortune from provisioning troops and settlements in Nova Scotia. He chose to sink his profits in coal, in south-west Wales. Neath and Swansea were two of Britain's leading coal ports, and the reserves of the hinterland, although not yet mapped, were known to be extensive. In 1748/49 he obtained leases to mine at Eaglesbush, just south of Neath, as well as in the Tawe Valley and the Llanelli district. Above Swansea, in roughly the area between Llansamlet and Birchgrove, he leased the coal reserves beneath the Morgans' Gwernllwynchwyth estate and, a few months later, in November 1750, he made a similar arrangement with the Mansels, owners of the Briton Ferry estate immediately to the south. With the leases, Townsend controlled the coal reserves on the eastern side of the Tawe. In 1762 he obtained from Sir E V Mansel a lease of all the minerals beneath the Stradey estate, Llanelli, and at Genwen he sank to the nine feet thick Great Vein.

To be sure of a steady demand for his Tawe valley coal, in 1755 Townsend built, in association with a group of London copper and brass manufacturers, a copper works on a parcel of Mansel land, known as Middle Bank, on the east bank of the Tawe across from Swansea. In the act confirming the lease, the Mansels noted that 'great quantities of coal must necessarily be used and consumed,' and stipulated that coal for the works be taken only from mines on Mansel lands. The lessor, Lady Louisa Barbara Mansel, who would collect both ground rent for the copper works and royalties on the coal consumed, declared that she was well satisfied with the arrangement. Two years later, in 1757, Townsend extended his manufacturing interests by building, in partnership with his son-in-law John Smith, the Upper Bank lead and spelter works. Lead ore for the works was mined at Llechryd, Cardiganshire, and the coal in coal works on Mansel land.

Townsend soon realised that, without a more efficient system of transportation than the pack horses and carts used by the Mansels, who had operated a number of coalmines, he would have difficulty moving his coal either to the works or to shipping places farther downstream. The Tawe is navigable for a few miles above Swansea but the tracks leading to the shipping places were deeply rutted and, in wet periods, they were quagmires. Like Mackworth, Townsend was attracted by the wagon-ways, made from wooden rails and wooden sleepers, that were an established feature of the Northumberland and Durham coalfield. He is said to have travelled to the north-east to look for an engineer who would build one and, at Gateshead, met and hired George Kirkhouse. Kirkhouse settled in Swansea, built a wagon-way, and introduced to Townsend's mines practices that had been proven in northern England. 'Townsend's Wagonway', as it came to be called, was a single a track line, with passing places, three and a half miles long. It ran from his mines at Llansamlet to the Upper and Middle bank works and then to a stone jetty that Townsend had built at Foxhole, opposite Swansea. At the end of the jetty was a 'trunk' or chute that delivered coal emptied from the wagons into the holds of waiting vessels. Both wagon-way and trunk were north country words. By 1770, sixty two-ton wagonloads of coal, roughly five times as much as could be carried by road, were moved daily, either to the Upper and Middle Bank works or to the wharf.

Offering smooth and nearly level footing, the wagon-way became a public thoroughfare and, as such, was the scene of one of the first fatal rail accidents. On a January evening in 1762, when riding home to Llangiwg, farther up the Tawe, David William Gibbs came upon an empty coal wagon drawn by two horses, heading back to Gwernllwynchwith from White Rock. He urged his horse into a gallop and, just as he was overtaking the wagon, the horse stumbled, throwing its rider onto the rails and under the wheels of the wagon. Injured about the head, David William Gibbs died instantly.

Although he is best remembered for his wagon-way, Townsend's consuming ambition was to mine deep. At Gwernllwynchwith, he sank three shafts into the Swansea Five Foot seam and brought two mines into production, but Townsend's holy grail was the Great Vein, later known as the Swansea Six foot or Graigola vein, known to run below the Five Foot seam. The Mansels before him had worked the vein at the Llanwern colliery, on the edge of the Crymlyn bog, but it had been lost through faults 'which were many fathoms in disturbance.' In Townsend's day, sinking was still a Herculean labour, fraught with risks, both physical and financial. The adoption of gunpowder, however, had made it speedier. To sink the air shaft demanded by Sir Humphrey Mackworth for the Trewyddfa colliery in 1728, Robert Morris sent to Cornwall for miners 'for blasting the rock call'd shooting.' He declared that 'Welsh colliers are ignorant of ye use of powder,' unaware that Mackworth had used it to level ground for a wagon-way as early as 1710. But not until 1719, according to Robert Galloway, the historian of mining, was gunpowder used to sink a shaft in Britain. The method was to bore a hole about two inches in diameter and thirty inches deep and charge it with gunpowder to a depth of several inches. A long pricker or skewer was inserted and the hole filled with marl or clay that was rammed tight with an iron rod. The pricker was then withdrawn and replaced by a straw filled with powder, to the top of which a piece of greased touch-paper had been stuck with a bit of clay. The touch paper was lit and the miner at the bottom of the shaft was drawn up as quickly as possible. The method was used only when the rock was extremely hard and, presumably, when the shaft was not too deep.

Sinkers were itinerant specialist workers, who lived in crude, shanty huts that they dismantled once the job was finished. With picks, hammers, chisels and wedges they gnawed at the underlying strata, in a space usually not more than six or eight feet across. Before attacking a difficult section of rock, they might weaken it by lighting a fire above it and, once the rock was hot, dousing it with cold water, hoping that the sudden temperature change might cause the rock to crack.. A more elaborate technique involved boring holes in the rock and then covering it with hot, or unslaked, lime that would expand and crack the rock when water was added. Working from timber staging built above the shaft, sinkers were winched downwards from the surface in the large iron bucket that was used to bring up the diggings. These were dumped in pyramids on the surface. The sinkers basic tools were picks, shovels, hand rock-drills and a plumb to ensure the verticality of the shaft. To protect themselves from falling stones and water, sinkers wore a distinctive dress: sturdy wide-brimmed hats and long, hard-wearing coats, reaching down to their ankles.

With or without the use of gunpowder, sinking – at the rate of about six feet a month at the end of the eighteenth century – was a slow process, and exceedingly so when hard rock was reached. The Rev Joseph Townsend recalled an exchange between his father and the foreman of the sinking crew at Pwll Mawr, Llansamlet, Townsend's final attempt, after many failures, to reach the Great Vein. The diggers had come to such hard rock (on which they were apparently reluctant to use gunpowder), that they informed Townsend that it was impossible to go any deeper. In reply, Townsend said to the foreman, 'Well, John David, can you bring up a bucketful of material in a day?' 'No, I cannot,' replied David. 'Can you bring up a hatful, then?' 'Doubtful,' was the answer. 'Can you bring up on a shilling as much as a shilling will hold?' 'We will try it, sir,' was the reply.' 'Very well, keep pegging at it if you cannot do more than trouble the water.'

The sinkers kept pegging until eventually they struck the Great or Six Foot vein 480 feet from the surface. It was the culmination of an almost twenty-year search and a record sinking for south Wales that was not surpassed until the sinking of a pit six hundred feet deep at Bryncoch, near Neath, in 1806. A survey made just after Townsend's death, in 1770, revealed that work had begun on another shaft and that there were plans to sink further shafts at 400 yard intervals. The coal was brought up in a large wicker basket fixed to a hempen rope. There were no guides in the shaft, and the basket, six to eight hundredweights (700-900 lbs) when laden, swung from side to side as it was hauled up the shaft. At the surface, the coal was dumped into wagons and taken by wagon-way to the jetty at Foxhole or to the Middle Bank works. Pitmen and boys were raised and lowered in the swaying baskets, and, if their basket happened to collide with one filled with coal, they could be dislodged.

Townsend invested his fortune (estimated at £30,000) into his Llansamlet pits, much of it into the 480-foot-deep Pwll Mawr. Like Jethro Tull, the zealous agricultural improver, who drilled away his fortune, Townsend bored and sank away his. When giving evidence to a House of Commons Committee, in 1810, his grandson Henry Smith remarked: 'I am certain my grandfather expended his whole fortune in it [Pwll Mawr] for he died without any property but that.' Even after the development of reliable boring equipment, sinking remained a laborious and risky business, and a successful sinking was a cause for celebration. When the owners of the Primrose Colliery, Pontardawe, struck the Swansea Six Foot seam at 1390 feet in 1863, the response, after several years of high costs and equally high anxiety, was explosive – literally. Cannon were fired and *cwrw da* [beer] drunk from a supply that, according to the *Cambrian*, seemed limitless.

Chauncey Townsend's drilling away of his fortune in the lower Tawe Valley may help to explain his puzzling neglect of his Llanelli coal leases. By 1762 he had, through a decade of careful – some would say shrewd – negotiation, acquired a near monopoly of the Llanelli coalfield from Sir Edward Vaughn Mansel. Only the leases west of the Lliedi river lay outside his control. Yet, at the time of his death, in 1770,

*Pit-sinking crew at Seven Sisters, in the Dulais Valley, 1872.*

he had worked almost none of the coal. In 1763, Daniel Shewen, Sir Edward's attorney and brother-in-law, wrote to Sir Edward urging him, as owner of the Stradey Estate, to press Townsend to begin mining. 'I wish you to write to Mr Townsend a few lines to let him know that by all accounts from the Country, the manner in which he carries on your collieries is astonishing to the whole Neighbourhood, particularly at a time when there's such a demand for coal and that he does not think them worth carrying on with some you desire he would give up his lease.' Between 1752 and 1762, Townsend had negotiated the leases of veins beneath the Stradey estate at extremely low royalties, in an agreement that required no minimum royalty clauses and no sleeping rents, so that there were no financial penalties if he failed to work them. Sir Edward was once described as 'a person of very weak intellect and incapable of transacting business.' Daniel Shewen, who expected to benefit substantially from Townsend's enterprise, had previously held some of the leases but, having no capital to work them, had surrendered them to Sir Edward so that all the coal under Stradey Park could be leased to Townsend. The most obvious explanation for Townsend's inactivity is that, like Shewen, he too was short of funds. An observation in a letter written in 1760 suggested as much: 'I should think money is very scarce with Townsend, for there is not a penny in wages in Cwm Ystwyth.' Other possible explanations are that he engrossed the Llanelli coal leases to forestall competition with his mines in and around Swansea or, alternatively, that with an eye to Sir Edward Vaughan Mansel's mounting debts, he hoped to buy the Stradey coal lands at knock-down prices.

Only after 1765 did Townsend, either through a change of heart or some improvement in his fortunes, begin to work the Llanelli coal holdings. In the Bynea area east of the town he began sinking pits, the deepest 240 feet down to the Old Golden or Great Vein, which he drained with a steam or fire engine. His grandson, some forty-four years later, referred to several pits and, although he had no documentation, a considerable expenditure. Yet there is no evidence of much production and, from Llanelli's point of view, as M V Symons, the historian of coalmining in the Llanelli area, has pointed out, it was a case of too little too late. Townsend's inactivity between 1752 and 1766 had inhibited not only the town's coal industry at a critical period but its industrial expansion in general. To add insult to injury, John Smith, Townsend's son-in-law, who took over the principal management of his collieries, did even less with Llanelli's coal reserves than Townsend himself. He did not deepen the fire engine pit at Genwen, and several sinkings were begun but never completed. As with Townsend, the inactivity is difficult to explain. He, too, may have wanted to keep Llanelli coal off the export market, and it is also possible that disagreements between Townsend's heirs may have stayed his hand. Furthermore, in the twenty years that elapsed between Chauncey Townsend's death and his own, the coal export trade, suffering from Britain's hostilities with France, did not encourage development. But neither an improvement in the market nor John Smith's death brought a change in Llanelli's coal fortunes. His sons, Charles and Henry Smith, inherited his four-fifths interest in the Llanelli coal leases but, instead of working them, they promptly set about regaining the missing one fifth that Chauncey Townsend had bequeathed to his daughter Charlotte and which, on her death, had passed to her husband. They won the legal contest that followed and, as the century ended, they were as firmly in control of the Llanelli coalfield as their grandfather had been with as, MV Symons has pointed out, no greater inclination to work it. The Townsend legacy in Llanelli, he concluded gloomily, was to hold back the industrialisation of the area by almost half a century.

Farther east, in and around Swansea, on the other hand, there was no lack of initiative and enterprise. The low-volatile, dry steam coals that lay between Neath and Swansea and a few miles to the north were coveted both at home and abroad. Until overshadowed in the 1860s by the smokeless steam coals of the eastern valleys, the Graigola mines at Birchgrove, north of Swansea, boasted 'decidedly the best steam coal in the world,' their agent listing the British Admiralty, various steam navigation companies, the East India Company, copper smelters, and large brewing companies among its buyers. Naval steam packets advertised specifically for Graigola coals. To handle the increased production and export of coal, John Smith replaced Townsend's wagon-way with a canal. On John's death, in 1797, his sons, Charles and Henry took over their father's Llansamlet mines and sank several more nearby. Charles, who was also known as 'Squire' Smith, was an excellent geologist and an accomplished student of the Welsh language. Under the pseudonym *Viator*, he was also a regular contributor to the *Cambrian*. Charles' son, Charles Henry Smith, carried on the business and, until his retirement to Pembrokeshire in 1870, he too was a prominent figure in Swansea affairs. As owners of the Hafod copper works, John Henry Vivian and his son, Henry Hussey Vivian, owned and operated several collieries in the surrounding district. To be closer to sources of coal, John Henry Vivian moved his smelters from Penclawdd to Hafod, on the lower Tawe. Also prominent in coalmining and the coal trade of the Swansea-Neath area were the Glasbrooks. John Glasbrook, a farmer's son, entered the coal trade after meeting the geologist and coal viewer Edward Martin. With his brother-in-law, Philip Richard, he worked coal reserves to the north and west of Swansea; by the 1840s, the best coal reserves in the lower Tawe Valley were nearing exhaustion. Like the Smiths, the Glasbrooks mined deep, striking the Five Foot seam in Gorseinon at more than six hundred feet and, in November 1860, the firm Richard & Glasbrook struck the Five Foot seam at Morriston after three years work. The celebratory dinner, which followed all deep sinkings, was, according to the *Cambrian*, a 'crack' affair that consumed 300lbs of beef, 12 hams, 12 legs of pork, 20 geese and a mountain of plum pudding.

# 'A COAL
# WITH A DIFFERENCE'

---

### Canals, railways and the move inland

> But here, although so fresh and fair
> The extended landscape may appear,
> The soil is poor, the culture rude
> Scarcely procuring daily food.
> Yet underneath are stores of wealth,
> Full deeply hid, yet man by stealth,
> Contrives to enter, make his own,
> And turns to gold, by forms unknown
> To former times, and ancient ways

> Wm Weston Young
> *Guide to the Scenery of Glynneath*, 1835

Dam the Canals, Sink the Coalpits, Blast the Minerals, Consume the Manufactures, and Disperse the Commerce of Great Britain.

(Toast of the Civil Engineers recorded in Robert Morris' Commonplace Book, 1774)

T APPING THE COAL RESERVES in the hinterlands of the coal ports, with packhorses and carts, over rough, unkempt roads, was analogous to draining water from a reservoir through a rusted, narrow-gauge pipe. The early roads, according to a wryly humorous Walter Davies, were of two types: '*deep* in the centre of the plain or valley, and *steep* up the brow of the hill: in the former case, the roads were public *ditches;* in the latter, public *step-ladders.'* Roads leading out of south

Wales were so hazardous that few, according to Davies, were prepared to take to them without first settling their affairs. Within Wales, farmers who lived near the ditch roads in the valleys, 'and possessed of strong teams and tender hearts,' could find employment many times a day by rescuing foundered carts loaded with a few bushels of lime, or a few 'hundreds' of coal. There were no turnpike roads in either the Nedd or the Tawe valleys, and the roads in general were so poor that one, leading from Ystradgynlais to Neath, was subject, in 1783, to an indictment presented at the Court of Great Sessions. Some anthracite was sent by packhorse down the Nedd and the Tawe valleys to Swansea and Neath, but, in general, coals distant from navigation, as Gabriel Powell had declared, were of almost no value.

The solution to the problem of the bulk movement of coal from

*The Tennant Canal from the Neath river bridge. Tucked under the left arm of the collier looking down on the canal and the barge is what amounted to a badge of office – a sawn-off pit prop used to make kindling. The painting is by Will Roberts. Private collection.*

places where there were no navigable rivers was, as the Duke of Bridgewater had demonstrated, the canal. In the early 1760s, the Duke and his engineer, James Brindley, built a canal from Bridgewater's south Lancashire collieries to Manchester. In south Wales, Thomas Kymer of Robeston Hall, Pembrokeshire, led the way. Convinced that poor transport facilities and a general reluctance to install machinery had led to the closure of a number of Pembrokeshire collieries, and determined that the same fate should not befall his own in the Gwendraeth Valley, in 1766 he obtained an Act, the first in Wales, to build a canal that would connect his mines and limestone quarries below Pontyates with Cydweli, four miles away. Small canals or waterways linking collieries with works had been built earlier, but Kymer's canal was the first in south Wales to link collieries with the sea, and the first to reach into the anthracite area.

Through the combined pressure of landowners keen to exploit their coal reserves, ironmasters seeking low-cost transportation to Neath and Swansea, and merchants in both towns looking to increase trade, both valleys became subjects of Canal Acts. Granted by Parliament, the Acts enabled canal companies to purchase land and raise funds by public subscription. The Nedd Valley canal was the easier project. The broad, flat floor of the valley, interrupted only by occasional moraines, its arrow-like straightness, and its gentle declivity were gifts to the canal engineer. In its passage across the coalfield, the Nedd falls fewer than two hundred feet, whereas the Rhonddas and the Taff, in their courses through the high eastern plateau, descend more than five hundred. The Neath Canal Act, sanctioned by Parliament in 1790, and receiving Royal assent in 1791, authorized the building of a canal from Pontneddfechan to the Melincryddan Pill, a distance of thirteen miles. Completed in 1795, the canal had nineteen locks and could accommodate barges carrying up to twenty-five tons. By contrast, the Glamorganshire Canal, connecting Merthyr Tydfil with Cardiff, would require fifty locks. To accommodate vessels larger than those able to make their way up the river to the Neath bridge, in 1799 the Canal Company, against the objections of the burgesses of Neath, built a two-and-a-half mile extension to the canal, from Melyncryddan, the site of Mackworth's copper works, to Giant's Grave, Briton Ferry, on the estuary of the river. To protect property values in Neath, a clause in the act authorizing the extension forbade building, other than farmhouses, on the east side of the river within a half mile of the termination of the canal. In the 1780s, according to the Collector of Customs at Briton Ferry, each year, between five and six hundred vessels, loaded with coal and culm brought down in river barges, sailed for Guernsey, Ireland, France and even the United States. In 1811, Rees Williams of Aberpergwm, on a visit to inspect his own coal stocks at Giant's Grave, found thirty vessels waiting to be laden.

Served by branch canals and tram roads, the canal brought coal from the upper reaches of the valley to Neath and Giant's Grave, and iron ore from outcrops on the sides of the valley to iron works at Cwm Gwrach, Melin y Cwrt, Aberdulais and Neath Abbey. The preamble to an 1800 Harbour Act characterized Neath as 'a Place of very considerable Trade and a great Nursery for Seamen.' The canal was a great success but, within a few years of its completion, there was conflict between the ironmasters on the one hand and the canal company and coal exporters on the other. In 1798 canal users complained of the practice of 'scouring', that is using a torrent from dammed-up surface water to expose the underlying ironstone and separate the ore from the clay. The lighter silts and clays from the loosened overburden silted up feeders to the canal and, eventually, the canal itself. The chief offenders, the Foxes of Neath Abbey, who owned minerals at the head of the valley, agreed to build a new feeder, but there was no general let-up in the practice. By 1811, silt and clays from the overburden removed by Francis Tappenden, owner of an ironworks above Glynneath, threatened to choke the headwaters of the canal and seriously inhibit traffic. The Canal Company brought charges and, after a two-year legal battle, won the case, but it was opposed by the whole body of ironmasters, who had hoped that custom would sanction and legalize the practice.

So obvious were the benefits of bulk transport by water that George Tennant, owner of the Cadoxton estate near Neath, was moved to extend them by linking the Nedd and the Tawe valleys. Nedd valley exporters would then have access to shipping facilities at Swansea as well as those at Neath. Tennant, a wealthy Londoner, moved to Neath in 1811, bought the Rhyddings estate and shipped coal from a colliery on the estate to the Neath wharf via an artificial waterway and an inclined tram road. To build his link, he acquired the lease of an existing canal built by Richard Jenkins, leaseholder of the Glanywern (the G was often omitted) colliery on the eastern flank of Kilvey Hill, to circumvent charges on the turnpike road between Neath and Swansea. The canal, thought to be an enlargement of a medieval drainage ditch, *Clawdd y Saeson*, crossed the Crymlyn Bog to the Red Jacket Pill – so called after the red-jacketed men who operated the canal boats – on the Nedd. It is graphically described by the Reverend Odisworth in his *Guide to Swansea*, 1802:

> Binding coals of very superior quality are here [at Glanywern] raised, and sold for exportation in the river of Neath, at a place called Trowman's-hole, whither they are conveyed from Llanywern by means of a canal, which in many respects is worthy of observation, and particularly as being the first that was ever made in Wales. Before this canal was cut, the coals were taken to Swansea river by a tedious and expensive land-carriage, and shipped at Fox-hole. It was found necessary to take the canal for nearly two miles through the midst of Crymlyn, or Crumlin bog or morass, the soft spongy ground of which rising up repeatedly after the surface was cut away, seemed to present an insuperable obstacle to the completion of the undertaking. The work was finished in the year 1790, and may be looked upon as not the least striking instance which this country affords of spirit and perseverance successfully exerted; the length of the canal being somewhat more than three miles, and the whole expense of the undertaking defrayed by a single individual.

After acquiring the lease of the canal, Tennant extended it westward to join a newly constructed pier at the entrance to the Tawe. He also built wharves to serve small seagoing vessels on a tidal inlet of the Tawe that still bears his name. By the summer of 1818, barges could drop down the Nedd with the tide, lock-up into the canal at the Red Jacket Pill, and cross the neck of land to the Tawe and Swansea harbour. So successful was the canal that Tennant proposed to create a direct link with the Nedd Valley canal by cutting a new channel, roughly parallel with the river, from a point near the Red Jacket Pill to Aberdulais, a village two miles above Neath. The new channel would join the Neath Canal via a ten-arched stone aqueduct across the river. Fearing congestion in their harbour, Tawe valley exporters and the town's Harbour Trust objected to the scheme but Tennant and his engineer, William Kirkhouse, persisted. Described as 'a bluff independent personality, strong in the knowledge of his abilities, and confident in his powers', Kirkhouse appears to have been cast from the same mould as the great nineteenth century canal and railway builders. He was the grandson of George Kirkhouse, the builder of Townsend's railway, and he apprenticed under his father, Bedlington Kirkhouse, an engineer and a sinker of pits in Neath, Swansea and Llansamlet. William Kirkhouse is admired for his aqueduct, in particular, but his finest engineering feat on the Tennant canal is out of sight: a massive, inverted stone arch five hundred yards long and thirty feet deep, built to encase the canal in its passage through a patch of quicksand near the Neath Abbey Iron Works. The sand, 'of the finest grain and most subtle nature,' was so restless that not even acutely-sloped banks could confine it, and so deep that no iron rod could reach its bottom.

Tennant applied for a Canal Act in the reasonable expectation that local landowners would be willing to invest in his project, but none were, so he was thrown onto his own, clearly considerable, resources. His 8.5-mile canal, which opened for both commercial and passenger traffic in late May 1824, is considered to be the most important canal in Britain built without benefit of an Act of Parliament. The opening, as the *Cambrian* reported, was a gala event highlighted by a flotilla led by a pilot boat, the *Countess of Jersey*, with a group of musicians on board. Following it were a handsome pleasure boat and a barge that had been converted into a floating battery. The pleasure boat carried the engineer William Kirkhouse, an agent representing George Tennant, and a group of local dignitaries; the barge was filled with masons and carpenters who, to the delight of the crowds on the town bridge and the banks, discharged cannon at regular intervals. Taking up the rear was a convoy of a dozen coal-laden barges, ten from the Nedd Valley and two from Neath Abbey. On arrival at Swansea, the flotilla, and the hundreds of well-wishers who had walked along the tow-path, were greeted with the ringing of bells, the firing of guns and a display of flags hoisted by all the vessels in the port. Tennant's workmen were treated to a feast of beef, mutton and beer. Weeks later, the excitement had scarcely abated:

'The Canal has been open seven weeks, and 376 barges with 5930 tons of coal and timber have already passed over its line. No inconsiderable number of passengers have been borne upon it, as the inhabitants of Neath and vicinity are allowed to navigate it with families, servants, shop goods and parcels, free of all charge... we have also great pleasure in being able to announce that during this period a larger quantity of coal and culm has been borne by the Swansea canal, and also upon the Neath Canal, than had ever before been carried by either of them within the same length of time.'

The most fulsome praise for the canal came in the form of a nineteen-verse ode from Elizabeth Davies, the Neath laureate, who kept a lollipop shop on Wind Street:

O! could I make verses with humour and wit,
George Tennant, Esquire's great genius to fit;
From morn until even, I would sit down and tell,
And sing in the praise of Neath Junction Canal.

To his noble genius, great merit is due,
The increase of traffic, he'll daily pursue;
Employ to poor Labourers, it is known full well,
He gave them by making Neath Junction Canal.

But I think that my duty I do not fulfil
If I pass Mr Kirkhouse's very great skill,
He exerted his talents as wonderf'lly well
In that great undertaking: Neath Junction Canal.

Elizabeth Davies, like so many others, was greatly impressed by William Kirkhouse's elegant arched aqueduct over the Nedd, enabling 'two crystal rivers in union [to] meet.' Others, however, were blinded to the aqueduct's elegance by the provenance of the stones; they were quarried from nearby falls on the Dulais River. Among the detractors was Captain Gronow, a renowned Welsh swordsman, who accompanied the poet Southey on a house-hunting expedition in the Nedd Valley. For Gronow, the aqueduct builders and their agents, the quarrymen, were simply vandals who had 'destroyed' a natural cascade.

The idea of a canal for the Tawe Valley was first aired by William Padley, a Swansea merchant and importer and an associate of the engineer and mineral surveyor Edward Martin. Martin, from Martindale in Cumberland, was mining agent to the Duke of Beaufort. Padley was distressed that ships which brought merchandise to Swansea often went home in wasteful ballast. To fill the empty holds, he lobbied for a canal that would bring the coal, iron ore and limestone of the valley down to the town. The lack of a turnpike road and the existence of an act to improve the harbour, passed in 1791, pointed, Padley argued, to the pressing need for a canal. Padley's advocacy and the passing of the Neath Canal Act in 1791 eventually engaged public interest and, after a number of Common Hall meetings early in 1793, attended by aldermen and burgesses, the Corporation resolved to hire a surveyor, petition Parliament for a canal bill, and solicit public funds. Among the original subscribers were six of the Neath Canal's managing committee. The Swansea Canal committee commissioned a report which recommended a route on the west side of the Tawe. An assenting Act followed in May 1794. Work began later that year and ended in October 1798. Built for barges sixty-five to seventy feet long and seven and a half feet wide, the canal was thirty feet wide and five deep. The barges had a carrying capacity of twenty-five tons. Those that traversed the entire fifteen mile length of the canal, from the town to Hen Neuadd, between Ystradgynlais and Abercraf, had to negotiate thirty-six locks over a rise of 363 feet. To span the tributaries of the Tawe required six one-arched aqueducts and, for the Twrch at Ystalyfera, one of four arches. The barges, like those on the Neath canal, were horse-drawn and, to prevent wash and erosion of the banks, their speed was strictly limited to two miles an hour when full and three when empty. The complete journey took eight to nine hours each way and, in a workful age, the work for the barge boys was comparatively leisurely. The laconic ten-

*A ten-arched stone aqueduct built across the Nedd at Aberdulais, linking the Tennant and Neath canals. Behind the aqueduct is a railway viaduct. NMW.*

year-old Thomas Williams shared the work of leading a horse with his elder brother: 'I drive with my brother, he is 16 or 17. We work from six in the morning... until six in the evening, and often later, but we do not work at night. I have good health, but am out in all weathers along the canal... I have met with no accidents. My work is not very hard. I go to Sunday school every Sunday.'

Although open to the elements and extremely slow-moving, the barges also carried passengers, women – presumably from the lower reaches of the valley – travelling regularly to Swansea to do their shopping. Every week, too, a barge laden with goods and provisions made its way up the canal to the valley towns. As bulk carriers, the barges were a great success,

*Abandoned barge in the Swansea valley canal at Ystalyfera, c. 1950. Brecknock Museum and Art Gallery.*

crowding facilities at the harbour and, in the early 1820s, raising doubts in harbour trustees and colliery owners about the harbour's ability to cope with the increase in traffic threatened by George Tennant's canal. Local farmers, who depended on the haulage of coal, iron ore and limestone to supplement the meagre income from their farms, were also deeply worried. When one horse could pull a barge of twenty tons what work would there be for packhorses or carts that could carry only a few hundredweights! But like George Stephenson's locomotive, which could haul several hundred tons, the canal, as Thomas Levi remarked in his 1865 essays on the Tawe valley, simply created more work for everyone.

Of the remaining valleys, only the Gwendraeth was canalised. Plans to build a canal along the Llwchwr valley from Llanelli to Pantyffynon never materialized. The idea of extending Kymer's canal up the Gwendraeth valley was first proposed in 1793 but there were no firm plans until 1812. A prospectus, issued after a meeting in Carmarthen, aimed to improve the harbour at Cydweli and build a nine-lock canal up the valley that would connect with tram roads to collieries at Cwm-mawr and on the Great Mountain. A branch from Kymer's canal, with accompanying tram road connections to neighbouring collieries, would also be built to Llanelli. Projections were for 200 tons of anthracite to be shipped daily from Cydweli and 100 tons of bituminous coal from

Llanelli. These figures compared with 300 tons daily from Swansea and 470 from Neath. An Act followed in 1812 and construction, with Edward Martin as one of two engineers, begun. Kymer's canal reached Pontyates, four miles up the valley, where it was joined by a colliery tram road from the north-west. Here, for lack of funds, construction stopped and the canal was not completed until 1825. In 1817 Alexander Raby sold his ironworks interests in Llanelli and concentrated on coalmining in the Gwendraeth. From the valley, coal was sent by barge and tram to Cydweli and Llanelli both for export and home consumption. Every year estate owners and farmers from Cardiganshire, Pembrokeshire and Breconshire sent carts and wagons to Llanelli to bring back a year's supply of coal. The coal-carrying occupied the best part of a week and was made the occasion for much feasting and merriment. As Elizabeth Phillips pointed out, it was the only approach to a holiday that the farm labourer of those days ever experienced.

The canals galvanized their respective valleys. Property owners took a hard look at their mineral resources and many saw, for the first time, the chance for substantial returns. The income from most estates was marginal; upland areas were suited only to summer grazing, and on the valley sides and floors the farms were small and husbandry generally poor. Rents were low and arrears were usually large and permanent. In Wales, unlike many parts of England, no disgrace attached to commercial or industrial enterprise so landlords could, without embarrassment, campaign in concert to assert the rights of property. Customary rights were re-examined and leases re-negotiated to give landlords greater control of their coal resources. Idle tenants were ejected. D Rhys Phillips cites the cases of Jones of Pentreclwyda, and Morgan, landlord of the Lamb and Flag Inn above Glynneath. Both had neglected their land and Morgan, who paid no royalties, was also guilty of cutting coal for sale rather than for his own use. To some extent, they were unlucky in their landlord. Both were tenants of Rees Williams, owner of the Aberpergwm estate who was also a shareholder in the Neath Canal Company. Realising that the Nedd valley was now ripe for exploitation, he employed an eminent solicitor, William Gwyn, to renegotiate the terms of all farm tenancies and to regain control of all coal and ironstone workings that had been leased to individuals and consortiums. By 1810 he had taken over all the Aberpergwm coal interests and, to ensure that his control did not end once the coal had been loaded onto the barges, he bought four parcels of land at Giant's Grave, the shipping place at the mouth of the river. He also bought out all the shareholders of the Aberpergwm Company. By 1811 the estate was shipping seven barge loads daily down to Neath and Giant's Grave. Only in Pembrokeshire, now the least dynamic part of the coalfield, were there no immediate changes. Leases there already favoured the landlord or the lessor, whose share normally yielded a quarter or a third of the receipts of the colliery after all expenses had been deducted.

Some landowners chose to mine their own coal but most were content to lease the mineral rights and, if they had woodland, to sell off the young trees as pit props. By 1800 squire-coal masters like the Mansels and the Popkins were rare figures. As enablers or facilitators, however, the role of the landlords and their agents was often critical. In remote areas in particular their chief concern was to smooth the way for the entrepreneur. Some went to the trouble and expense of proving the coal under their lands while others, to attract an investor or clinch a lease, offered to build tram roads from the mine to the canal. In their advertising landowners stressed the advantages of working by drift, rather than shaft, as this meant a lower initial investment and cheaper operating costs. Haulage would be easier, drainage might be natural, and there would be relative freedom from gas. Because they were not risking capital, and because, in the last resort, they could always insist on the terms of the lease, landlords could afford to be generous. In negotiations they were always in the stronger position and were able to offer leases which gave some protection to the lessee and which at the same time safeguarded their own interests. Once the initial investment had been made, lessees were more likely, as the agent to Lord Dunraven remarked, 'to proceed in hopes of better success… than sustain a certain loss.'

For the colliery and associated headworks land was usually granted rent-free. Coal used in steam engines and furnaces at the colliery was, as a rule, also exempt from royalty payments as was the coal issued free to the colliers. In slack periods, rents might be waived, and even cancelled if the quality of the coal deteriorated or a seam ran out 'through unavoidable convulsions of nature.' Royalties were lower for small coal and culm and were a safeguard against a seam of large coal disintegrating into small. Thus Richard Lockwood, John Lockwood and Robert Morris paid the Duke of Beaufort half-rate on small coal fit only for lime burning. But such concessions could expose landlords to trickery. In 1808, Rees Williams of Aberpergwm sued a lessee, a Birmingham company, for breaking large coal into small and paying a royalty of three pence instead of a shilling. At the subsequent trial, the ruling was in Williams' favour. The company was assessed a penalty of almost five thousand pounds and thereafter ordered to weigh the coal and culm separately. To prevent similar subterfuges on his properties, the Duke of Beaufort reserved the right to appoint a 'landsman', paid by the lessees, with a right to inspect the colliery and check the accounts. Other landlords went further, appointing – again at the expense of the lessee – a watchdog at the wharves to ensure that the amount of coal shipped corresponded with the amounts on the way-bills presented.

By the beginning of the nineteenth century, most landlords had learned how to protect themselves not only against the machinations of unscrupulous lessees but also against leasing rights of exploitation to a non-renewable asset. Leases for a fixed annual rent, without payment of royalties, were now a rarity and to ensure that collieries were worked regularly, landlords fixed a 'dead or sleeping' rent, a minimum sum below which royalty payments could not fall in any one year. Entrepreneurs unwilling to pay a dead rent for a property that they were not ready to develop, and anxious to forestall rivals, could sometimes buy the coal outright for a fixed, and usually large, sum. To ensure the vigorous working of a colliery, the landowner could also insist that the lessee employ no fewer that an agreed number of colliers, twenty in the case of the lease of a Llansamlet colliery in 1750.

In the absence of reliable geological maps, most landlords were also wary of dishonest sinkers and unreliable mineral surveyors. But many were gulled, as De la Beche's field geologists discovered in the 1840s, into sinking shafts in strata where there was no possibility of finding coal. On the other side of the coin, landowners anxious to increase the sale value of their properties urged field geologists to suggest the possibility of minerals where none were known to exist. Where the workings extended beneath more than one estate, and where there was only one shaft for raising the coal, landowners also had to be vigilant to prevent coal from being taken literally under their noses. Every three months, surveyors from the Evans and Bevan mines in the Dulais valley met with surrounding landowners to overlay tracings of pit plans against estate plans to calculate how much coal had been taken from each property and the payment due. In such cases coal carried underground across property lines might be charged a way-leave rent, by the landlord granting the right of way, and a shaft rent for raising it to the surface. In cases where mine workings could not be extended beyond particular farm or estate boundaries, the costs of producing coal increased inevitably. A new mine on a neighbouring property meant a new shaft and new schemes for drainage, ventilation and haulage.

To safeguard land for future agricultural use, agreements often stipulated that shafts and gutters be filled as soon as possible after the closure of the colliery and, to prevent subsidence, that the lessee 'maintain proper and sufficient pillars for supporting and protecting the super incumbent strata from falling.' On the other hand, so as not to deprive the landowner of royalties, no coal was to be left behind that could be taken 'in the ordinary way of working.' In other leases, the lessees were expressly prohibited from removing topsoil and overburden by 'scouring and streaming.'

In both the Nedd and the Tawe valleys there were two distinct phases of development. Outcropping on the slopes of the main and tributary valleys were large runs of virgin coal that could be could be worked from drifts. But in the steam and semi-bituminous belt farther south, where all the easily-won coal had been taken, new winnings called for deep shafts, extensive workings, and very large amounts of capital. The shaft of Pwll Mawr, sunk c.1806 at Bryncoch, two miles above Neath, by William Kirkhouse, the canal builder for the Quaker ironmasters of Neath Abbey, was 600 feet deep and that of the Primrose Colliery, near

Pontardawe, sunk c. 1838, almost 1400 feet. To reach the Six Foot seam at Pontardawe was a two-year labour. Sinkings in the valley bottoms were shallower, but when digging through the alluvium, the sinkers had to contend with washouts of sand and gravel. The ground on the floor of the Nedd valley was said to be of the most 'restless' character, and very large tree branches had to be lashed behind the uprights to keep back the sliding shingle. At Pontardawe, a borehole on the valley floor, fifty yards from the side of the valley, passed through twenty feet of gravel and 110 feet of quicksand without reaching bedrock. Two shafts protected by cast-iron tubbing were sunk, but at fifty feet the tubbing caved in and the sinking had to be abandoned. New shafts were sunk in bedrock on the side of the valley.

On the valley slopes upstream and on the northern outcrop, however, the investment was relatively small and coal winning could begin as soon as the seam was cleared of overburden and a tramway laid to the canal. Business or professional men with a little capital to spare, or the means to borrow, could take a lease of a coal-bearing property, or a share of one. Among them were Edward Martin, the mineral surveyor, who opened three levels in the Twrch valley, and Thomas Sheasby, the canal's surveyor. Sheasby's partner was George Haynes, proprietor of the *Cambrian*, Wales's first English-language newspaper, and until 1810 part-owner of the Cambrian Pottery. Daniel Harper of Tamworth in Staffordshire, who was one of the proprietors of the Tawe Valley canal, bought existing collieries in the Ystradgynlais/Ystalyfera district in 1801 and opened several others, including Lefel Harper, farther up the valley. But not all investors were respectable business or professional men. William Arthur, who also invested in coal in the Twrch valley, was a reformed and once-daring smuggler. In 1786, inside his hideaway near Pennard, in Gower, he and a large number of armed henchmen, 'a body of desperate fellows,' repelled an attack by a posse of a dozen revenue officers. A report of the incident concluded that nothing short of a military exercise would avail 'against so popular and daring a freebooter.' In 1788, two expeditions set out to corner him, the captain of one of them (the Cardiff collector of customs) asking for an extra cutter and a party of sixty light-infantry men.

# A Coal With a Difference

The Nedd and the Tawe valleys also attracted distant investors. In response to energetic canvassing and advertisement by the Neath Canal Company, a number of prospectors from Cornwall, Bristol, Birmingham and Gloucester took leases on coal areas in the valley. In 1795, a year after the passing of the Tawe Valley Canal act and three years before the completion of the canal, James Lewis from Monmouth and Richard Griffiths from Cardiff leased land from Richard Gough Aubrey for the express purpose of exploiting the coal on the Ynyscedwyn estate. Aubrey was one of the directors of the Swansea Canal Company and one of the few landlords to engage directly in mining. The lease heralded something approaching a coal rush into the anthracite tract. The following year, five companies described as 'opulent' were working, or intending to work, the stone coal. In 1804 the canal carried about 54,000 tons of coal and culm, the main traffic; in the mid 1820s annual shipments averaged 130,000 tons. So critical was proximity or access to the canal that, in descriptions of their collieries, owners seldom failed to cite their distance from the canal and from the wharves at Swansea.

In both valleys the pattern of mining was the same. Collieries were connected to the canals by tram roads and branch waterways. The loaded trams ran downhill to the canals, where they were tipped into waiting barges and canal boats; horses drew the empty trams upslope back to the collieries. Edward Martin built a tram road from Lower Cwmtwrch to the Gurnos wharf on the canal and later extended the road to the upper parts of the valley. Unlike the old tram roads, which were usually makeshift, some of the longer, newer ones were surveyed. Martin's road could accommodate four or five wagons, the loaded ones descending on the brake, with an empty wagon at the end carrying two horses for the uphill journey back to the levels.

Occasionally the drifts were extensive but as these involved high costs for haulage and underground roadway maintenance it was usually cheaper to drive a fresh drift into the hillside than extend an existing one, even though there might have been plenty of coal left. The collieries were small, employing no more than a few hundred men, and each had a separate owner. As a result, the hillsides were riddled with tunnels. During his second walk through Wales, in 1794, the Reverend Richard Walker came upon a typical arrangement: 'Passing on for half a mile [from Aberpergwm], we crossed a rail-road along which the stone-coal is brought from the works... to the side of the canal. The mine lies at some distance to the left hand, and may be entered through a long level.' As well as noting that the vein was nine feet thick and dipped to the west one yard in twelve, he also gave, if his reporting was accurate, some indication of the profits to be made: coal cut and delivered at the mouth of the level for one shilling a ton could be sold at the Neath wharves for ten shillings and sixpence. The sixpence was a gift to the masters of the coal vessels, and an inducement to return.

In his economic and agricultural survey of south Wales, 1815, Walter Davies noted, perhaps disapprovingly, that, 'Pits will never be sunk in quest of coal where levels answer every purpose.' Levels presented little challenge to the mining engineer and prompted no improvements in technique. Only near the coast, where most of the easily-won coal had been taken and demand was greatest, had they been extended. At the time of Walter Davies's survey, however, mining in the anthracite region was about to enter a second phase of development. There, too, most of the easily accessible coal had either been won, or leased, and new winnings required the sinking of shafts, often of three hundred feet or more, and much heavier investment. Among the new pits, one was exceptional. In its day, Hendreforgan was one of the largest collieries in the upper Tawe valley and, in most eyes, the most progressive. By its own estimate, it was, if an 1831 *Cambrian* advertisement offering the colliery for sale is a fair measure of self esteem, 'The most complete and valuable colliery in the Principality,' and 'in a high state of perfection.' The colliery was named after a ninety-eight acre farm in the parish of Llangiwg and it opened, in 1814, under a ninety-nine year lease to John and George Evans of Llansamlet. George Evans quickly dropped out of the partnership, to be replaced in 1816 by James Cox, an attorney with connections in Dorset and London. The new partnership was sealed under a lease of, from the point of view of the lessees, remarkable laxity. In a district where a royalty of one shilling a ton was standard, it granted the lessees the right to work any quantity of coal, however large, for a fixed annual payment of 180 pounds. The smuggler William Arthur and his partner, the Swansea grocer Thomas Walters, were extended similar terms by, one assumes, an equally inexperienced lessor. Their 1798 lease called for a fixed rent of forty-seven pounds and for this they could work as much coal as they chose.

Except for a general interest in the coal trade, no one knows what attracted Cox to Hendreforgan. But whatever his motivation, he was determined to run the colliery as efficiently as possible. He had no tolerance for local mining practices and quickly unburdened himself of his partner John Evans, whom he regarded as incompetent: 'I do not hesitate to say that Mr Evans could never have carried it on.' He also removed his manager for a similar reason ('the improper manner in which the levels of my colliery were marked'), and replaced him with William Stewart, a north-eastern English engineer recommended by George Stephenson of railway locomotive fame. 'You will perceive,' Cox wrote to an English associate, 'that we have a predilection for Newcastle men, for the Welch do not or will not understand or attend to their business and to say in short, if they did, they are a century behind you.' In 1818 Stewart and Cox sank downcast and upcast shafts to the Great Vein, about 150 feet below the surface. A steam engine was installed above the downcast shaft, to pump the water out and wind the coal up. The coal was then taken along the Palleg tram road, the first mile of which had been built by Edward Martin, to the Gurnos wharf and then barged down the canal to two Hendreforgan coaling wharves at Swansea, each capable of stockpiling 50,000 tons. According to Stewart, Hendreforgan coal was of excellent quality but the pit was far gassier than any of its neighbours. An underground furnace at the foot of the upcast shaft increased the draught and the rate of expulsion of stale air, but the arrangement, which was standard practice in northern English mines, could not be maintained. The Great Vein dipped more sharply than had been predicted and could not be worked by headings driven horizontally from the foot of the shaft. Two headings, each nearly five hundred yards long, followed the dip of the seam, and to pump them dry and haul the coal 'up the deep' to the base of the upcast shaft, Cox installed a steam engine bought from George Stephenson in

1820. It was probably the first application in Wales of steam power to underground haulage. Once Stephenson's engine had been installed, there was no longer any need for a ventilation furnace because the fire under the boiler of the engine, and the exhaust steam from the engine itself, were more effective at despatching stale air than heat from the furnace alone.

Until 1827, the Great Vein was the only seam worked but as the headings lengthened and pumping became more difficult the decision was made to sink to the next vein down, to the Milford seam, thought to be about fifty feet below the Great Vein. In actuality, they sank to two hundred and twenty feet before they reached it, encountering on the way a ten foot thick seam, which quickly thinned to two and a half feet, and 'as full of gas', according to Stewart, 'as you ever saw an egg full of meat.' To work the Milford seam without sinking a ventilation shaft, Stewart bratticed, i.e. divided, the single shaft with partitions, using one of the vertical sections as the downcast shaft and the other as the upcast. In order to provide ventilation for the Milford vein, he then led a pipe from the boiler of the Stephenson engine, on the Great Vein, that expelled a jet of steam at high pressure (fifty-six psi) into the upcast shaft. The effect was to augment the force of the air current in the upcast shaft already produced by the exhaust steam from the engine. The result was a draught so powerful that it ventilated both the Great Vein and the Milford Vein. The system, which operated from 1828 until 1833, is thought to have been the first application in a colliery of steam jet ventilation, as distinct from allowing exhaust steam to escape and force stale air up the shaft. In 1835 Sir Goldsworthy Gurney, who had experimented with steam jets as a way of improving the draught in locomotive boilers, would recommend the system to the Select Committee on Accidents in Coalmines. The Committee approved of the system but reversed its opinion when tests indicated that a doubling of coal consumption, *vis-à-vis* furnace ventilation, was not accompanied – Hendreforgan's experience to the contrary – by an appreciable increase in draught.

Most of the stone coal and culm, which constituted the bulk of the canal traffic, was sold to the customary buyers: greenhouse operators, lime burners, hop driers and maltsters in the West Country, London, and south-east England. 'This stone coal,' trumpeted Richard Gough Aubrey of the Ynyscedwyn Estate, in 1799, 'is equal in quality to the Tenby, and the culm superior to any ever produced in this country for burning lime... Masters of the vessels applying for this coal and culm will find it everyways worth their attention.' Coal and culm from the Aberpergwm colliery, near the head of the canal, nine miles from Neath, which had not 'hitherto [been] shipped either Oversea or Coastwise', caused consternation among Neath customs officials who, accustomed only to the bituminous coals of the lower valley, were unfamiliar with culm and were uncertain as to how it could be used or classified. The Collector of Customs had it tested on a smith's fire and then pronounced: 'Will not burn without a mixture of clay or other substance: produces neither flame nor smoke; used for burning limestone.' Within a year, the colliery at Aberpergwm was shipping coal to Ireland and the west of England, its exports of coal and culm increasing from 8,250 tons annually in 1796 to 38,500 tons in 1811. In Cornish markets, coal and culm from Swansea and Neath, which enjoyed cheap coal freights on the returning copper ore boats, had no competitors. Walter Coffin, the Rhondda colliery proprietor, was well aware of the advantages of a return cargo: 'Swansea must have the entire supply of coals for their engines, because they have it as back carriage.'

After the building of the canals, the movement of anthracite down the valleys increased from the merest trickle to a respectable flow. But the torrent that the landlords, miners and merchants might have hoped for did not materialize. The demand for anthracite had increased as populations grew but the range of uses had changed little since the Middle Ages. Aside from heating the boilers of steam engines, the chief uses in Britain were still the heating of greenhouses, the drying of hops and malt, and the burning of lime. In the domestic heating department, because of the difficulty of igniting and burning it in unenclosed grates and hearths, anthracite hardly registered. In his *Geology* (1813), Robert Bakewell could remark that, 'A considerable part of the coal in South Wales is of an inferior quality, and is not at present burned for domestic use.' In some areas hard, unbroken lumps of anthracite were so little regarded that they were thrown away as incombustible refuse. In the 1840s, the Millbrook Iron Co. of Swansea patented and attempted to market an iron grate suitable for burning anthracite but with, it would seem, little success. In February 1841 it opened its warehouse on High Street for the inspection of grates constructed, so it claimed, on an entirely new principle – one that 'combined great power for warming rooms, neatness, economy, safety and consuming only a small quantity of anthracite coal in a week, and also a perfect cure for smoky chimneys.' Later in the century, anthracite would finally make headway in the domestic fuel market but in the first half of the century the only hope for increased demand lay with industry.

In both the Nedd and the Tawe valleys, iron ore had been smelted since the seventeenth century. Clay ironstones, or clay band ores, are a constituent of the coal measures and initially there was no shortage of wood for making charcoal. Limestone, needed in the furnaces as a flux to separate the gangue or waste products from the iron, was readily available at the heads of both valleys. The sulphur in coal, which made the iron brittle, ruled out raw coal as a possible fuel, and Abraham Darby's coking process applied to steam coals only. Anthracite contained too few gases to be successfully coked, so ironmasters in the Nedd and Tawe valleys were faced with the dilemma of iron ore interbedded with vast deposits of a highly calorific coal that they could not use to smelt it. In 1804 Edward Martin built an experimental furnace in which he used stone coal, but a report in the *Cambrian* claiming that the quality of the iron exceeded that made with coke, and equalled that made with charcoal, proved to be premature. There were further trials in 1824/25. Thomas Harper, the son of the coal owner Daniel Harper, experimented with a furnace at Abercraf but he was no more successful than Edward Martin. Thomas Harper's legacy was cultural rather than technical. Immersed in the language and culture of the district and the country, he was described as 'the best Englishman who ever came to Wales.' In 1824 James Ward built a furnace at Hen Neuadd, near the head of the canal, but it also failed to produce iron of acceptable quality, and continued to fail when taken over by William Walters, whose fortune it is said to have drained.

The galling dilemma presented by an abundant local fuel that could not be used to smelt local ore was finally resolved largely through the efforts of David Thomas, the young manager of the Ynyscedwyn Iron Works, near Ystradgynlais. Thomas, who subscribed to the idea of design or purpose in nature, rejected any suggestion that the conjunction of anthracite and iron ore could have been simply accidental. He was born to a farming family at Bryncoch, a village just above Neath and, owning to a far greater interest in machines than ploughs, he apprenticed at the Neath Abbey Iron Works nearby. As well as producing iron from, as Richard Walker described them, two 'immense blast furnaces' blown by iron bellows operated with a Boulton & Watt double engine, the works was also one the largest builders of mining machinery and Cornish pumping engines. From Neath Abbey, David Thomas moved, in 1817, to the Ynyscedwyn Iron Works at Ystradgynlais, where he was appointed steward of the company's blast furnaces and iron and coalmines. Iron ore and limestone were available locally but coke or coking coal had to be brought by barge from the Graigola colliery, Clydach, lower down the valley. As the young, ambitious manager of coalmines and an iron works he had to confront daily the anomaly of shipping a local coal, anthracite, down the canal and hauling coke and coking coals up.

In his experiments to smelt the clay band ironstones with anthracite, which were no more successful than previous ones, Thomas found that the coal would not burn at a temperature high enough to liquefy the metal in the ore and allow it to flow out of the furnace for casting. He then experimented with mixtures of anthracite and coke and although some of the results were encouraging, frequent failures disheartened the men. These, not sharing Thomas's belief in the providential pairing of anthracite and ore, attributed the failures to the fuel, not the methods of smelting. 'The men,' Thomas reported, 'became so prejudiced against it that I had to give it up. Still, every year I would try some experiments with it.'

If anthracite was to be used in smelting, then it had to be made to burn at a higher temperature. The solution, as events unfolded, lay in substituting a hot blast for the customary cold blast in the smelting furnaces. In Glasgow, in 1834, James Neilson, a Scottish gasworks engineer and friend of an ironmaster who complained of the amount of coke consumed by his blast furnaces, discovered that by heating the blast before it entered the furnace, the coke burned hotter and more efficiently. The process became known as Neilson's hot blast. Credit for the perception that a hot blast might solve the problem of smelting with anthracite is the subject of some dispute. George Crane, the colourful – he wore a yellow hat – and eccentric owner of the Ynyscedwyn works, claimed it as his own. Crane was the son of a Midlands clockmaker and, before acquiring the Ynyscedwyn works, he had been a hardware merchant and a nail manufacturer. One evening, as he recounted the event, shortly after the news of Neilson's discovery had filtered to Wales, he took his bellows to pieces of anthracite laid on a parlour fire previously made up with bituminous coal. Some of the pieces were already burning well but, on blowing hard with the bellows, he noticed the appearance of a black spot on one of the coals, and on continuing, he 'blew the fire out of it.' By substituting in his mind's eye a furnace for his parlour fire, and industrial bellows for his household ones, he concluded that the cold blast used to drive air and fire through the mass of dense materials piled high in a blast furnace might, instead of encouraging combustion, actually discourage it. A hot blast, he reasoned, might have the opposite effect. According to Edward Roberts, Thomas's biographer, however, Crane and Thomas were together in the parlour and it was Thomas not Crane who remarked that a blast of warm air might have the desired effect: that it would make the anthracite 'burn like pine'. Attributing the intuition to Crane, Harry Scrivenor, an American commentator, remarked how years of frustration had been ended by the 'idea… that a heated blast, upon the principle of Mr Neilson's patent, might, by its greater power, enable him to complete the combustion of this peculiar coal.'

Whatever the actual provenance of the idea, it was David Thomas, the metal maker, not Crane, the former nail manufacturer, who left for Glasgow to inspect Neilson's hot blast technique. He returned to Ynyscedwyn with a licence from Neilson to use it. He also brought with him a mechanic who knew how to make the wrought-iron ovens for pre-heating the air, and together they connected the oven to an anthracite-burning furnace. The hot blast raised the temperature of the furnace and at the same time speeded up the smelting process. The higher temperature also allowed sulphur from the fuel to be removed as calcium sulphate in the slag. The first hot air furnace was blown at Ynyscedwyn in February 1837 and it cast the first iron ever smelted with anthracite.

By 1853 there were six furnaces in operation and an iron pig from Ynyscedwyn had been displayed at the Great Exhibition, Crystal Palace, in 1851. At Ynyscedwyn and elsewhere in south Wales the immediate reaction to David Thomas's new furnace was cool. A hot blast contradicted the lore that smelting furnaces burned hotter, and produced better quality iron, in winter than in summer. What ironmasters failed to realise, however, was that it was the additional moisture in the summer air, not its temperature, that affected the heat of the furnaces and the quality of the iron. The iron from the new anthracite-burning furnaces was reputed to be far superior to any produced previously at the works, and that it was as good as any iron being produced anywhere. John Rowe Richardson, a chain cable manufacturer, declared that a three-quarter inch bar of Ynyscedwyn iron broke at nineteen tons whereas bars made with iron from conventional furnaces broke at sixteen and a half. David Rosser, an in-house master blacksmith at Ynyscedwyn, pronounced that it was the best iron he had ever worked. George Cottan, an engineer and general iron founder, also testified to its strength – a standard bar (one inch square and four feet long) of ordinary iron broke at 440 pounds whereas a bar made from anthracite-smelted iron could withstand pressures of almost 600 pounds.

The significance of the Ynyscedwyn achievement did not escape mine and property owners. In June 1838, anthracite proprietors met at Swansea to form an association, the object of which was to demonstrate the applicability of anthracite 'to those purposes to which it had been lately applied.' At the Swansea meeting, a Mr Johnson observed: 'It is difficult for anyone not acquainted with the vast abundance of this material, and often in situations where no other description of fuel is to be found in proximity to the ore, to conceive the vast accession to our national resources that must result from its successful application to the manufacture of iron.' Within five years the hot blast method had become standard in the ironworks of the anthracite region, and by 1856 there were twenty or more anthracite furnaces in the area, extending from Saundersfoot in the west to Abernant, in the Nedd valley, to the east, each one consuming approximately twenty-five hundredweights of anthracite for every ton of pig iron produced. The main concentrations were at the head of the Tawe valley, with by far the two largest works at Ystalyfera and Ystradgynlais. Between 1801 and 1851, Ystradgynlais's population increased from fewer than one thousand to more than three and a half thousand. There were smaller works at Abercraf and Brynaman, at Onllwyn and Banwen in the upper Dulais Valley, at Abernant and Venallt in the Nedd Valley and at Ponthenry and Trimsaran in the Gwendraeth valley. Most of the ironmasters were also colliery owners. It was, however, a brief and inconsistent flowering. Most of the works were short-lived and production was intermittent; only the works at Ystalyfera and Ynyscedwyn could be described as successful and these had to blend some bituminous coal with the anthracite. But not even Ystalyfera and Ynyscedwyn could withstand changes in the technology of iron making. The new Bessemer converter, invented in 1856, required a higher grade of ore than the local ironstones, and the works in the anthracite district were too far inland to make the hauling of ore worthwhile. The production of pig iron peaked in 1857, and declined slowly thereafter.

Tinplate manufacture, however, which had developed as a subsidiary of the iron industry, continued to thrive. It may not have been a significant consumer of coal but south-west Wales, to which the industry gravitated after 1850, had fuel to operate the rolling mills, limestone for fluxing, water for washing the plates, and – as a by product of the copper industry – sulphuric acid for 'pickling' or cleaning them. There was also a long tradition of working with metals, and as copper and iron making declined in the second half of the nineteenth century tinplate was able to absorb the surplus labour. Most of the works were in the coastal belt between Cwmafan and Llanelli but there were a number in the Tawe and the Amman valleys that, once the local smelting furnaces had shut down, imported pig and bar iron and, as technology changed, steel bars. American protectionism, in the form of the McKinley tariffs, 1891, virtually closed the American market to foreign tinplate and in the process crippled the Welsh industry. Imports to the United States, the chief market for Welsh tinplate, fell by 80 percent and more than two hundred Welsh tinplate works, just under half of the total, were forced to shut down. The depression in the industry lasted for most of the decade, lifting only when beef canning in Argentina, fruit canning in Australia, sardine canning in Portugal and Spain, milk canning in Switzerland and petroleum canning worldwide presented new markets for Welsh tin.

The Neilson-Thomas hot blast furnace was a godsend to anthracite mining in south Wales, but its most lasting impact was in the United States, where coal owners in the vast anthracite field of eastern Pennsylvania were said to be 'watching like cats at mice-holes' for any application that would create a demand for their coal. Unlike products, useful foreign technology was not subject to tariffs. American ironmasters, too, were anxious to find a substitute for charcoal. American coals did not coke well and to fuel a furnace for twenty-four hours consumed in charcoal the equivalent of an acre of hardwood forest. George Crane, still claiming the hot blast application as his own, reported the discovery at the 1838 meeting of the British Association for the Advancement of Science, at which there might have been American delegates. Developments at Ynyscedwyn were also covered by articles in the London *Mining Journal* and the *Journal of the American Institute*. The Neilson/Thomas or the Neilson/Crane hot blast furnace was the opening the Pennsylvania cats had been waiting for. Before the end of the year the Lehigh Coal and Navigation Co. had offered David Thomas all the capital and resources he would need to build an ironworks on the banks of the Lehigh. It also offered a generous salary, with the proviso that, if the works failed to make a profit within five years, the company would pay the cost of moving him and his family back to Wales. Thomas, who was then forty-four, left Wales in June

1839 and in January 1840 he blew the first anthracite furnace in the United States. By 1856, anthracite furnaces were producing one half of the USA's pig iron. One leading iron master, who told Thomas, 'I will eat all the iron you make with anthracite,' was invited to a dinner cooked, so it was said, in the new furnace. In America, David Thomas received the acclaim that Crane and his subsequent move overseas appear to have denied him in Wales. In 1874 he was elected president of the American Ironmasters Convention, and, after the Civil War, he ran as a Republican candidate for Congress.

In Wales, efforts to extend the market for anthracite continued, its promoters dismayed that so remarkable a coal could have such limited market appeal. To sell a truckload of anthracite in the first half of the nineteenth century, lamented W H Jones, the historian of the port of Swansea, took as much effort as to sell a thousand tons of steam coal. An obvious avenue to explore was steam-raising. Anthracite was used in stationary steam engines at the anthracite collieries, yet all efforts to extend that use to mobile engines – the logical next step – had failed. The first trial was in 1804, when anthracite raised the steam for Richard Trevithick's patent engine at Penydarren. The *Cambrian* reported that the engine ran 'with the greatest of exactness' for six hours, consuming less than two hundredweight of coal. But Trevithick's locomotive was so heavy that it broke the rails and was declared impractical. Thirty-four years later, anthracite was used on a trial run of the Manchester-Liverpool Railway. The coal was found to do 'very good duty,' neither blocking the pipes and tubes, as was the case with coke, nor requiring much, if any, stoking. It was also economical; when hauling loaded wagons, the locomotive consumed five and a half hundredweights of anthracite against the customary seven and a half hundredweights of coke. Yet neither the Manchester-Liverpool nor any other railway company, possibly through inadequate publicity, made any move to adopt it. The results were noted in the press but had such little impact that even owners of Welsh steam and semi-bituminous coals complained that trials in which their coals were held to be superior were of little benefit to them.

For steamships, anthracite appeared to be an ideal fuel. It produced only small amounts of ash or clinker, was clean to handle and, unlike the more sulphurous and more friable bituminous coals, it was unlikely to combust spontaneously. As a hard, dense coal with a high calorific value, it also took up much less stowage space than most other coals, it would not crumble under the constant attrition from the movement of a ship at sea, and in the tropics it would not deteriorate. And, finally, if used in Admiralty vessels in wartime it would leave no tell-tale plume of smoke to give away the ship's position. In anticipation of a demand for steamship coal at Milford Haven, Dr Edward Frankland, an eminent Victorian scientist, who would found the Institute of Chemistry, was asked in the early 1850s to assess the steam-raising power of anthracites from Saundersfoot and the Gwendraeth valley. He concluded that their capacity to evaporate water, and produce steam, was as great as that of the best steam coals. In his tests, Saundersfoot anthracite scored only fractionally lower than the steam coals of Neath Abbey, and it did so without stoking. Under working conditions, he inferred, anthracite would score higher because stokers could not be expected at all times to keep steam coals burning at maximum efficiency.

The first attempts to use anthracite for steam navigation in Britain, of which few records have survived, were on a small vessel, named *Anthracite,* on the Thames, in 1835. The first large scale attempt was on the *Washington*, an American Line steamship plying between Southampton and New York. Loaded with 600 tons of anthracite, the vessel left Southampton in 1847, under what were described as magnificent, fan-driven fires, but within a few hours she had to turn back, her furnace bars destroyed by the great heat. In 1853 and 1854 anthracite was used without artificial draught in the *Liverno* and *Genova*, two steamers owned by a Liverpool company that traded with Mediterranean ports. The company reported a great success: 'Anthracite has proved to be a twofold saving in regard of economy of space, and to a very large saving in the consumption.' The saving of stowage amounted to 20 percent and the reduction in consumption to 40-50 percent, thus scotching the charge that steamships would be unable to carry enough coal to complete long voyages. But not the least of the benefits of anthracite, the report continued, was 'its great cleanliness and entire freedom from smoke.' The Mediterranean trade, however, proved unprofitable and after two years McLarty and Co. discontinued the service.

Anthracite was also used on HM yachts *Fairy* and *Victoria and Albert* on voyages between Holyhead and Dublin. On 7 July 1853, the *Times* reported, ponderously: 'Her Majesty and the Court, as well as the officers of the yacht, will have a more comfortable voyage this trip than hitherto, owing to the use of the anthracite fuel with Colonel Coffin's steam jets fitted to her furnaces, by which no smoke or ashes issue from the funnel, thus abolishing the nuisances of smuts in the eyes and on the clothes of all on deck, and covering the decks with the dust from the flues which the ordinary coal throws upon them.' The Queen was said to have been so charmed with the clean-burning attributes of anthracite that she forbade the use of any other fuel when she was on board.

Other steamships also experimented with anthracite but in no case was use of the fuel continued. In 1866, J M Child, owner of the Bonvilles Court Colliery, Pembrokeshire, reported that I K Brunel's *Great Britain*, loaded with Saundersfoot anthracite, had steamed to Australia and, on arrival, had nearly enough coal for the return voyage. He also accused the owners of the steamships the *Royal Charter* and the *Faith*, in which anthracite was reported to have been used successfully, of having interests in steam coal collieries. But in spite of these apparent successes, the bitter truth seems to have been that to burn well Welsh anthracite needed either an artificial draught, in which case it burned so hot that it melted the bars, or a grate or burning surface so large that ships and locomotives could not easily accommodate it. Several patents involving circulating air or water for protecting the grates and bars, were registered in the middle years of the century. In 1847, Messrs. Kymer and Kirk, owners of an anthracite colliery in the Gwendraeth Valley, took out a patent for a water grate in which the grate and the bars were cooled by circulating water. But the design was not practicable and there were few, if any, takers. Thirty years later, in a series of trials at a foundry in Swansea, fans and steam jets forced cold air through the hollowed, perforated bars of specially constructed grates. The cold air was meant to cool the bars and the blast to aid combustion. The patentees reported that several works adopted their patent for their stationary engines, but there was no general application.

In Great Britain, the blow that ended all hope for using anthracite in steamships was delivered by the Admiralty in 1880. After a series of trials, it concluded that anthracite was suitable only for stationary engines where all that was required was a good general draught. At sea there was not enough fresh water to supply both the boilers, that provided steam for the engines, as well as cooling mechanisms for the bars and grates of the furnaces. Yet, while most of the efforts in Britain to increase the use of anthracite either failed or were thwarted, across the Atlantic anthracite had become a celebrated fuel, widely used in blast furnaces, locomotives and steamships as well as in stationary engines and domestic cook-stoves. Chemical analysis, appearance and general physical characteristics indicated that Welsh and Pennsylvanian anthracites were similar, suggesting that the contrasting fortunes of the coals might have little connection with their chemical or physical make-up. As a possible explanation of the anomaly, John Percy, an eminent chemist and metallurgist with close connections to Swansea and the copper industry, pointed to the property of decrepitation, or crumbling, that some varieties of Welsh anthracite possessed 'in an extraordinary degree.' By blocking the grate, ash and crumbling coal might have impeded the draught. But even allowing for John Percy's caveat, it seems likely that culture and need, a combination of nineteenth century American 'can do' attitudes and a relative shortage of good steam coal, were stronger determinants than differences in the quality of the coals. The vast anthracite fields of Pennsylvania that the geologist William Logan, on a visit in 1841, declared could power the entire industrial world, could not remain fallow indefinitely. American steamship companies reported marked successes with Pennsylvanian anthracite, and the new Bessemer furnaces, which revolutionized the making of steel, were fuelled by it. To provide the larger grate surface that anthracite needed to burn without an artificial draught, Americans designed the camel or hump-backed locomotive that allowed the grate to be positioned above, rather than between the frame and the wheels. The smaller sizes of anthracite did not burn well in the long, narrow fireboxes located between the frames. The new arrangement, which burned culm as well as small coal, meant that the driver had to sit in front of the firebox furnace, above the whirling side rods, while the fireman stood on a narrow platform at the back, with very little protection from the weather. The first Camelback reported annual fuel savings of two thousand dollars, more than thirty thousand in present-day money. After a journey on the Delaware, Lackawanna & Western Railroad, known colloquially as the Lackawanna or Anthracite Road, Mark Twain reported that his white duck suit was just as white at the end of the journey as at the beginning. The company siezed upon the image of sparkling whiteness and, substituting a demure 'Gibson Girl' for Mark Twain, produced a seemingly endless series of jingles for a memorable billboard campaign:

> Says Phoebe Snow,
> About to go
> Upon a trip
> To Buffalo:
> "My gown stays white
> From morn till night
> Upon the Road of Anthracite"

And:

> This is the Maiden all in Lawn
> Who boarded the train one early morn
> That runs on the Road of Anthracite

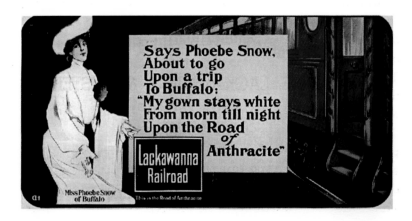

and when she left the train that night
she found to her surprised delight
hard Coal had kept her dress still bright

The closing of the ironworks and the rejection of anthracite by the Royal Navy and British steam shipping in general were blows from which anthracite did not recover until late in the century. But more important in the long run than the loss of one market and the failure to find new ones,

**Lackawanna Railroad**

THIS IS THE ROAD OF ANTHRACITE

This is the Maiden all in Lawn
Who boarded the train one early morn,
That runs on the Road of Anthracite
and when she left the train that night
she found to her surprised delight
hard Coal had kept her dress still bright

was the concurrent development of a system of transportation that allowed anthracite miners and entrepreneurs to penetrate previously inaccessible areas. And when the market did eventually turn in anthracite's favour, it allowed them to increase the volume and tempo of shipping to the ports. Canals had served the industry well, but as a means of transportation they were obviously limited. Movement was slow, and unloading was both cumbersome and labour intensive. The remedy, provided first by Trevithick and then by George Stephenson, was to apply steam rather than horsepower to the wagons on the tram or railroads. Although tram roads had shown that heavy loads could be transported with far less effort than before, most people looked on them simply as a way to move produce to the nearest canal. While steam engines were used to draw water and coal up mine shafts, no one, until Trevithick and Stephenson, conceived of a mobile steam engine that could pull trams or wagons along a track. The benefits of a railway to the Tawe, and by extension to all the valleys, was the set essay subject for the 1860 Ystalyfera eisteddfod. The prize-winning essay, printed in the popular magazine *Gardd y Gweithiwr*, was a ringing condemnation of the limitations of canals. At the best of times, according to the author, canals were slow and cumbersome and, at the worst, they were unusable. Summer droughts could beach the barges in shallow water and heavy winter frosts, such as those in 1854, could lock them in ice for days or even weeks at a time. Cargoes could also be damaged from exposure to heavy rains or by water bursting into the boat. For coal, this was not a serious hazard but for imported foodstuffs it could be ruinous. Most damaging to coal was the handling required. Coal was inevitably broken, and the small lost, when barges were loaded either by chute or wheelbarrow. After a few miles, and several locks, the small, which accumulated at the bottom of the barge, would be sludge and therefore useless for the furnace and of no interest to the exporter.

The Nedd, the Tawe and the Gwendraeth Valleys would have railways by the 1860s, but the earliest ones were to places which the canals and tram roads had not served. The first was a line along the Llwchwr valley from Llanelli to Pontardulais, built in 1839, that in 1842 reached up the valley to Pantyffynon and Ammanford, and along the Amman valley to Garnant and Brynaman. The rich outcrops of the Amman had previously been worked only in small patches and by a handful of small levels. The line opened up the valley for the first time and, to the consternation of Swansea, converted Llanelli into a coal port. In 1851, the Vale of Neath Railway Company opened a broad gauge line from Neath to Aberdare, and shortly thereafter to Merthyr. The main object was to wrest from the port of Cardiff some of the steam coal trade of the Aberdare valley. Whereas the Neath canal, with its locks, horses and barges, had been a bucolic, Constable-like addition to the valley, the railway was a harbinger of the new industrial age. An old manservant of Ynysygerwn prophesied that the cows would withhold their milk, the calves would die, and the hills turn red from drought:

> Ni fydd dim llaeth gan wartheg mwyn
> Daw'r twyni'n goch gan sychyn;
> Yn lloi yn feirw ar a waen
> O ofn y tram a'r injin!

Likewise, the landlord of the Plough Inn at Abertwrch thought smoke and steam passing so close to the house would destroy the horses in the stables, while Sian Glover, who lived in a cottage at Pont Walby above Glynneath, feared that the puff of the engine would sour the contents of the milk pails from Llanfaglan at the mouth of the valley to Pencaedrain at its head.

In 1860, the Swansea Vale Railway Company opened a line from Swansea to Pontardawe and the following year extended it to Ystalyfera. In 1862 an extension along the Twrch valley met the Llanelli line at Brynaman. It took mining into the heart of the anthracite region and, by tapping Amman valley coal, solidified Swansea's position as the anthracite port. A line from Neath to Coelbren, built by the Neath and Brecon Railway Company in 1867, opened the Dulais valley, while a branch line from Coelbren to Ystalyfera connected the Dulais and the Nedd with the Tawe. A tramway had been planned to run from the Neath canal up the Dulais valley toward Creunant, and although authorized in 1826, the tramway was never constructed and the Dulais valley was left comparatively remote and untapped. The Gwendraeth valley, the last to be canalised, was also the last of the main valleys to be served by a railway. In 1869, the Gwendraeth Valley Railway Company opened a line, built along the old Gwendraeth valley canal, from Burry Port to Cwmmawr, at the head of the valley. The railways eventually brought into production the remote eastern reaches of the anthracite region with the building of a line from Briton Ferry to Abercregan and Glyncorrwg, in the upper reaches of the Afan valley. Faulting had preserved an anthracitic inlier of the lower coal series but the coals weren't mined until 1905. The railways, too, as had the canals before them, also stimulated production of the bituminous and steam coals nearer the coast. Smelters and steam engines at home and abroad had always generated a steady demand, but with easier access to the coast, exports from Swansea and Llanelli increased substantially.

The greatest beneficiary in the long run, however, was the anthracite trade. With a comprehensive network of rail lines, complemented by improvements in the docks at Burry Port, Llanelli, Swansea and Briton Ferry, the anthracite region was poised for export to world markets. The canals were taken over by the railway companies, and if not filled in – like the Gwendraeth canal – had comparatively little use thereafter. Encouraged by the tentacle-like reach of the railways, developers, between 1870 and 1873, opened new drifts on the east side of the Gwendraeth valley, where the seams of the Lower Coal Series dip toward the centre of the basin beneath the Pennant sandstone. At the same time, the first deep shafts were sunk in the Dulais valley, where there had been a small coal and iron industry. The first struck a serious, but unspecified, disturbance at sixty feet, and had to be abandoned, but the entrepreneur, David Bevan, whom the *Cambrian* described as the 'enterprising and spirited proprietor of the Cadoxton Steam Coal Collieries,' was not discouraged. In March 1872, his eldest daughter, Isabella, cut the first sod for a new shaft two hundred yards farther down the valley, within a mile or so of Onllwyn. The district, of scattered farms, was known simply as Cwmdulais, the earlier small industrial population having dispersed following the collapse of John Williams' iron enterprise in 1861. Miss Bevan's implement was an inscribed silver spade and her accompaniment the brass band of 17th Glamorganshire Royal Volunteers. The band, playing against a backdrop of showy bunting and the firing of artillery, 'rendered', so one report ran, 'the otherwise lonely valley quite jubilant.' Sinking was completed in 1875 with the striking of the nine foot seam at a depth of 630 feet. The new pit, whom some wanted to name Brynycae, in acknowledgement of the topography, was named Seven Sisters after David Bevan's seven daughters. The Seven Sisters pit was the beginning of the 'down-dip' migration of anthracite mining, the movement away from outcrop working on the northern edge of the coalfield, and in the river valleys, to exploitation of seams in the lower coal measures near the deep centre of the coal basin. The Seven Sisters sinking was followed in the early 1890s by the sinking, through the Pennant cover, of the Glyncastle pit in a tributary valley of the Nedd east of Resolfen. Located in a valley bottom where the Pennant cover was at its thinnest, Glyncastle was the first pit to break through the half-mile thick sandstone barrier. At roughly the same time, there were also sinkings at Great Mountain in the Gwendraeth Valley, and at Gwauncaegurwen in the Amman Valley, to exploit seams that could not be reached by drifts.

Yet in spite of the opening of new drifts and pits, in the late 1880s neither the demand nor the output of anthracite in south Wales was commensurately greater than it had been in the 1850s. While investment, spurred by the endorsements of the Admiralty and steamship owners, poured into the steam coal region of the eastern valleys, anthracite remained a comparative Cinderella. Most of the collieries were still small-scale drifts, employing at most a few hundred men, and the market remained a specialised one. At the 1880 British Association meeting at Swansea, Charles H Perkins could speak of a magnificent fuel 'shunned and despised.' The south Welsh anthracite field was by far the best source of good anthracite in Western Europe and all parts of it were within a short rail haul of the ports, distances seldom exceeding twenty miles and often as short as ten. With 90 percent of the British production – Scotland was its only competitor – it also had a virtual monopoly of the anthracite trade of western Europe. Perkins disparaged the English prejudice of according comfort only to a blazing fire in an open grate, and referred to Hussey Vivian's efforts to promote the virtues of the Canadian stove in his *Notes on a Tour in America*, published in 1877. Like Perkins, Vivian was dismayed by the neglect of Welsh anthracite. On the tour, he visited the great anthracite fields of Pennsylvania, noting that their one disadvantage was distance from navigable water. We, on the other hand, he asserted, possess the finest anthracite in the world, and although within sight of the sea, it lies almost unworked. Vivian examined metal stoves and, in Pennsylvania, he visited 'the great anthracite consuming city of Philadelphia,' contrasting its relative smokelessness with London's pollutant-laced air.

In Canada, he spent some time in Hamilton, Ontario, the 'Swindon of Canada', as he described it, and the home of a self-feeding anthracite stove that burned little coal with even less attention. Lit in the Autumn and put out in the spring, it threw out a great and uniform heat. And if placed in the passages and entrances of houses, and the pipes carried through the living rooms into the chimneys, it would heat the entire building. The loudest praises came from his landlady in Hamilton, a Lancashire woman who had lived in Brecon and emigrated to Canada two years earlier. Like Charles Perkins, she thought that abundant and uniform heat were a lot to give up for that curiously English pleasure of poking the fire. Vivian urged Welsh anthracite colliery owners to promote the Canadian stove and added that he had done his bit by ordering several that he hoped would arrive and be in full blast in his home before Christmas. Ironically, the conversion from the European ceramic stove to the enclosed anthracite-burning metal stove had been made possible by the invention of cast iron, a product readily available in the Welsh coal-mining valleys. Strong, and able to withstand high temperatures without damage, cast iron, which is also an effective conductor and radiator of heat, was an ideal material for stoves. A skilled patternmaker could also make a stove as intricate and as attractive as one wished. 'To this day,' remarked Charles Perkins, nonplussed by the British resistance to anthracite and stoves, 'the use of anthracite in this country is practically confined to malting, hop drying, and lime burning.'

But within a few years of the 1880 Swansea British Association meeting there would be a great expansion of the export market. According R L Sails of Swansea, the first break in the European resistance to anthracite as a domestic fuel occurred in 1883, with the discovery that it was ideally suited for closed Scandinavian stoves. It ushered in a change from the marketing of large, unbroken anthracite, which formed the bulk of the trade, to sized anthracite, broken and graded for both domestic and industrial consumers. The first consignments were small parcels of 'nuts', broken with hammer and chisel, hand screened and packed in sacks that were then sent as samples to Berlin, Hamburg and Cologne. They were distributed free in order to demonstrate the great heating and lasting power of Welsh anthracite. These were followed by shipments to Sweden, France, Holland and Denmark in 1885, and later the Channel Islands. The hand-breaking of the large coal, which produced a great deal of small, was quickly superseded by machine breaking that reduced the amount of waste. The expansion of the European export market owed much to Fred Cleeves, 'father of the anthracite trade', who in the 1880s and 90s was the sales agent for the Gwauncaegurwen collieries.

The next major change came when importers abroad found it to their advantage to break the coal at the home port. After the stresses of the voyage, in which there was always some breakage, the coal had to be screened again anyway, and, with the breakers at the port of importation, the coal could be broken into the sizes required by the market. In France, the largest of the European importers, most of the sizing occurred in merchants' storage yards at Le Havre and Rouen. French consumers preferred the coals of the Gwendraeth Valley. Breaking produced large quantities of small or duff, which the French made into briquettes known as 'boulets'. For the greenhouse markets of the Channel Islands and Holland, large anthracite was preferred, for its slow-burning qualities. Sails observed, disappointedly, that the British had contributed little to the renaissance, even though an ordinary grate with brick sides and back, close bars and a fair draught could produce as cheerful a fire as could be desired. Even without help from the home fires, anthracite production increased from 360,000 tons in 1865 to more than 1,500,000 in 1895. By 1913 this had increased to almost 5 million and markets extended to places as distant as the Near East, West Africa and Central and South America. There was an accompanying increase in employment, the number of miners doubling from roughly nine thousand to more than eighteen thousand. But, according to the industrialist Sir Alfred Mond, whose combine (Amalgamated Anthracite) would control the anthracite industry by the late 1920s, more needed to be done. Addressing the Swansea Chamber of Commerce in 1922, when he was then Minister of Health, he pronounced that the difficulties of marketing anthracite, which heated the furnaces in his nickel refinery at Clydach, could only be ascribed to inadequate promotion and the absence of an 'eloquent mouthpiece'.

In response to Sir Alfred's challenge, and the promotion of his own anthracite combine, the 1920s saw the dramatic opening of a major new market. In 1913/14, the Canadian market, of 50,000 tons, was so small that H S Jevons, in his book on the British coal trade, 1914, did not mention it. By 1923 exports had risen to more than one million tons, and kept on rising. Canada's coal resources were considerable but, in British Columbia, Alberta, Saskatchewan and Nova Scotia, they were half a continent away from the urban-industrial heartland of Southern Ontario and southern Quebec. On his return to Canada in 1842, as the founding director of the Canadian Geological Survey, William Logan had been pressed hard to find coal, but he could find none closer to the country's heartland than Nova Scotia. Much more convenient to the towns and cities of southern Ontario and southern Quebec were the coalfields of Pennsylvania, and Canadian consumers, who favoured anthracite almost exclusively, for the most part burned Pennsylvanian coal.

A series of strikes in eastern Pennsylvania, however, combined with the aggressive marketing of Welsh anthracite by Dominions Secretary J H (Jimmy) Thomas and the anthracite companies, turned Canadian attention towards south Wales. In 1922/23, tours of Canada and the eastern United States by one of Fred Cleeves' 'best men', and by Sir D R Llewellyn of the Firm Llewellyn, Merret & Price, secured contracts for Welsh anthracite and led to the construction of breaking and sizing plants in Montreal and Quebec. Cleeves now represented the Mond Combine, and the salesman whom he had despatched to Canada was soon followed by Sir Alfred Mond himself. In 1924 Welsh and Canadian interests combined to found the Canadian Welsh Anthracite Company that built its own sizing and screening plant in Montreal. In an equally bold move, Amalgamated Anthracite, in 1924, invited 170 Canadian newspaper and magazine editors to Swansea so that they might view collieries and examine the quality of the coal. In that same year, Amalgamated Anthracite also exhibited at Wembley.

In the North American market, Welsh anthracite producers held two advantages, one real and the other debatable, over their Pennsylvania rivals. Welsh anthracite could be delivered by ship and it was considered superior to the Pennsylvanian. The cities of the north-east lay either on the eastern seaboard, or along the St Lawrence River and the Great Lakes. Bulk freight rates by water were so much lower than overland rates that it was, for example, far cheaper to send coal by ship from Swansea to Quebec or Montreal, a distance of 2800 or 2900 miles, than by rail to London. Delivery of Pennsylvanian anthracite by rail to Ontario and Quebec cost $4 a ton, while Welsh anthracite shipped via the St Lawrence and Lake Ontario from Swansea or Llanelli to Quebec City, Montreal and Toronto cost $2.50 per ton. So competitive were transatlantic shipping rates with American rail rates that Welsh exporters were able to undersell Pennsylvanian anthracite in New Brunswick and the New England states, despite lower production costs in the thick, relatively undisturbed Pennsylvania seams.

The Canadian trade, confined to the ice-free season, when the St Lawrence was open and the North Atlantic relatively tranquil, also dovetailed nicely with the chiefly winter trade to Europe. To ensure that there would be no seasonal lay-offs at the Tumble colliery, the surface superintendent at the mine built a reinforced retaining wall between the railway embankment and the mine to create a storage space for hundreds of thousands of tons of coal. As soon as the St Lawrence opened, streams of coal were directed down long lengths of corrugated sheeting into waiting trucks. To reduce turn-around times for the coal-carrying vessels, each day trainloads of coal left for Llanelli and Swansea. A priceless asset of the Canadian trade, as of the Cornish copper ore trade two centuries earlier, was the availability of a back carriage: in this case, hard wheat from the Canadian prairies that had been stockpiled in granaries and elevators over the winter. Like hard wheat, anthracite was not affected by deep cold and, unlike the softer coals, it did not break down in the wind and the rain.

Like the Europeans, Canadians preferred sized anthracite, chiefly of the smaller kinds, but in all countries there was a preference for graded and washed varieties. Washing, to remove clay, slate and coal dust, gave anthracite a clean, shiny, more metallic look that, so the promoters fervently hoped, would suggest to consumers that hard coal was superior to soft. The lumps were tailored for specific energy needs: nuts for stoves and cookers and domestic central heating furnaces, grains and peas for large central-heating plants. Other sizes were egg coal, rice coal and buckwheat coal. Canadians and Scandinavians perfected the cast-iron anthracite stove, embellishing it with fittings of copper, nickel and brass and using it for cooking and heating water as well as primary heat. Feet could be warmed on the surrounding chrome rails and spirits raised by the sight of glowing coals behind small windows of mica or isinglass in the doors. Only admirers of female beauty complained, the poet and writer Arthur Hugh Clough attributing the parchment-like skins of aging American women to long exposure to the dry heat given off by anthracite furnaces and stoves.

The effect of burgeoning new markets was to attract investment, primarily from limited liability companies who acquired existing collieries and opened new ones. Unlike the tidal wave of capital that engulfed the eastern, steam coal valleys, amounts and enterprises were small at first. Most companies owned only one colliery. But the steady expansion of the anthracite market after World War I induced a change that had been threatening for twenty years. Anthracite, as the economic geographer I L Griffiths pointed out, was a coal with a difference. Smoke-free, highly calorific, and clean to handle, it was unique among coals, and 90 percent of British production was confined to a corner of south Wales. Conditions were ripe for combination or amalgamation. From being an industry of generally small, individually owned collieries – in 1921 there were eighty-four collieries owned by fifty-three different companies – it became, through a series of amalgamations between 1924 and 1928, a virtual monolith, with 70 percent of production under the control of a single company, Amalgamated Anthracite.

With capital to invest, the amalgamated companies revived the quest for south-west Wales's equivalent of El Dorado, the rich anthracite veins of the lower coal measures that lay beneath the thick cap of Pennant sandstone. The Glyncastle sinking in the Nedd valley in the early 1890s had been the only down dip sinking to break through the Pennant barrier. Boreholes were sunk at Cwmgors, some three miles south of Gwauncaegurwen, and in the lower Dulais valley, a mile and a half downriver from Creunant. No shaft was sunk at Cwmgors, despite favourable borehole results, but in the Dulais valley the sinking eventually struck gold. In 1926, Amalgamated Anthracite of Ammanford took over the sinking operation at Cefn Coed, where three earlier attempts had failed to break through the hard Blue Pennant Sandstone, and raised its first coal in 1930. Tapping seams down to 2500 feet, half a mile below ground level, Cefn Coed was the deepest anthracite mine in the world. The mine prospered for twenty years, but mining at those depths in a very gassy pit took an inevitable toll. Firedamp explosions, roof falls, and shaft accidents were commonplace at first, picking off colliers at a rate that earned it the nickname 'The Slaughterhouse'.

The years immediately following World War II saw the completion, kingdom-wide, of the processes of rationalization and amalgamation. In 1947, the Labour Government nationalized the entire British coal industry. In south-west Wales, the closure of inefficient collieries continued, but at a faster pace. Many of the old drifts, badly laid out and, because of the long roadways, increasingly difficult to maintain and ventilate, had been extended well beyond their economic limit. The long-term solution was to close the inefficient collieries, improve the still viable ones, and revive efforts to tap seams beneath the Pennant sandstone; the latter required capital investment on an unprecedented scale.

The sinkings at Cynheidre, in the Gwendraeth valley, and at Abernant, just south of Cwmgors, were the largest single investments ever made in mining in south Wales. Boreholes at Cynheidre were sunk in 1949 and shaft sinking began in 1954. Two shafts were sunk to 2280 feet and coal was worked both at this level and in seams at 1680 and 1980 feet. Abernant, just a mile south of Cwmgors, was a similar development. Between 1955 and 1958, shafts were sunk to a depth of more than three thousand feet and the coal, as at Cynheidre, worked on several levels.

Although smaller collieries managed to coexist with the Leviathans, many were closed, including most of those in the Gwendraeth valley. Many minuscule, private operations, however, employing fewer than 31 men, were allowed, under special licence, to operate beneath the wing of the National Coal Board. With a small outlay, a strictly local market, and sometimes intermittent working, they perpetuated the part-time farmer-miner tradition of the anthracite coalfield. But the general effect of the closures and the opening of giant mines was to change wholesale the pattern of employment. Whereas in the past each colliery had drawn its workforce from the village or the neighbourhood, the reach of Cefn

Coed, Cynheidre and Abernant extended to Swansea, Morriston, Neath and Port Talbot, drawing colliers from the semi-bituminous region whose mines, closely tied to the non ferrous metal industries, had suffered setbacks during the interwar years. The Leviathans may have eased a redundancy problem in the coastal belt, but they were, as the manager of a small, locally-manned colliery, remarked, 'collieries without a heart.'

# THE COLLIER
# AND CONDITIONS
# OF WORK

WHILE DIGGING FOR COAL was seen as a country, or bucolic, activity, mining suffered no stigma greater than that associated with all forms of manual labour. On landed estates in coal-bearing districts, the labourers and tenant farmers were often part-time colliers. To guarantee labour for their collieries in the 1770s, the Phillips family of Picton Castle, Pembrokeshire, insisted in their leases that tenants, when needed, should work in the landlord's mines. Just as horses were expected to haul coal and culm as well as pull harrows and ploughs, so men and, in places, women combined work in the fields and in the collieries. The account books of Rees Williams of Aberpergwm, in the Nedd valley, show that in the 1790s he gave occasional employment to men both on his farm and at his colliery. Evan Richards, in 1799, earned fifteen shillings for six days mowing and one pound ten shillings for fifteen days coal work. In early days, there were even suggestions of a feudal relationship between master and man: '*Pan own i'n gwithio Aberpergwm*' (When I worked at Aberpergwm), was often the proud as well as identifying prelude to an anecdote about mining. In the neighbouring Dulais valley, the owner of the Onllwyn colliery, when he had orders to fill, had to go around the farms to ask farmers and labourers to come to work. In Pembrokeshire, the most agricultural of the coalfield counties, the farmer-collier dualism persisted until the late nineteenth century. The collieries were small and, because many were worked intermittently, it was possible to combine farming, or farm work, with mining. At a typical small mine, as on a small farm or smallholding, the whole family participated: the men and boys worked underground and the women wound up the coal and unloaded it.

Because Pembrokeshire had no canals, carters from the farms also carried coal to the ports. The result of these interchanges, Herbert Mackworth, HM Inspector of Mines, remarked in 1854, 'Is that the Pembrokeshire collier differs but little in any respect from the agricultural labourer, and his gains but little exceed the payment for work on the surface of the ground.'

But in the larger and more heavily capitalized mines of Carmarthenshire and west Glamorgan, there was a greater dependence on full-time, specialized workers. Gerald Gabb, the Swansea historian, has found evidence in church and civic records to suggest that by the late sixteenth century a class of colliers was emerging. Churchwarden accounts for 1558 and 1584 contain entries for the wives of coalminers; one refers to the wife of John Morice, 'colyer', and the other to the wife of Griffith, 'colier'. In sixteenth and seventeenth century leases, several Neath and Swansea lessees are described as colliers, and by 1747 John Grey could claim that he had been a collier for thirty years, working first for the Mackworths and then for Robert Morris. Other Swansea men avowed that they had been 'coalworkers since the beginning of their labours.'

From the outset, wage-earning coal workers were regarded with suspicion. Many had come from the Midlands and the North of England, and at Neath they lived apart in the Mera, in cottages known as Miners Row, which had been built for them by Sir Humphrey Mackworth. As strangers, they were sitting targets for disgruntled and malevolent natives. At Neath, in bad times, they were vilified as drunkards and 'disorderly livers' with no other ambition than to impregnate local women. At Swansea, too, relations seem to have been uneasy. In February 1627, 'Mychell the colyer and his wyff' were among twenty strangers expelled from the house of Will Dene. In cases of suspect lessees or employees, it was customary for the landlord or employer to act as guarantor. In November 1609, Robert Rogers agreed to reimburse the Swansea corporation for any expenses incurred against the corporation by Evan ap Owen, collier and his family. In August 1624, Rowland Rees and Roger Miricke provided the same service for 'William Edwardes, colier'.

# The Collier and Conditions of Work

Full-time colliers worked underground in pits and drifts, not in surface diggings, and in time they took on the colour of their product, both literally and metaphorically. Faces and hands and, if they worked with their shirts off, even bodies became permanently stained with coal dust, and, no matter how skilled the collier, he would never command the respect accorded the ore miner and the metalworker. Coal was simply an unimproved, degradable fuel, whereas the mineral ores, which were scarcer and more difficult to find and to mine, commanded the attention of near shaman-like metalworkers. Coalmining, on the other hand, was noted for its danger rather than its skill. Finding the buried seams, judging the quality of the coal, interpreting the throws or faults, and dialing or laying out the mine, might have been regarded as arts, but the work itself was seen as toil. For more than five hundred years the tools and the techniques of mining hardly changed. An account book for the lordship of Gower, 1400, has expenditures for the mending of barrows, the making of picks and the refitting of old ones, and for candles. Add a shovel, an axe, a hand-borer for drilling holes and you have the toolkit of a nineteenth century miner. The miner in the famous sixteenth century Miner's Brass at All Saints Church in Newland, Gloucestershire, has a hod and a pick and, in his mouth, a candlestick. A collier's tallow candle was three to four inches long and provided light for an hour or two; larger candles, often in clay shields to protect them from draughts, lit the roadways and lasted for a shift.

In south Wales, as elsewhere, the collier was the lowest paid of the industrial workers, ahead of the common labourer and the farm worker but behind the copper man, the iron and the tinplate worker. He was not a member of Hobsbawm's aristocracy of labour. On his way to work, when there were few people about, he might have been sprightly, fresh and clean but on his return, in the days before pithead baths, he was blackened with coal dust, red-eyed and leaden-footed. In summer, he trudged home in broad daylight. In 1910, six Glasgow miners, accused of violating a corporation by-law, pleaded guilty to a complaint by a tram conductor that they were travelling 'in clothing which... might soil or injure the car or the dress of the passengers.' Working in Stygian darkness hundreds of feet below the surface, and at coalfaces that could be a mile or two from the entrance to a drift or the bottom of a shaft, colliers appeared to live troglodytic lives, surfacing periodically for air and sunshine. Even William Cobbett, who understood labour and labourers, assumed that colliers lived at least seasonally underground. In the coalfield itself, 'underground' was a freighted word, signifying a private, enclosed world made up of networks of great complexity and sometimes astonishing length. It is said, for example, to have been possible to walk underground from Bryncoch colliery, just west of Neath and on the eastern side of the Drumau mountain, to Glais in the Tawe valley, via the Main, Cwmdu, Birchgrove, and Graigola collieries, emerging at the surface through one of the drifts at the latter, a distance of ten miles. When referring, in an essay written in the 1860s, to miners at the head of the Tawe valley in the late eighteenth century, Thomas Levi found it necessary to add – for readers outside the coalfield – that the miners were not dwarves or pygmies, but men of normal stature and strength. To emphasise the point he presented an anecdote involving two mythically strong miners of that time, who rode to Neath and, returning later than they intended, found the toll gates shut and the gate-keeper in bed. They resolved the dilemma by joining hands under their horses' bellies and lifting them over the gate. The perception that miners occupied a subterranean world from which they seldom emerged persisted until the end of the nineteenth century. At a pub in Kent, John Wilson, the Durham miner's union leader, is said to have surprised the barman with the disclosure that he did not actually live underground.

Distinctiveness of dress or habit might have given the collier more cachet, but his standard work clothes in the nineteenth century and for much of the twentieth were a cloth cap, an old scarf or muffler, a worn suit jacket and waistcoat, flannel shirt and hard-wearing trousers, moleskin for preference, and strong boots. Good Welsh wool flannel, which was sold at the spring and autumn fairs, absorbed sweat and did not, unlike some of the shoddier shop flannel, become clammy and cold. Inside his coat were sewn big pockets to hold his food box and water jack. To make kneeling easier, the trousers were tied with a piece of string below the knee and held up by a leather belt. For women, who worked on the screens and the spoil banks, the standard dress was boots, black stockings, a long flannel dress and a large apron. To protect their hair from coal dust, they tied scarves tightly across the forehead and down to the chin. There is no evidence that Welsh colliers, unlike English pitmen and Andean copper miners, ever indulged in colourful holiday dress. Until greyed over by Methodist piety, on Sundays and statutory holidays, Northumberland pitmen are said to have worn flowered waistcoats, 'posy vests' cut short to show an inch or two of shirt over the waist-band, plush or velveteen breeches fastened at the knees with coloured ribbons, long coloured stockings of pink, purple or blue, clocked up to the knees, and stout shoes or laced boots. Younger colliers curled their hair at the temples, by turning it around pieces of lead tied with paper, and – leaving a fringe of curls – covered their heads with a headscarf or a round hat.

Popular misapprehensions of the coalminer in the nineteenth century were reinforced by writers obliged to produce dramatic copy. Among the most culpable was J R Leifchild, author of books on both coal (*Our Coal and Our Coal-Pits*, 1856) and copper mining. Leifchild's

*Colliers at the Seven Sisters Colliery, 1908. SWCC, Swansea University.*

*Colliers at the Cwmmawr Colliery. SWCC, Swansea University.*

miner is a gargoyle: 'His [the miner's] stature is diminutive, his figure disproportionate and misshapen; his legs being much bowed; his chest protruding... His arms are long, and oddly suspended. His countenance is not less striking than his figure; his cheeks are generally hollow, his brow overhanging, his cheekbones high, his forehead low and retreating; nor is his appearance healthful; his habit is tainted with scrofula.' While allowing that people may be shaped by their labours, Leifchild's description is revealingly eugenic. The long, oddly hung arms, the high cheekbones, the overhanging brow, and the low retreating forehead place the miner disturbingly close to the anthropoids. Most misshapen of all, to Liefchild's eyes, were the men who worked at the coalface: 'A hewer will be distinguished by his incurvation of body, inclining to the shape of a note of interrogation. His legs will have a graceful bow, only it will be in the wrong direction. His chest will protrude like that of a pigeon. His eye will have the glance of a hawk half-awake, and his face somewhat the look of a pound of candles.'

Just as dismissive of the collier was Swansea's Dr Thomas Williams,

*Colliers at the Brynhenllys Colliery. SWCC, Swansea University.*

an expert on diseases of the lungs who, a year before the publication of Leifchild's book, had been asked by the Council of Health in Hamburg to prepare a report upon the effects of copper smoke on health. Williams may not have been directly in the pay of Swansea's copper masters but he knew on which side his bread was buttered. In his report, he whitewashed the smoke, finding no connection between high rates of consumption, asthma and chronic bronchitis, and working twelve hours a day in dust, smoke and sulphur and arsenic-laden fumes. Copper workers were notoriously thin, wiry and sallow-faced but Williams found them of easy carriage, firm and confident step, and manly upright gait. They were also made nimble by the demands and dangers of their work: ladling, raking, and shovelling hot and molten materials in furnace heat called for lightness of foot. Colliers were the copper-mens' foil. Subjected to close, poisoned air when below ground, and to cold, damp mountain air when above, they were stalked by pestilence and disease. Among them tubercular and scrofulous diseases were 'frightfully prevalent'. Physically, they were lumpen figures, their

*Group of unidentified colliers. NMW.*

bodies – and here he agreed with Leifchild – misshapen from being bent and constrained in unnatural positions for long periods. 'Like the tailor, his body is bent in a constrained and unnatural attitude, he can use freely only a limited group of muscles.' Work in the dark and confined spaces of a mine would, of course, encourage careful and deliberate, rather than quick and nimble movement, just as working continually in crouching positions along low seams also made some miners bow-legged. But Williams, like Leifchild, was drawn to caricature. 'Sailor-like,' he continued, [the collier] 'slouches from side to side, the knees awkwardly bend beneath the weight of the body, the carriage is singularly ungraceful, and the attitude always uncomely. In the march there is no firmness. The head stoops forward in stupid modesty, the physiognomy lacks animation, the eye intelligence, the ensemble the charm of fearless manliness. He evidently stands a full degree below the copperman in the ethnologic scale.'

Equally damning in Thomas Williams' eyes was the collier's unrelieved Welshness. By the middle of the nineteenth century, the descendants of the English immigrant miners had been thoroughly assimilated. Outside Swansea, the general population, including most of the miners, were Welsh-speakers, many of them monoglot. Swansea then was one of the most anglicized towns in Wales, and London-trained Thomas Williams was a committed and undisguised anglophile. Colliers lived beyond the pale, in a benighted Celtic hinterland. While the copper workers lived in neat company houses, colliers and hill farmers were condemned to conditions that were 'truly Celtic'. In the coalfield villages, 'The miner's cot exemplifies still the rude architecture of another age. The thatched roof, the cold, damp, chilling earth-floor, the large, open chimney and fire-place, through which alike the wind gusts, the frost bites, and the sun-light gleams; the cheerless solitary apartment, the unceilinged roof, the small windows, the mud walls and the single room, proclaim still the absence of the material requisites of health and decency.' Williams' descriptions of the working environment were just as dramatic: 'Immured in darkness and pestilence, in a close poisoned air, in a climate chilly at all times and damp, far down from the cheering influences of the sun's rays, under an augmented weight of barometric pressure… clad in black dirty rags, gritty with coal dust, matted with filth, the eye regaled only by the miserable light of a farthing rusher, or the muffled luminescence of a 'Davy'; the ear, weary with the sepulchral monotony of a subterranean silence, broken only by the hollow clang of the cutter's pickaxe… companionizing with maneless, tail-less, broken-kneed, coal-besprinkled horses; now horror-smitten by an army of overgrown *rats*, and now disgust-stricken with the lazy hoppings of hideous *toads*.'

Work below ground, in dark, cramped, foul-smelling and frequently wet conditions did not need the garnish of lazily hopping toads to render its difficulties, dangers and discomforts. The nature of the work, and working conditions, had changed very little since the days of George Owen. Even in places where the seams were relatively thick and the headings and the roadways generous, the miner's world was remarkably confined. The manager of the Nolton colliery, Pembrokeshire, told RH Franks, who was investigating conditions in the mines, that children under twelve were not required in the Nolton mine because the vein was four feet thick. Almost every task underground was made infinitely more difficult by having to be performed in tight spaces, where every edge could cut and bruise. Hewers at the face moved around doubled-up or stooping, while in the lowest headings the young carters scampered on all fours.

Nor had methods changed markedly. In the middle of the nineteenth century, the hewer still worked in stalls, George Owen's 'sundry holes', the longwall system never having been popular in south Wales. In longwall workings the hewers advanced along a wide front, removing all the coal. The access roads were at each end. As the face advanced, the hewers and their helpers propped up the roof with temporary timbers and packed the space behind with the 'gob' or 'goaf' (thought to be from *ogof*, the Welsh for cave), a mixture of small unsaleable coal and rubble and stone from roof-ripping and roadway-cutting operations. It is thought that the longwall system may have originated with miners of metallic ores, who were unwilling to leave any of their valuable product in the ground. Early in the nineteenth century, R J Nevill of Llanelli offered to lend Sir John Morris two or three immigrant colliers, 'who are used to longwork... for as much time as may be necessary to instruct your men.' But Welsh colliers, fearing for their safety and disinclined to work in groups, were never tempted or persuaded, although in many places they were forced to use modified longwall methods. In 1859, however, Lionel Brough, mines inspector for south Wales, could report that longwall was still in its infancy. The system worked as long as each man, or each pair of men, worked at the same rate, but if some were faster than others the workface became irregular and the uneven pressure on the roof could cause it to break. At the Stepaside mine, at Kilgetty, in Pembrokeshire, where the system was used at the end of the nineteenth century, each pair of men was given about twenty-five feet of face to work, so that there was a continuous 'breast' of several hundred feet. But the difficulty of keeping the face continuous and more or less straight caused frequent disputes, which the manager or his assistant had to settle. The solution was to give the slower cutters a shorter working face, so that they could keep pace with their neighbours. James Thain and his mate worked beside a pipe-smoking 'old fellow' and his son, who were no match for them. Between them developed a 'rib' of uncut coal, which Thain was compelled to work. Thain often remonstrated with the old man but to no avail, until one day a fall of slate from the roof, some of it in large pieces, virtually buried him. But the old man was unrepentant. On being dug out and revived, by a bucket of water poured over his head, his first words were, 'Where is my pipe?'

When opening a mine, the usual practice was to drive a roadway in the direction in which the coal might be most easily worked and, at distances of about 120 yards, cut crossheadings at right angles to the roadway if seams were level, but if the seams inclined steeply they were cut at an angle to reduce the gradient in the heading, allowing the ponies to bring down the drams on fully spragged, or braked, wheels. The hewers' stalls were then cut out of the coal, parallel to the main roadway, on each side of the cross headings. Where the cross headings were only sixty yards apart, the stalls were driven from one side only. The dimensions of the stalls and the size of the pillars to be left were matters of judgement, determined by the depth of the workings and the nature of the roof. The more secure the roof and the more timbering used, the wider the stalls. At the Old Pit in Cwmgors, very little timber was used to support the roof, so pillars about four yards wide were left between the stalls. With a good roof, the pillars might be three yards wide, and six yards with a bad one. The great length of the stalls and the relative smallness of the pillars were a feature of south Welsh mining until late in the nineteenth century. In shallow mines, stalls could be a hundred yards long and from five to nine yards wide, with, to support the roof, a bottleneck entrance. Such length was possible only where the mines were relatively shallow; the deeper the mine, the more danger of falls, from irregular roof pressure and from creep, the rising of the floor. As a mine aged, and the limits of exploitation were reached, colliers worked backwards, removing coal from the pillars and letting the roof collapse behind them. Owners were reluctant to leave coal in the ground, and for the miners cutting coal from the pillars, working 'in the broken' was easier than hacking it from the coalface. Miners, however, who were paid by their output, were always tempted to take more coal than safety decreed, so that unsanctioned cutting, 'robbing the pillars', was not uncommon. At R J Nevill's Bryn Colliery,

Llanelli, the pillars at first were four yards square and the openings four yards wide, an arrangement that allowed extraction of about two-thirds of the coal. Before closing the mine, Nevill removed one half of the remaining third by, as he put it, 'splitting the pillars'. Split pillars, like robbed pillars, could be dangerously fragile.

In the pillar, or post and stall system, the usual practice was for two or three workers to occupy a stall: a leading collier and his assistant or 'butty', and a boy to move coal to the trams in the heading and roadways. Whereas the width of the stalls was a matter for judgement, the height depended on the thickness of the seam. The system worked best where the seams were several feet thick. In thin seams (in Pembrokeshire some were only 18-24 inches thick), or in places where the roof was particularly strong, the longwall system, or some variation of it, was more practicable. In thin seams, the collier had to rip or blast away enough of the top rock so that he could kneel or crouch or, failing this, lie on his side with enough space to swing his pick or mandril. In anthracite mines, where the seams were thinnest, short handled tools were preferred: a small flat shovel, and a mandril, which (to prevent inadvertent injury to a workmate) might have only one pointed end. Unable to move freely, the hewer often had to crouch or lie for several hours in one position. But whatever the thickness of the seam, undercutting the coal face was standard practice and it could be done only by kneeling or lying on one's side. Few physical labours have been more demanding. B L Coombes, a celebrated miner/author and a former farm worker, who came to the Nedd valley in the 1920s, wrote that it took him many weeks to learn the way, when lying on his side, of swinging elbows and twisting wrists without moving his shoulders.

Aside from the physical discomfort, chipping away at the coal face, or the underlying fireclay, fraction by fraction, until a groove an inch, then six inches, then a foot deep, had been cut, was deadly monotonous work that left pads of hardened skin on the hips, elbows and shoulders. When the cutter was forced to rest, or move, water was thrown into the groove to soften the coal before the next attack. Undercutting might continue until the depth of the groove equalled the full length of the pick handle and the hewer's arms. Wooden 'sprags' supported the undercut coal until the collier was ready to let the overhanging coal fall under its own weight or, failing this, pry it loose with steel bars and wedges. In places where the coal was particularly hard, or stiff, and where there was no gas, it might have to be brought down with explosives but these, because they smashed the coal and produced a great deal of small, were not popular.

B L Coombes worked for some time in an eighteen-inch seam. To measure the height of a post, he and his mate would press their elbows on the floor as they were lying down and clench their fists; the distance from elbow to fist was the height of a post. To work in spaces that were no higher than the bottom of a chair, they sawed their mandril handles short and took out the handles of the shovels, replacing them with a little crutch on the end of the steel blade. With neither space nor power to lift stones or lumps of coal, they pushed these ahead with their hands, getting power by bracing their legs against some solid object. In unguarded moments, they might study the roof and wonder what would happen if it lowered a few inches – which was not impossible. Only during their quarter hour meal breaks were they able to stand up or kneel. At the beginning of each shift, Coombes and his mate massaged each other with oil and, at night, their wives put ointment on their grazed backs and raw knees.

Hewing or cutting, however, as E D Clarke had noted on a visit to 'Mr Morris's mine' in 1791, was not just a matter of straining muscle and sinew. 'Their method of cutting is ingenious as it saves a great deal of labour. They first place strong props of wood against the vein and cut out a small quantity from the bottom and from each of the sides, the supporters are then removed and the whole gives way and by this means 15 or 20 tons of coal are obtained.' The objective of all hewing, the miner being paid for the quality as well as quantity of his coal, was to bring out the large coal with the minimum amount of waste. Like an experienced quarryman at the rock face, the hewer had to be able to 'read' a seam, determine its direction and how, by detecting lines of weakness, it might be broken down. In the anthracite collieries, the coal was arranged in segments or slips, not in more or less continuous layers. Each slip was made up of leaves, varying in thickness from

*Undercutting, 1898. NMW.*

*Two colliers 'holing' or undercutting, 1906. NMW.*

three or four inches to a yard, and all slanted in a particular direction. John Williams of Banwen, in conversation with the distinguished oral historian George Ewart Evans, explained the approach: 'Now you'd go into the corner now [of the stall] about five yards and work in, advance in. When you were working in that direction, digging under, you were putting in a *sprag* [a short wooden support] to hold that while you were doing it. Then you knocked out all the sprags and the whole of the coal would fall. Now you had to be taught those things. A stranger coming in, however scientific he was, he'd have to be taught that. You were trained to understand the layering of the coal, to know where to look for it, and how to go at it when you find it.' By working upward through the coal seam, cutting and wedging – with hammers and a crowbar – and by using natural roof pressures, a skilled hewer could bring down the coal without 'putting the powder in.'

Even the use of the pick and shovel, now the least regarded of tools, had to be learned. 'If you didn't know how to shovel,' John Williams continued, 'you'd kill yourself in about five minutes.' Shovelling hard lumps of coal on a rough, uneven floor was not simply a matter of

*Collier viewing or 'reading' a coal seam. NLW.*

*Edmund Jones, apprentice craftsman, Skewen Main Colliery, 1902. NMW.*

thrusting in the shovel and lifting. The shovel, small-bladed and sharp, had to be 'worked in'. For loading coal into carts or drams from a rough floor there was no better instrument and attempts to replace it with the curling box, in the 1920s, incensed the miners. Owners complained that shovelling the coal into the drams introduced too much small, for which, in a depressed market, there was little demand. The curling box was an iron scoop eighteen inches to two feet wide, with a handle on each side, that could only be filled by hand from a stooping position. If care were taken, the small could be left on the floor of the stall. The miners objected to the boxes because, as in the case of all tools, they had to pay for them and, more important, because they considered them unsafe. In thick seams, the coal could break away from the face or sides of the stall, and might crush or engulf a boy as he bent over to scrape the coal into the scoop. In anthracite mines, where the coal was arranged in slips, or leaves, this was seen as a particular danger. The miners, alas, were proved right. At the Seven Sisters pit, in 1921, a lad, bending over his curling box, was killed by a falling stone that landed on his back, crushing his body and impaling him against the sharp edges of the box.

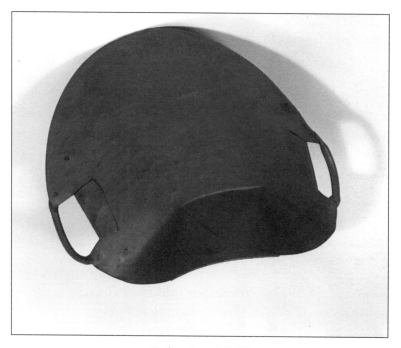

*Curling Box. NMW.*

The use of the boxes continued for a while, but stopped completely when the demand for small coal rose again.

Through walking and working in confined, rough-edged spaces, miners developed bat-like antennae that saved their heads from cuts and bruises and, when needed – Liefchild and Thomas Williams to the contrary – nimbleness of foot to dodge projections from the walls or the roof. When walking along a roadway in a mine that was new to him, B L Coombes followed the collier ahead, a former boxer named 'Crush' Williams. When they came to a piece of projecting timber at about eye level, Williams called out: 'See that bit, just a flick of the head and a step sideways. But allus keep your balance; that's ringcraft, that is.' In stall work, the Banwen miner John Williams remarked, that you hardly ever saw a man hitting his head against the roof. 'Instinctively, like a bat, he knows, *this is low*, without ever having to think about it.' Those same antennae, the miner's 'instinct', also enabled him to anticipate danger, to know when new supports were needed and, in case of trouble that couldn't be anticipated, how to get out of it. Anecdotes abound of miners who, in obedience to some sixth sense, or in response to some slight, hardly registered movement in the roof or the face, or the faint creak of a timber prop, moved away from a workplace seconds or minutes before the roof or the face collapsed. The verse that follows is from the Durham coalfield but the sentiment expressed is common to coalmining districts the world over:

> Jowl, jowl and listen lad
> And hear the coalface workin
> There's many a marra [mate] missing lad
> Becaas he wadn't listen lad

In places where the roof was unstable, or where the pillars were being cut back, the hewers and their butties had to install supporting timbers. Some mines, too, were subject to 'squeeze' or 'pooking', when pressure from above could lower the roof, raise the floor, and force out the sides. Pressures were sometimes so great that openings in the coal or in surrounding strata might immediately begin to squeeze or close up. In the Timber vein at Hook, Pembrokeshire, a roof nine feet high could be reduced to four in a fortnight, and in a disused roadway at the Pentremawr colliery, the floor rose to within six inches of the top of a ten foot arch. At the same colliery, a tub left in a stall at the end of a shift was found the following day, wedged fast against the roof. Horses caught in tight headings or roadways also suffered, having to force their way through lower or narrower spaces. Movement usually began with the curving, then cracking of the floor, then the compression and crushing of the pillars. Safety in the mine, and even survival, clearly depended on the skilled handling and dressing of timber. To take the pressure of the roof, or from the floor, the uprights had to be perpendicular and the tie beams or collars dead level, otherwise, when the pressure of the roof came on, they would just roll off. The collier worked without a level or a set square and the joints or notches were cut with an axe, kept, in the case of good timbermen, 'as sharp as a lance.' In Pembrokeshire, if the roof was particularly unstable, branches of hazel and willow, known as 'drivers', were woven into the roof supports to contain falls.

As well as keeping their timbers square, good face workers also kept their workplaces as uncluttered as possible, removing the waste or gob and packing it in places where the seam had been worked out. A collier's stall, as Edmund Stonelake pointed out, was his domain and he worked it in his own way and at his own speed, brooking interference from no one, not even the manager. In 1871, Alexander Dalziel, an official of the Coal Owners Association, remarked with, one suspects, grudging admiration, that in south Wales all the rules of the pit were in restraint of production. The cutters might chivvy the carters but in the stalls, noted Dalziel, it was a point of honour with them not to hurry.

The hewer, or the face worker, was the aristocrat of the mine and all other workers served his needs. His immediate servants were the boys who carted the coal to the tubs or trams in the main roadways. These were paid by the collier, whose earnings depended upon the amount of saleable coal (measured in tons) that reached the weighbridge at the head of the shaft, or the mouth of the drift. As a result, the boys worked to the incessant call of the carts and the needs of the face worker. Carting was generally regarded as the hardest work in the mine. Hezekiah Williams, a noted Tawe valley poet and author, who wrote under the pseudonym of Watcyn Wyn, described the tyranny he felt as a ten-year-old:

> Cart, cart, cart
> Before the break of day,
> Cart, cart, cart,
> When night has come to stay,
> Cart, cart, cart,
> The cart is never out of sight,
> In dreams throughout the fitful night,
> I push the cart with all my might,
> Cart, cart, cart.

If there were no tram roads in the headings and stalls, the coal was dragged or pushed along the rough, planked floors on sleds or in wooden boxes about three feet long and a foot and a half high, fitted with iron shoes for easier travelling. The normal load was about 1.5 cwt. A commissioner reported in 1842 that at the Loughor and Broadoak collieries boys drew the carts by means of a hook along the bottom stone of the vein to the main roadways, where they were emptied into horse-drawn wagons. In roadways which were too low for horses, boys trammed the coal from the face all the way to the bottom of the shaft. Boys, who were often the children of face workers, were the cheapest form of labour and, as important, they were small enough to manoeuvre in narrow seams and passageways. Most worked barefoot, boots being considered burdensome in confined spaces. Richard Hare, agent for the Kilgetty colliery, Pembrokeshire, reported to R H Franks, the Children's Commissioner, that he employed children to pull small wagons in seams not more that two feet high, and in roadways of only three and a half feet. One of his carters, Elias Jones, a veteran at fourteen, hauled with a girdle that passed around his body and a chain attached to the cart between his legs. He dragged, on all fours, for sixty yards in veins between two and three feet thick. 'It is very hard work… for we work like little horses. I cart for two colliers and I load five drams, each weighing 18 cwt.' John Williams, also a Pembrokeshire carter, told Franks: 'I creep on my knees, and often on my belly.' Ben Thomas, eight years old, a hauler of skips or drams in a pit near Begelly, told the Commissioner: 'Began working 12 months ago. Work seven and eight hours. Father dead. Mother winds below with my sister… The boys do not wear shoes in our pit.'

Conditions in small collieries had not changed greatly by the 1930s. The boys were older, and they wore boots or shoes, but the work of carting was the same. At a colliery in Pembrey, O J Anthony recalled that the wooden handcarts moved on skids 'just like a sledge' and could hold several hundredweights of coal. On each end was a U bolt, for pulling by chain. The boys wore a harness, known as a 'dress', made by cutting a rubber tyre to fit around the waist. From the dress a metal chain passed between the boy's legs and hooked to the U bolt of the cart.

# The Collier and Conditions of Work

Until mining legislation could be enforced, late in the nineteenth century, the youngest carters were eight or nine years old and the oldest about fifteen. Usually, the carters were unable to keep up with the cutters, and worked a longer day, perhaps eleven or twelve hours against the cutter's nine or ten. The carters were left to clear up. Also last to leave the shift in the first half of the nineteenth century were the door boys, who were the youngest workers of all. They started at the age of seven or eight, graduating in a few years to some form of hauling. Sitting alone in the dark with, it was often said, only the rats for company, the door boy's function was to open the ventilation doors along the airways, to allow the passage of the trams. According to J H Howard, the boys got used to the squealing rats scrambling over their clothes and stealing their food and candles. They were alarmed only by swarming rats, which were known to attack humans and animals, and by the sighting of a white rat, regarded as a sure sign of an accident. But if rats could be tolerated, boredom and deprivation could not. Some, according to a mine visitor in 1851, bought a 'farthing's worth of happiness' by taking to work a piece of chalk and covering the doors with recollections of life above ground. Ben Davies, a noted poet, wrote how, as a door-boy 'buried in that grim blackness', he would conjure up images of mountain streams and sunlit fields. But longings had to be contained. The door boy's task was to prevent long interruptions in the movement of air, and to prevent trams on a down slope from smashing through the doors. To accomplish this, they had to listen carefully for the approach of a 'journey' of trams, opening the doors by pulling on a string just as the trams approached, and closing them immediately upon their passage. At the Broadoak colliery, Loughor, the trams, as John Owen explained to the commissioner, 'Come along every quarter of an hour. I do not stay quiet but run about to keep warm but I must mind the door. They are very particular about the door; it keeps the air right.'

Boys also helped to keep the air right by tending the fires and furnaces at the base of the upcast shafts, sometimes working with men too old or too worked out to cut coal. One ten-year-old worked with 'old David Jenkins' at the Landore Colliery: 'I go more for company for the old man than to work.' For the Great Exhibition, 1851, Robert Mills, a Northumberland-born manager or, in the terminology of the north-east, 'viewer' of mines at Llansamlet, submitted an 'ingenious contrivance' of self-acting doors, which opened and shut by the mere passage of trams through them. Mills was awarded a medal but details of his invention have not survived and there is no evidence that it was ever implemented.

For the door boys and carters, who were constantly on call, there were no set breaks or mealtimes. Bread and cheese, kept in a bag or tommy box to protect them from marauding rats, and water from a tin jack, were eaten and drunk, one-handedly, on the run. A sit-down meal or, an even greater luxury, a rest or lie down, according to J H Howard, was quite impossible. Thomas Jenkins, aged ten, snatched a few mouthfuls of bread and cheese, washed down by cold tea, while riding in an empty coal cart pushed by his workmate from the main roadways back to the coalface. Once home, they would get broth or tea and bread and butter, but seldom butcher's meat. Only on Sundays, their one day of rest, might they get bacon meat. In the late eighteenth century, colliers and collier boys in the upper Tawe valley ate barley bread, made from barley ground in Clydach, and, from time to time, a boiled or a fried egg. The food was carried in little canvas sacks tied with linen and slung over their shoulders.

For the children of collier families, childhood was a chimera, no sooner entered than it was over. Keir Hardie, the labour leader, who worked in pits from the age of ten, described himself as, 'One of the unfortunate class who has never known what it is to be a child – in spirit I mean.' One of R H Franks' respondents, William Richards, an air-door boy of about seven or eight (he was uncertain of his age), was in his working gear when interviewed: 'His cap,' the commissioner recorded, 'was furnished with the usual collier candlestick and his pipe was stuck familiarly in his buttonhole. He said he smoked half a quartern a week.' Len Ley, an Ystradgynlais historian, noted how the responses of the interviewees were delivered in the low key, matter of fact manner of children who had known nothing but drudgery. He quotes Margaret Thomas, an eleven-year-old who came with her parents from Tredegar to Ystalyfera: 'I was at school a little at Tredegar, but I can't read. I go sometimes to the Sunday schools here. I go to work with my father and sister every morning before six o'clock. We go from the house at five and we come out of the level about four in the evening. I carry the tools out, and sometimes come out before my father and sister. I don't know how many hours I work, but I am almost 12 hours from the house. I don't know what wages my father gets. I have wet feet today, but I do not get them wet every day. I don't work barefoot, I always have shoes... I sometimes stay at home to help my mother in the house. I do not know which I like best, whether working in the house with my mother or on the level with my father. I am more used to work on the level.' Margaret Thomas probably worked as a carter.

Once at the main roadway, the coal was dumped from the carts into trams and hauled or pushed on rails to the mouth of the drift or the bottom of the shaft. In the hard coal district, the final loading, in a technique known as 'racing the dram', was done carefully. Without using timber, a wall of coal about a foot high, and stable enough to prevent any loss on the journey to the weighbridge, was built above the top of the tram. Where the roadways were not large enough for horses or ponies, the coal was moved out by 'trammers', older boys of 15–18 and, in Pembrokeshire, by women and girls, who pushed and pulled the laden trams. Tramming was a stage up from carting. In western Glamorganshire and Carmarthenshire, according to Commissioner Rhys William Jones, women were scarcely ever permitted in what he called the subterraneous departments; the work there, he remarked, was considered unsuitable for the sex. If the haul was up a steep rise, as it often was in the steeply inclined seams of Pembrokeshire, it was done by a windlass operated by older girls and women. Where the seams were worked at different levels of the mine, a windlass also raised the coal from one level to the next. Before the introduction of steam winding in the 1840s, women also worked the windlass in the main shaft. Hannah Brown, 16, windlass girl at the Broadmoor colliery, Begelly, worked from seven in the morning until three in the afternoon, hauling daily up to 400 loads weighing from 1.5 to 4 cwt.

For older boys, underground, the most sought after job, until they could graduate to the coalface at nineteen or twenty, was that of haulier. In south Wales there was no orderly system of training, but for suitable boys there was a gradual movement from the trap-doors toward the coal face. In drifts where the seams were thick or where the roadways had been ripped out to depths of five or six feet, horses and ponies provided the draft for the drams. The ponies were blinkered and were fitted with a leather cap designed to protect the head. To save the expense of enlarging roadways, grooves were sometimes cut in the roof to allow passage of the pony's head and steps cut in the floor between the sleepers to accommodate its feet. Only after the introduction of steam winding and cages in the 1830s, could ponies be lowered into pits. They were kept in brick-lined stalls, lime-washed to discourage bugs or insects that might spread infection, and they were well fed, but there, according to B L Coombes, good handling stopped. Although hauliers were chosen from the steadiest and best-tempered boys, they were not, as were farm wagoners, well-trained in the handling and care of their charges. To keep pace with the trammers and cutters, they often had to goad the horses to move quickly through narrow, rough-walled passageways, where bumps, cuts and scrapes could not be avoided. An entire shift, too, might go by without the horses being watered. Only if they worked in levels, when they were taken outdoors after the shift, did they ever see daylight and taste fresh grass.

Lord Shaftesbury's report on the employment of children in mines, 1842, which he based upon the findings of the royal commission that he had been instrumental in founding, shocked early Victorian society. Against the concerted opposition of mine owners, he presented a bill that would outlaw the employment underground of children under the age of ten, which was soon amended to thirteen, and of women and girls. There were, however, too few inspectors to enforce it and too many desperate collier parents who, needing the additional income, were prepared to lie about the ages of their children. Coal owners in general were opposed to any change in the employment of children because of the costs of raising the height of roadways and headings to accommodate youths and ponies. Hugh Owen, trustee to the Sir John Owen estate in Pembrokeshire, expostulated: 'I am of the opinion

*Pit pony. SWCC, Swansea University.*

*Underground stable. NMW.*

that a limitation of the age at which children should work in mines is not necessary, as they are not tasked above 10 hours either night or day.' Sixty years later, in 1900, when the age limit had been raised to thirteen, there could still be a poignant sense of loss when a boy went underground. On his first day at the Banwen colliery, in 1928 or 1929, Hywel Jeffreys (Jeff Camnant), received this elegiac benediction from an older miner, who shook his hand and said *'Mae dy haf bach wedi passo! Mae'n rhaid i ti weithio nawr'*. (Your short summer is over; and now you must work).

In the years following the Children's Commission report there were many improvements in underground haulage. Main roadways were enlarged, tramways were relaid, and steel trams introduced. An iron bar attachment to the tram, the 'shaft and gun', made braking easier and prevented the tram from colliding with the hind legs of the pony on downward slopes. Previously, the trammers could exhaust themselves in their efforts to hold the trams back. In the 1830s, James Watt made an engine in which power could be applied to both sides of the piston alternately, providing a continuous cycle of operation and the steady pull necessary for all winding operations. By 1836, a system of winding with cages and shaft guides had been devised in northern England that allowed drams, or tubs, to be wheeled into the cages and lifted up the shafts. At the same time, stationary, steam-driven hauling engines equipped with cables or wire ropes, powered by steam or compressed air were built to pull trains or 'journeys' of drams to the base of the shaft. These, in combination with the winding engines, reduced the costs and greatly increased rates of moving the coal. Steam winding roughly doubled the quantity of coal that could be lifted at any given time and steam haulage halved the costs of horse haulage, even though in many mines pit ponies still hauled trams from the work places to the main roadways. Each horse required its haulier, and every year, on average, one third of the horses had to be replaced.

At the coal face, the great technological change was the replacement of hand cutting by machine cutting. The longer the cut, the more efficient the machine, so, in mines where machines were introduced, long wall cutting replaced the hewer in his stall. Stalls survived only where seams were too thick – about six feet – to be cut by machine, and where the seams were too disturbed to allow a long cut. By 1939, machine cutting dominated only in the large mines of the Neath and Dulais valleys, where conditions approximated those of the eastern coalfield. West of the Dulais, only seven out of roughly seventy anthracite mines had machine cutters. While coal was cut by hand in stalls, mining was still a craft, symbolized by the hewer's provision of his own tools. Men like Hywel Jeffreys of Banwen, who were renowned for their skill as colliers and who, as big hewers, would have been chosen to drive 'hard headings', were reduced to 'hands', the servants and operators of machines. George Ewart Evans compared the skilled hewer, who kept his heading straight and his stall clean, to a ploughman known for the straight, clean look of his furrows.

By cutting along the face of the coal seam, the machines were able to cut in a few minutes what might take a hewer an entire shift. After the cut, the coal was simply shovelled unsorted onto a conveyor belt so that greater amounts of waste and small reached the surface. Under the new system, each man was responsible for a section of the face but he now had little control over it. To get to the machine cutters he had to scramble over mounds of 'duff' (small coal thrown back by the cutter) and the conveyor itself. If it was a two-shift system he also had no idea what to expect at the beginning of his shift. All workers dislike rubbish underfoot and in the stall system it was possible to maintain a relatively clean station. The more careful the collier, the easier the work. If the tram rails came right up the heading to the stall, he could sink the rails a little lower to ease the loading and if there were moments to spare he could do some timbering.

As well as eliminating craftsmanship, mechanized cutters and conveyors also nullified the miner's antennae, the early warning system that detected faint sounds from movements in the roof, or from the extra pressure on a prop, that might herald a fall. The first conveyors were long structures made from shallow, metal pans – replaced later by more or less noiseless rubber belts – which moved the coal forward in a series of spasmodic jerks. The clanging and rattle of these, the roar of the cutting machine, and the noise of men shovelling masked any sounds from the roof. Hywel Jeffreys elaborated: 'I felt very unsafe when I went on a conveyor. There was something you said, Ifan, about the noise of the conveyors: I didn't realise how much we were depending on our ears when we were working: little cracks in the top, or little flakes dropping by here – things like that, rumbling. So much easier when you were working in a stall. You could say when a place was squeezing, when it was preparing to collapse, settling down or something. You were careful when you heard that. And you could listen for the coal working, and find exactly where was the easiest place to go and pull out a dram of coal. This business of listening: when you are knocking the top. We used to have to hold the mandril firm and tap the top with it; and we could say whether the top was safe or not, just by the sound. The only thing we had to watch for were the bells.' Bells were compacted balls of iron ore that would give a solid sound, and still drop without any warning. Some of the older miners were so unnerved by the noise of the cutters and conveyors and – because of the depth of the undercut – by the extent of exposed and unsupported roof from which there were no audible sounds that, if there were stalls in the mine to which they could go, they refused to work near the machines. 'I was happy underground,' remarked a retired Dulais valley miner, 'when we had our own place to work. You had your freedom... But when the conveyors came in you had to keep up with the machine... Under the old method you set your own pace. No, I wouldn't want to go back to it like it is now.'

Along with mechanical cutters and conveyors, and the need to keep them working, came the two or double-shift system. According to B L Coombes, objections to it were general but were strongest in mines where the stall system still operated. A one-shift system allowed time for the workings to be aired out, to be cleared of powder smoke and the heat produced by the bodies and breath of men and horses working vigorously. It also allowed the workings to rest and settle for a period and, because there was always pressure from the roof on the edge of the unworked coal, some coal might be squeezed free by the time men returned to work in the morning. In the anthracite mines, an experienced collier would encourage the process by trimming and cleaning the slips of coal, so that they would slacken more readily and give him 'easy' coal for the morrow. The slips lay on one another like the leaves of a book and sometimes, Coombes remarked, they would work out 'like a tide'. A careful workman would also put his timbers in where needed and would see that they were solid and well sloped. In the double-shift system, there was no guarantee that the timbering left by one shift would not be abused by the next. The good workman was at the mercy of the poor one.

But Coombes, who had spent countless hours undercutting while lying on his side in narrow seams, was no sentimentalist. When machine cutting eased the work without adding to the risks, he welcomed it. At first, the machines produced choking clouds of dust that, at the end of a shift, had to be removed from clothes and faces with a sweeping brush. To suppress the dust, long holes were bored into the face, filled with jets of water, and then plugged. The water worked its way between the slips, where the dust collected, and at the same time loosened the coal. More effective, however, were sprays of water fed by tanks placed above the cutting chain that prevented the dust from rising. Some miners complained of the muck and muddy conditions which inevitably resulted, but for B L Coombes, being able to see a lighted lamp from a distance of forty or fifty yards, or his mate next to him, not shrouded in clouds of dust, was a fair exchange. When the old, trough-type conveyors were replaced by comparatively quiet belts, to greater visibility could be added a degree of quiet that may still have muffled the telltale sound of falling fragments of rock, or a creaking prop, but gave some reassurance to the older miners. 'Let them cut, I say,' was Bert Coombes' verdict, provided it could be done without jeopardizing safety or health. Older miners, born to mining and whose status in the mine and in the community had depended on their skill as hewers or timbermen, were less sanguine. When, late in his working life, Hywel Jeffreys, a legendary big hewer in the upper Dulais valley, went to work in the deep, mechanized mine at Cefn Coed, he found himself – his main strength gone – simply one of a gang pulling on a rope that moved machinery.

The tension between colliers anxious to protect customary methods of working, and owners determined to maximize output and profits, was felt throughout the coalfield but probably most acutely in the south-west. Until the 1920s, many of the anthracite drifts were essentially village enterprises. They were owned by local landowners in partnership with business and professional men, and worked by men and boys from the locality or adjacent counties. Owners, for the most part, did not challenge the methods and customs of the miners and, because they were not answerable to boards of directors and shareholders, they were not driven by the need for ever increasing returns. From time to time, however, there were disputes but usually they were resolved in context, either by the miners' lodge committee, which determined the conditions of work, or by the lodge committee and management. Writing in the 1930s of his youth in the Llansamlet of the 1890s, J H Howard offered this observation: 'Colliery proprietors and workmen knew each other; they were neighbours, lived in the village, attended the same chapel, spoke the one language, and were interested in each other. The manager was approachable, and that without a go-between agent or committee; we were a family with mutual interests at the pit.' Reasonable doubts that Howard's view might have been heavily nostalgic were partly allayed by a 1925 report of the Government Inspector for the Swansea region: 'Officials and workmen live in a common community, are often related to each other by blood or by marriage, and their familiar association breeds affection and loyalty.'

In the Inspector's comment on worker/management relations there is, perhaps significantly, no reference to the colliery proprietors, only to officials and workmen. In the anthracite district, the once-comfortable, if not always amicable, relationship between miners and mine owners began to deteriorate in the 1920s and broke down completely in the year of the Government Inspector's report. By 1924 most of the anthracite mines had been acquired by two large combines, Amalgamated Anthracite and United Anthracite, who, under pressure to maximize profits, took a more calculated view of custom and tradition. They had bought at a time of booming prices for anthracite, when the collieries

*Locked-out colliers at the Soviet Level, Glynneath, during the 1926 general
strike. SWCC, Swansea University.*

were overvalued, and they had based their takeover bids on potential monopoly profits rather than actual ones. Dividends were low and the companies, who had to answer to shareholders, were understandably anxious. 'Working conditions,' as F A Szarvasy, the chairman of United Anthracite, remarked unequivocally, 'had to be rearranged before satisfactory profits could be earned.' Conflict was inevitable.

In an article for a 1926 issue of *Colliery Workers Magazine*, D J Williams, a miner from Gwauncaegurwen and the future Labour MP for Neath, (1945-1964), set the stage: 'The growth of these powerful Combines effects a complete revolution in the relations of capital and labour in the coal industry. Time was when the colliery worker knew his employer personally. In those days it was the custom of the owner himself to come round to the faces to consider allowances, prices, special job rates, and to meet in person the workers and their representatives. Such is not the case now. The old relations of persons have given way to the new relation of things. The Combine is a vast machine and the worker is merely a cog in it. He does not know his employers; probably he has never seen them. But the struggle between labour and capital still goes on, only it is now fought in a more intensive form.' It was not just the colliers who resented the change but the overmen charged with executing the instructions of the company. One commented on the wholesale change in atmosphere: 'I used to love to go to work, but now I hate it like poison, not because of the work itself, but the drudgery, the slave-driving methods… that are being introduced.' When Welsh mettle failed, or refused to acquire the desired degree of hardness, local overmen were sometimes replaced by English imports: '*Am fod mwy o'r bwli yn perthyn iddynt*,' (there are more bullies among them) was a workers' refrain.

The danger of surrendering customs to the will of the combines did not escape Llanelli's *Labour News*: 'If the men will but preserve their customs, they can withstand the Trusts: once they lose their customs, the Trusts will do what they have done in the Rhondda.' The customs or practices at issue were the 'stint', whereby the miners to a large extent controlled the output and the conditions of each workplace, and the Seniority (last on, first off) Rule, *Rheol Blaenoriaeth*, which prevailed throughout the anthracite district. To undermine the stint, the combines introduced to each pit, if they were to be had, miners and officials ignorant of, or indifferent to, local customs. At Ammanford No 1 Colliery, United Anthracite immediately appointed a new manager, who threatened to eliminate the New Year's Day holiday, the Good Friday holiday, the short Saturday shift, free or cheap house coal for miner lodgers as well as the householder, and cheap coal for colliers unable to work because of sickness or injury. Colliers absent through sickness were cut off after a few days. Also at risk in the combine collieries were the 'price lists' which, through negotiation, fixed the rates for cutting the coal and for jobs such as driving airways, timbering, and hauling and ripping the top in places where the seams were narrow. Most prices were quickly settled but discussions over the cutting price for coal could be prolonged. In the anthracite field, where the geology was complex and unpredictable, price lists protected a collier's income. Coal cut from seams that were difficult to work qualified for a higher rate of return than from seams where the cutting was easier. The combines pressed for, and in some mines succeeded, in setting a uniform rate fixed at the lowest level; that is, where the coal was thick and the cutting easy. Other allowances that were threatened or eliminated were the extra half shift's pay for working in wet places and extra pay for working on a Sunday night. But perhaps the most grating of all the changes, actual or proposed, was the threat to the 'old spells'. At mid shift, hewers and their butties, working in the same level, would leave their stalls and gather to eat. For the combines it was a time-wasting practice, but for the colliers it was a ritual, an important part of the society of the mine and, of an ownership that would seek to eliminate it, a damning indictment.

Most of these practices were, in effect, privileges, sanctioned by long use but unprotected by a written agreement. The Seniority Rule, as Hywel Francis has pointed out, was the product of a close knit society, a workforce that was largely local, and a pattern of work that tended to be seasonal. When the anthracite trade slackened during the summer months, miners, in collieries unable to stockpile coal, were in the habit of tramping over the mountains to the 'Steam', i.e. to the steam coalmines of the eastern valleys and returning to their old work places when trade revived. The Seniority Rule ensured that during the temporary lay-offs all men were treated equally and laid off in order of seniority, without reference to the grade or quality of work and, on their return, reinstated in the same order. The Rule was a reward for service as well as a safeguard against older and less productive workers being turned off. For militant workers, whom the company might want to be rid of, it was also protection against victimization. From the point of view of the combines, however, the Rule was an umbrella that protected not only the old and the militant but gratuitous troublemakers, the plain idle and the incompetent. The advantage clearly lay, and perhaps unfairly, with the workers: Dai Dan Evans of Abercraf, who knew both the western and the eastern coalfields, made no bones about it: 'In the anthracite area, if you wanted to dismiss a man who was a bit of a troublemaker, they would have to take possibly a hundred men out before him… [Consequently] you see you had lambs roaring like lions in the anthracite whereas in the steam coalfield,' he continued, 'they had to be a lion to bloody well roar like a lion.'

The test of the Rule occurred during a dispute over a change in methods of work and rates of pay in the Boxer section of the Ammanford No 1 Colliery, a difficult to work, unprofitable and traditionally militant district of the mine. In response to a change in methods of working, the men demanded a minimum wage instead of the piece rates offered. The colliery agent gave notice to all 116 men in the section. The miners' lodge, presumably accepting the need for some lay-offs, offered a seniority list but the management insisted that the original 116 be made redundant. Tempers rose at this challenge to a near-hallowed custom and the animus generated provided the tinder for a now-famous strike. The spark, or incident that fired the tinder was the combine's disregard of yet another valued safeguard. Custom decreed that a hewer could have his son work with him, provided his regular partner, or butty, agreed to work elsewhere. The arrangement, however, had to be sanctioned by a general meeting of the colliers because it affected the custom of the *tro* or turn. Workplaces were allotted by rotation, a practice that in theory ensured that everyone had a share of the good and bad workplaces. The *tro* prevented the company or management from reserving the better workplaces for the younger, more productive workers. At Ammanford, management ignored the procedure, attempting to move the man in question, Will Wilson, to another place without the approval of the workers. Wilson refused to move without the workers' sanction and was dismissed. The miners met later that day and sanctioned the move, but when Wilson turned up for work the next day the company refused to reinstate him.

The miners regarded the Boxer incident, the bypassing of the general meeting, and the dismissal of Wilson as frontal attacks on the custom of the mine and, by extension, of all the anthracite mines. When, in April 1925, the Ammanford No 1 Lodge decided to strike, they were joined by the lodges of four other mines in the neighbourhood. By 30 June, the *Western Mail* reported that the whole of the anthracite district was about to come out on strike. By 14 July, all the anthracite miners were out, except for those in the Nedd and Dulais valleys. The Dulais valley miners continued to work because they were employed by Evan Evans Bevan and not by the combines. The distinction, however, was lost on the incensed Amman and Tawe valley miners, who arranged a mass meeting at the Glanaman football ground, to decide on a means of bringing the recalcitrant collieries to heel. Thousands attended and resolved to confront the Dulais Valley miners on their way to work the following morning. The first group left Ammanford at 10.40 pm, led by the Ammanford Band, and marched up the valley, where they picked up the Cwmaman section, also headed by its band, and so on to Gwauncaegurwen and Brynaman. Others marched up the Tawe valley, joining the Amman valley marchers on the Ystradgynlais Common. From there, several thousand marched through the night until they reached Creunant, in the Dulais valley, 21 miles from Ammanford. The march, referred to as *Ar Hyd Y Nos* by the *Llanelli News*, became part of the folklore of the Amman Valley. At Creunant the marchers met the workmen's trains coming up the valley from Neath. Trouble began only, so it was said, after a knife or knives were drawn by the miners wishing to go to work. The picketers hauled the resisting Neath men off the platform, gave them a '*cwpl o bunts*', and told them to walk back to Neath. About twenty policemen appeared, 'quaking in their boots' and 'absolutely cringing and begging the crowd to go away', according to one account. After further scuffles at the Brynteg Colliery, Seven Sisters, and another 'momentous' open-air meeting, all the Dulais valley miners joined the strike.

The marchers, however, had not finished. One pit in the anthracite district – the Rock Colliery at Glynneath – was still working. The following day, in what became known as the Battle of the Rock, the Dulais valley miners joined the thousands from the Tawe and the Amman valleys in marching over the Hirfynydd Mountain, near Banwen, to picket the Rock miners. They were led by a band and followed by a crowd of schoolchildren whom no classroom could hold. At Glynneath, unlike at Creunant, the police were organized and resolute. They had cordoned off the entrance to the mine and the marchers, according to one participant, found themselves walking into the jaws of a lion. The police let some of the marchers through and, at the sound of a whistle, one hundred other policemen, who were hiding in a ditch, emerged and, for ten minutes, it was said, all that could be heard was the thud of batons on heads, arms and shoulders. One of the strikers, a veteran from the Great War, sounded a charge on his bugle but the miners were in disarray and could not respond. There were no fatalities and, given the numbers involved and the temper of the two sides, relatively few casualties. One policeman, a boxer and an international rugby forward, was badly mauled and sixteen miners were bloodied and bruised, one so badly that he spent a long period in hospital and never worked as a miner again. The policeman who administered the beating, another rugby player, was a marked man and not forgotten. In his next game against a Swansea valley side, he was injured so badly, or so painfully, that he, too, never played rugby again.

With all the mines closed, the strikers decided to strengthen their position by calling for the withdrawal of the safety men (firemen and pumps men) who were guarding the pits and keeping them dry. Feelings ran so high that the safety men were compelled to call a district meeting, at which they voted overwhelmingly to join the strikers. The combines responded by using 'volunteer' – blackleg to the strikers – pumps men and enlisting extra police from neighbouring counties. In late July there were skirmishes at five collieries. The *South Wales Daily Post* reported that a crowd of colliers, some with hoods over their faces, rushed the Gelliceidrim Colliery, where 'mob law' prevailed for a time. At Saron Colliery, officials were attacked, shots fired, explosives discharged and a man hit by a bullet. There were further demonstrations at Penygroes and Cross Hands, where a crowd, led by the local check-weigher, 'terrified' the police by singing Joseph Parry's *Aberystwyth*. At Betws, Wernos, Pantyffynon and Llandybie, baton charges were necessary, to disperse miners protesting against the use of blackleg safety men. A week later, 5 August, followed the 'Battle of Ammanford', when crowds lined the streets, prepared to march on Ammanford No. 2 Colliery, where an electrician was said to have been smuggled into the mine on the pillion of, presumably, a police motorcycle. The local police, who were concealed inside the colliery premises, were joined by 200 Glamorgan policemen, who were billeted in the Gwauncaegurwen brewery. These were rushed to Ammanford by bus, surviving an attempt to ambush them on the way. Warned of their approach, miners rained stones and boulders on the buses from an embankment beside the road, and although they smashed most of the windows, the buses got through. The skirmish lasted from 10.30pm until 3am, with reportedly heavy casualties on both sides.

Alarmed by the violence, and fearing for the safety of the mines, the combines yielded, agreeing to reinstate Wilson and to the continuation of the wages and conditions that prevailed before the strikes. In short, the Seniority Rule was saved. But there were repercussions. Ammanford No 1 Pit was closed permanently and 198 miners were arraigned, 58 of them receiving sentences, which the Home Secretary refused to lighten, of from one to eighteen months. The trials were held at the courthouse in Carmarthen and every day busloads of miners and their families travelled to Carmarthen, where, accompanied by a brass band and in a highly charged atmosphere, they sang hymns and the *Red Flag* outside the courtroom. The trials were perceived as class warfare, aggrieved miners on one side and on the other the combines, supported – this was the general perception – by a jury of Carmarthen gentry. The foreman was the estate agent to Lord Cawdor, and among his fellow jurors were two colonels, two majors, a captain, a knight and a parson. The judge, who seems to have been a scold, advised the miners not to congregate in future and to be thankful for the fair way in which the prosecution had handled their cases. On their release, prisoners were awarded a medal and scroll by the International Class War Prisoners' Aid Society.

The gaoling of some of the strikers and the closure of the Ammanford No.1 Colliery meant that both sides had saved face, but at the cost of an easy and, to some extent, trusting relationship between owners and employees. Because of the anthracite miners' semi-rural way of life, observers would continue to regard them as more peasant than proletariat, but the miners had been politicized and none henceforth would regard himself as the mine owners' man. Just as, centuries earlier, new field systems, new crops and new machines had swept away the customary rights of the mediaeval manors, so the combines and capitalistic enterprise in general would erode custom and practice in the mines. By World War II, except in small mines, the days of the big hewer, the individual stall, and the independent miner were over, and they would never return.

# ACCIDENTS AND OCCUPATIONAL DISEASE

O, collier, collier, underground,
In fear of fire and gas,
What life more danger has?
Who fears more danger in this life?
There is but one – thy wife!

(W.H. Davies, *The Collier's Wife*)

THE AUTHORS OF THE 1842 report on the employment of children in mines listed the ten most common ways in which miners could be injured or killed: 1) Falling down the shaft. 2) Being struck on the head, by something falling, when descending or ascending the shaft. 3) Breaking of the rope or chain that raised or lowered the basket, bucket or cage. 4) Being drawn over the winding pulley and dashed to the ground or precipitated down the shaft through the neglect of the engineman. 5) Something falling from the roof of the mine. 6) Being crushed by a fall of coal at the face. 7) Suffocation by carbonic acid gas (chokedamp). 8) Suffocation or burning by firedamp. 9) Drowning from sudden break-ins of water from old workings. 10) Injuries from horse or carriage.

Only winter sailing in cold Atlantic waters presented as many dangers. Friedrich Engels, however, would brook no comparisons: 'In the whole British Empire there is no occupation in which a man may meet his end in so many diverse ways.' J U Nef, the great American historian of British coalmining, considered that subjecting men, women and children to labour in mines was equivalent to sending raw, unarmed troops into battle against a trained and well-equipped enemy. He could well have been echoing a sentiment expressed by one of the 1842 commissioners, who remarked that, to judge from the conversation in certain mining communities, 'We might consider the whole of the population as engaged in a campaign.' The military metaphor was also adopted by Lionel Brough, Government Inspector of Coalmines for the Western District, in his report for 1864. 'This account of death, contusions, fractures, amputations and surgical operations, altogether sounds like the description of military movements in the field rather than the report of industrious and peaceful pursuits.' By the time of World War II, mining was a far less dangerous occupation than it had been a century earlier, but miners still suffered from tensions, similar, according to B L Coombes, to those that affected soldiers. As members of a reserved occupation, miners were not conscripted, but in the bus taking them to their shift, as Coombes described them, hewers, fitters, labourers and repairmen '[sat] silently as if they were being carried to a battle.'

In mining, as in war, to extend the military metaphor, near misses were so common that they hardly registered. 'If you are nearly run over by a car,' Hywel Jeffreys remarked, 'you remember it for the rest of your life [whereas underground], it's as if we, well, expected to have narrow shaves.' In stall-work, when Jeffreys was in his early twenties, a shotsman, Evan Jones, fired a shot that unintentionally blew out a supporting post about eight feet high. While he was replacing the post, Hywel Jeffreys heard a shout from the shotsman and he felt his shirt tear. A stone six feet long, a yard wide and a foot thick, with razor sharp edges, had fallen and taken a piece from the shoulder of his loose-fitting flannel shirt. Evan Jones insisted that he sit down for a while, but, by the end of the shift, the incident was so far out of mind that Jeffreys didn't even mention it when he got home. Only when an older brother, who had spoken to Evan Jones, returned and remarked: '*G'est ti gynnig heddi!*' (You had a close shave today!) did he think of it again. Injuries and deaths from everyday accidents were so commonplace that, to extend Nef's metaphor, they were as unremarkable as casualties in military skirmishes. Most went unrecorded, and if recorded, the reports were perfunctory. Thus, 'Thomas Morris, single, collier of Winifred Road, Skewen, was killed at

No. 7 Pit of the Main Collieries at Skewen early this morning. Deceased was buried under a fall of about two tons of coal.'

The frequency of narrow shaves, injury and death resulted from the extraordinary conditions in which colliers worked, combined with poor management and an indifference to safety that, to Joshua Richardson, a Neath civil engineer and author, appeared 'almost incredible.' In a privately undertaken 1848 monograph on the prevention of accidents in mines, Richardson pointed to an inverse relationship between precaution and the degree of danger. In spite of dangers ten times greater than in almost any other line of work, he found that there were fewer safeguards in collieries than in any factory he had ever seen. His contemporaries, the geologist Henry De la Beche and the chemist Lyon Playfair, concurred. Asked by government in 1846/47 to inquire into the causes of gas-related accidents in coalmines, they concluded that working conditions and working practices in the mines of south Wales were not only among the worst in Britain, but were 'as bad as they can well be.'

For the pitman, the hazards began at the shaft: 'A collier,' as one respondent to the 1842 Children's Employment Commission remarked, 'is never safe after he is swung off to be let down the pit.' In the category of day-to-day accidents, deaths from shaft accidents were second only to falls of rock from the roof or, in places where the seams were thick, of coal and rock from the coal face. If, as in early days, the descent was by ladder, men, and the boys clinging or tied to their backs, sometimes fell to their deaths through a loss of footing or, as happened from time to time, through an accumulation of chokedamp in the shaft. At Llanelli, where ladders are said to have been in common use in 1842, they were placed perpendicularly down the side of the shaft and divided by stages or platforms every twenty or thirty yards. Falls could only have been fatal. After the introduction of the windlass and the horse-driven whim gin, colliers descended and ascended either by standing in a basket or tub, or simply by hooking a foot or leg through a loop of the rope or a link in the chain. If hooked in series they looked, as one observer remarked, like a string of onions or, where each man was holding a lighted candle, like a chandelier. In shallow pits, the raising and lowering was by hand windlass, and in deep ones, by horse gin. The colliers held on with one hand, leaving the other free to guide their bodies away from the sides of the shaft. Boys, who often sat astride the knees of the men, could be dislodged by bars or timbers projecting from the side of the shaft. In 1771, at a pit in Landore, a spike projecting from a plank, according to the coroner's report, '… catcht the deceased's waistcoat and he fell down the pit.' In 1785, a collier at work in the coal works of Gruffydd Price, Pentre, when going up, 'struck his head against a piece of timber in the middle of the pit and he lost hold.' In 1769, Thomas Llewellyn, described as an 'infant' and employed at Craig Trewyddfa near Morriston, 'slipped from the chain' and fell back into the shaft. There was an identical accident at Llansamlet, in 1781; when 'coming up by rope about 5 o'clock this morning his [a lad's] foot slipped in the chain which is fixed to the same rope and falling, was dashed to pieces.' In the Seigneury of Gower, between 1700 and 1832, out of 290 recorded fatalities, at least 48 occurred in the shaft.

Ascending or descending in baskets or tubs was less hazardous than hanging onto a rope, but whether filled with coal or colliers, the tubs, without guides to restrain them, could swing from side to side in the shaft. Nor, too, was there any protection from projectiles from above. In December 1815, a basket being lowered down a shaft at Llansamlet was struck, when about 120 feet from the bottom, by a falling stone. One of the two men in the basket fell to the base of the shaft, while the other, suspended by a leg, was saved only because two boys who were also in the basket managed to hang onto him. Ropes and chains were of uncertain quality and strength and, in the days of hand-winding, the only brake, before catches were fitted to prevent the windlass from winding back, was the physical strength of the winder or winders. From time to time, a rope or chain would break, or the operators of a windlass or horse-driven gin, through a miscalculation of the weight, would lose control. The breaking of a windlass handle in 1753 resulted in one of the first recorded deaths of a woman in a mine in Wales. The victim, Prudence Hopkin, was a winder at the Brynhir Colliery, Llanrhidian, when the handle of her windlass 'broke in her hand and she fell into the pit eight or nine fathoms deep.'

After the introduction of steam winding in the 1830s, 'over winding' could be added to the list of causes of fatal accidents. Unless the winding stopped at the top of the shaft, the cage or the container carrying the colliers could be drawn up into the winding wheel, throwing the men off, as one report put it, like monkeys. The winders were often boys, hired at one fifth of the rate of grown men, who at times were inattentive. In the report of one shaft fatality, the winder, a boy of nine, was said to have been distracted by a mouse. After the Coalmines Act, 1842, no one under fifteen could be left in charge of a winding engine, and after 1860, the minimum age for anyone controlling a steam-driven engine was raised to eighteen. The invention of a shaft-guided steam winding engine in the late 1830s reduced the number of accidents, but until the installation of a fence which closed automatically when the cage descended, jerking motions of the cable could still tip colliers down the shaft. A safety cage was introduced in the 1850s and a mechanically controlled gear to prevent over winding in the 1870s. After 1858, too, new shafts had to be lined, but in 1879, at the newly opened Seven Sisters pit, the descending cage somehow snagged on the side of the pit, tilted, and sent three men crashing to their deaths.

Many shaft accidents were the result of the breaking of chains and ropes. In his 1847 monograph *On the Prevention of Accidents in Mines*, which drew heavily on the reports of the 1842 Commissioners, Joshua Richardson considered chains to be 'peculiarly unfitted' for the purpose of winding. Whether examined by eye, or struck with a hammer, the soundness of the links was difficult, if not impossible to determine. A link that gave out a clear ringing sound when hammered could break without warning. Ropes were safer than chains because they usually frayed before breaking, but old ropes could also snap, and fraying served as a warning only if the ropes, as rarely happened, were inspected regularly. The solution, which came from northern England, was a flat rope made of three strands of ordinary rope laid parallel, and then stitched together strongly. At the Ynysygeinion colliery, Ystalyfera, the rope was ten inches wide by four thick, and the shaft 149 yards deep. Any weakness in a flat rope could be detected as easily as one in a standard rope and the probability of all three strands breaking at once was small. But however safe the ropes and, latterly, steel cables, and however reliable the lifting and lowering mechanisms, many colliers never became accustomed to the cage, pausing on the last step before climbing into it. The sensation of stepping onto a platform over a shaft hundreds of feet deep, the swift fall of the cage, the brakeman's practice of applying the brake halfway down to slow the momentum and the gravity-defying sensation this gave of travelling upward when, in fact, the cage was still going down, tested the strongest stomachs and even the weakest imaginations. Following a disaster at Trimsaran, in 1923, even the journey by slow-moving 'spake' up or down steeply inclined slants could create anxiety. A spake was a wooden frame conveyance fitted on tram wheels and axles. Colliers, usually eight to a spake, sat on each side of a bar or hand rail that ran down the centre. In 1923 a chain link broke on a journey drawing men and tools up the slant. Five of the spakes careered off the rails, dislodging their passengers and hurtling them to the bottom of the slant. Seven miners were killed outright and two died on their way to hospital.

Haulage was also a frequent cause of injury and death. Unlike the hewers, hauliers were paid by the day and, in theory, need not have taken unnecessary risks, but in practice they were, like the carters,

*Descent of the spake, Cwmgwili. NMW.*

*Arrival of the spake, Cwmgors, 1910. NMW.*

under the whips of the hewers. Coal had to be moved from the face to the shaft, or the opening to the drift, as quickly as possible. Boys who helped the hauliers could be killed from a 'crush of trams' when trying to hold back trams on a downslope, or when trams ran out of control. A cause of many deaths was the practice of riding on the 'gun', a bent iron bar that attached the tram to the limbers of the horse. If for any reason the haulier fell off then he could be crushed by the following trams. From time to time, also, the shackles and the pins broke, injuring not only the haulier but the horse. Main haulage roads that followed the contours of the seam were often switchbacks, the trams labouring uphill and then plunging down. Due either to poor initial laying, or to subsequent shifts or squeezes in the floor, tramways often zigzagged instead of running straight. Runaway trams invariably flew off the rails, crashing into the rough sides of the roadways and often bringing down timbering and, with it, the roof. In August 1894, the hapless Philip Jenkins, a young trammer at Pencoed Colliery, was killed when walking beside a tramline at the end of his shift. He had a lamp in each hand and, beneath one rounded arm, a large tin jug. The clearance between the tram line and the wall of the roadway was about two feet. The boy was either far from a 'manhole', a place where he could shelter as the trams were passing, or he felt that there was enough clearance between him and the sidewall. As a journey passed, however, one of the trams caught his extended arm, rolled him along the wall and at the same time reduced the jug to metal shards that pierced his body.

At the coal face, there was danger both from roof falls and falls from the face itself. Careful propping or timbering would have prevented many falls but because face workers in south Wales were paid by the amount of coal they cut, timbering was often neglected. And however careful the collier, tops were deceptive. When the roof was clearly unstable, when it was 'sly', or when there was 'clod' above, the men might put in a post every yard or so. Rock tops, which appeared safer, were timbered more sparingly and, as a result, could be more dangerous. A roof with no visible lines of weakness and which rang as soundly as thick cast iron could collapse without warning. In 1866 Lionel Brough, a mines inspector, reported that the worst roofs in the world were in south Wales, '… so complete with 'bell moulds', joints and 'grimes' that perhaps a minute after trying or sounding, a fall, without the slightest warning in the world, will take place, and then those planes and surfaces of structural division are clearly enough seen, many of them as smooth and polished as plate glass.' In 1897 John Henry Richards at Glynea colliery was killed by a stone, nine feet long, six feet wide, two feet six inches thick, and weighing five tons, that fell minutes after the roof had been tested. To break up the stone and free the body took six men an hour and a half.

Like many miners, B L Coombes preferred working beneath a weak or friable roof: 'Better to work in a bad top… then a chap is always careful.' He also disliked working in places where the roof was so high that both testing, with hammers and mallets, and timbering were difficult. Six feet, he reckoned, was about right for mining. Then, a collier could fix supports against the roof and test it for weakness. A higher roof meant a struggle with long, heavy timbers and constant testing for pockets of methane that might have collected in high cavities. Heavy timbers, however, were not always proof against even heavier stones. B L Coombes tells of a three-ton stone snapping a high oak collar and falling with such force that it pushed up the ground around it. A fall of a large stone from a high roof meant almost certain death for the collier below. Coombes' irreplaceable chronicles of coalmining were prompted by a fall that killed two of his workmates. They were clearing a roof fall that had blocked a tramway, when a massive stone fell on them from a height of eighteen feet, killing them instantly. At the inquest, Coombes discovered that neither the coroner, the solicitors, nor many of the attending public had the least idea of what happens underground. He spent the next thirty years informing them.

Fatal falls could occur even in the narrowest of seams. In 1909, John Jones, also at Glynea, when working on his side in a two foot three inch seam, was killed when a stone broke free from the roof and crushed him. His brother managed to pull him free but John Jones died the following day. The examining physician found bruises on both hips and concluded that he had died from abdominal injuries. Death could also come from the walls as well as the roof. In 1919, David Williams was killed by a 'slip', an eight hundredweight stone falling from the side of a heading or roadway. Even cuts and bruises could kill. Daniel John, a road repair man, struck and cut his head against a roof timber in October 1923. The roadway in which he was working was four feet high, but during the shift a 'squeeze' reduced the height of a section of it by almost a foot. John, his miner's alertness dulled by repetition, struck and cut his head; a few days later he died from septic meningitis.

Even without falls from the roof, the standard method of working the coal face, undercutting, could injure or kill, especially when seams were thick. The usual practice was to prop up the face and then remove the props when the cutter judged that the coal was ready to come down. The propping was not always adequate and, if the face seemed particularly strong, it was dispensed with altogether, sometimes with fatal consequences. A coroner's report for 1776 reads: 'Deceased at work in Watch Pit, Gwernllwynchwith, and undercutting a large body of coal when same fell on his head.' And another, for 1788: 'At work at the Church Pit, Llansamlet... he put up a stick to support coals but the coals gave way and fell on the deceased.' Unusually elaborate was an 1853 report of an accident at the Emily Pit near Llansamlet. 'We [Edward Rosser and William Howell] cut under the coal at the bottom of the whole width of the heading, from five to six yards. We were both on our knees at work when the coal suddenly gave way, and [covered] both the deceased and myself. I extricated myself, but was much hurt about the head arms and body. The deceased [William Howell]... was insensible. His right thigh was fractured, and there were some other injuries about the head. In about a quarter of an hour the deceased recovered sufficiently to speak, but died shortly afterwards.'

In the aggregate, falls of ground, haulage and shaft accidents, the day-to-day penalties for coalmining, were the greatest threats to life and limb, but they were so frequent as to be almost beneath notice. Chokedamp and firedamp, on the other hand, which were more likely to ambush companies of colliers than pick them off singly, commanded attention. Although not always fatal, chokedamp could kill, or render senseless, quickly and silently. 'Neither visible nor noisome,' wrote Robert Plot, these damps 'are suddenly mortal,' overcoming so quickly that the collier was 'without access to cry but once, 'God's mercy.' Matthias Dunn, a colliery manager and the author, in 1844, of a book on the coal trade, averred that 'a single breath of it when pure is almost certain death.' Even those who escaped 'absolute suffocation' might, according to Mr Jessop of Yorkshire in 1675, suffer violent convulsions and 'some lightness of brain thereafter.' Heavier than air, chokedamp lingered in pockets and old workings not reached by the ventilation system, and which miners entered at some risk. The seventeenth century remedy for colliers overcome by what in England was known as the smothering damp was, 'To dig a hole in the earth and lay them on their bellies, with their mouths in it; if that fail they tun them full of good ale; but if that fail they conclude them desperate.'

At the Primrose Colliery, near Pontardawe, in October 1858, eleven men, a twelve-year-old boy and seven horses were killed by an invasion of chokedamp into the 'Old Machine Level'. Someone had opened or unlocked a door, inadvertently diverting the normal flow of air, and allowing chokedamp to invade the level. On hearing of the accident, sixty-year-old William Lewis and eighteen year old Griffith Gibbs plunged into the heading and were also suffocated. A further eight attempted entry and, of these, five were overcome and had to be pulled quickly out of the level. When the fourteen bodies were eventually brought up, all, so it was reported, appeared to be sleeping. Chokedamp's ability to fell miners without damaging or destroying the works, made it an object of, in Joshua Richardson's phrase, 'great and culpable negligence.' Because the mine and its equipment were not at risk, in mines where it was the only, or the prevalent gas, ventilation systems were seldom adequate to deal with it.

Firedamp, on the other hand, which killed and maimed violently, and usually with severe collateral damage to property, was another matter and in collieries 'infested' with it the ventilation systems, Richardson declared, were the most perfect. Pure methane is not flammable, but, mixed with air at proportions ranging from 5 percent to 14 percent, it may ignite and explode. The necessary ingredients were enough oxygen to support combustion and enough methane to cause an explosion. At best, the latter might be a rapid 'inflammation' and, at worst, a blast of enormous violence and velocity that could inflict fearful injuries. The usual sequence was an initial out rush of gases followed by a secondary inrush or 'after blast' to fill the partial vacuum. Explosions often occurred at times of abnormally low barometric pressure, when gas was able to escape more easily from the seams. Ignition might be triggered by sparks from a mandril striking a stone, a fall of hard stone from the roof, the firing of a shot or, more often than not, by open flames.

The earliest description of a firedamp explosion is found in a paper presented to the Royal Society in 1675. In a shallow pit at Mostyn, Flintshire, sunk in 1640, the miners discovered that firedamp began to 'breed' once the workings had moved some distance from the air supply at the bottom of the shaft. At first, the colliers began toying with it with their lighted candles, but play stopped when, one morning, the first man down was knocked over and 'singed' so severely that he was unable to work. Thereafter, a 'fireman', covered in wet rags, went down first to fire or explode the gas. At Mostyn nothing more was heard of firedamp until 1675, when the owners sank a shaft from the bottom of the mine (a staple or blind pit) to a seam below. The sinkers were soon troubled by firedamp but managed to sink to a depth of forty-five feet. On returning to the pit one Monday morning, they discovered that so much gas had accumulated that it had to be fired with a long pole and lighted candles. The explosion was so violent that the sinkers were reluctant to return to work. After a three-day work stoppage, the steward of the mine and two men descended gingerly, but before they could report on conditions below, several of the colliers decided to follow them. One, described as more indiscreet than the rest, '... went headlong with his candle over the eye of the damp pit.' The damp 'immediately catched, and flew over all the hollows of the work, with a great wind and a continual fire, and a prodigious roaring noise.' The men fell on their faces and hid as best they could behind timbers and in the loose slack, or small coal on the floor. The afterblast was even more violent: 'The damp returning out of the hollows, and drawing towards the eye of the pit, it came up with incredible force, the wind and the fire tore most of the clothes off their backs, and singed what was left, burning their hair, faces, and hands, the blast falling so sharp on their skin as if they had been whipped with rods.' Some of the men were thrown fifteen or sixteen yards against walls and timbers and the lucky ones lay 'a good while senseless.' Leaving a tangle of wrecked timbers, overturned trams, and the mangled and dismembered bodies of men and horses, the blast headed toward the day shaft, leading to the surface, and ascended with 'such a terrible crack, not unlike, but more shrill than a cannon,' that could be heard fifteen miles downwind. A horse gin, above the shaft, was blown aside and pieces of it, 'though bound with iron hoops and strong nails,' rained on neighbouring woods. One man, who must have been standing or sheltering near the eye at the bottom of the shaft, was, as later accounts would describe such events, 'blown up the pit' to a height of more than a hundred feet into the air.

In south Wales, firedamp was at its most dangerous in the volatile bituminous and semi-bituminous districts. In one incident at Wern Ffraith colliery, Neath Abbey, in 1758, seventeen men were killed by fire damp in one pit and were buried in rows the following day, in the Cadoxton churchyard. In June 1770, at the same pit, a further ten men lost their lives to 'wild fire'. Seventeen years later, in August 1787, a similar firedamp explosion killed eleven men at John Smith's colliery in Llansamlet. About an hour after the explosion, fourteen men went into the pit to recover the bodies but were down for so long that colliers and agents at the surface feared that they had been asphyxiated, which was in fact the case. A second group descended, cleared an airway, and recovered the fourteen bodies. The men had been felled by oxygen-deficient afterdamp (carbon monoxide) and, when brought to the surface, they were described as 'dead cold', with no pulse and no visible signs of breathing. It so happened that the surgeon called to the scene, Dr Thomas Williams, had recently attended a course of lectures on 'suspended animation' and with the help of an assistant and several volunteers, one of whom was the mineral surveyor Edward Martin, worked on the bodies for an hour and was able to revive eight of them.

Disturbed by the frequency of explosions as mines deepened, in 1815 the Sunderland Society for Preventing Accidents in Coalmines asked Sir Humphry Davy, Britain's most eminent chemist, if he could make a safe miner's lamp. All previous efforts at safe illumination, such as reflected light from mirrors and phosphorescence from the scales of rotting fish, had proved inadequate. Davy visited a gassy northern pit, examined an experimental safety lamp, and very quickly made one of his own from glass tubes and heat equalizing metal gauze. The gauze was of such fine mesh that the flame could not pass through it and, by quickly dissipating the heat from the flame, it kept temperatures on the surface of the gauze below the ignition point. As well as providing a safe source of light, the lamp also detected both firedamp and chokedamp. Chokedamp dimmed and snuffed out the flame, while firedamp gave it a blue mantle or hood. To test for firedamp, the wick of the lamp

An early Davy lamp. The early lamps were simple affairs: a brass oil container, a length of gauze, two vertical rods, and a carrying ring at the top. NMW.

was lowered until the luminous portion almost disappeared, and on being raised into a mixture of firedamp and air a pale blue cap would be seen burning above. From the shape, height and colour of the flame, a trained eye could tell how much methane was present..

The Davy lamp's one failing, that proved deadly for some, was that it produced far less light than an ordinary candle. The original lamp had no glass and the only light available filtered through the gauze. With the addition of glass, the lamp provided about half the light of a good candle but, unlike a candle, it could not be stuck into a convenient niche or hole where the collier worked. Inured to risk, and paid by the amount of coal they cut, colliers did not take to it and, in one of the industry's tragic ironies, the lamp was used in a way that its inventor never intended. In nine cases out of ten, miners used the lamp not to work by but to test for the presence of firedamp before work began. The tests were conducted by a fireman, who then fired the gas so that the men could work by candlelight.[5] Even when the lamp was used, there was a constant temptation to take the cap off, to get more light. As a result, tobacco smoking and the use of unguarded flames continued and became entrenched in the vernacular, the usage persisting long after open flames were forbidden. The collier's expression for let's take a little spell: *'cawn ni mwcin bach'*, originally meant let's stop for a smoke.

While admiring Davy's inventiveness and the intentions of his sponsors, Joshua Richardson considered the introduction of the lamp to be little short of catastrophic. It was the right invention but made, or rather presented, at the wrong time. Conditioned to danger and driven by want, colliers in general were 'so notoriously careless and fool-hardy' and owners generally so greedy that neither, in Richardson's view, should have been entrusted with the unregulated use of so 'dangerous' an instrument. The early lamps were easily fractured, but the greater hazard, given the habits of the colliers and the predilection of the owners, was that they would be subject to misuse. Instead of being used as an auxiliary to good ventilation, the lamp became a substitute for it, taking work into fiery regions of collieries that had been unworkable before the invention. Disarmed by an exaggerated notion of the protection given by the lamp, caution was abandoned. Quoting the findings of a select committee of the House of Commons, 1835, Richardson noted that deaths from explosions in the Durham and Northumberland coalfield, where safety standards were much higher than in south Wales, had actually increased since the introduction of the Davy lamp. In the eighteen years before the invention, reported deaths from explosions numbered 447; in the eighteen years following, 538. Richardson applauded Davy's invention, and urged the use of the lamp in all fiery collieries, but he had no faith that, without compulsion, miners would ever act in their own interest, or owners, despite the public opprobrium periodically heaped upon them, be moved to consider the safety of the miners first. In the face of blanket resistance from the colliery owners, he lobbied for much stronger government regulation in the operation of mines.

Herbert Francis Mackworth, the first government inspector of mines in south Wales, urged the adoption of locked safety lamps, but locking mechanisms were not always effective and Welsh miners, who seem to have been particularly lawless, were adept at opening them. Lock-picking 'contrivances', according to mine officials, were sometimes found in the pockets of dead miners. Had Herbert Mackworth not died in 1851, only seven years after his appointment, his influence on the mining industry might have been as great as that of his forebear, Sir Humphrey Mackworth. He studied science at King's College, London, and worked as a railway engineer, making tunnels, before going into mining. Had his hope for a mining school in Swansea been realized, one of its leading tenets would have been that, in a well run mine, discipline should be observed as scrupulously as in a good regiment. In the steam coal districts east of the Nedd valley, where there was greater risk from firedamp explosions, discipline appears to have been reasonably tight, but in the hard coal districts of the west, where even elementary precautions were considered unpitmanlike, discipline was a chimera. Among the first victims in south Wales from the failure to use the Davy lamp were three colliers at the Old Church Pit, Llansamlet. To the report of their deaths, in 1827, the *Cambrian* appended a cool rider: 'We are credibly informed that the proprietor has furnished the colliery with the Davy lamp, but the men, with fatal obstinacy to their own safety, refuse to use them.' The same reluctance accounted for the deaths of six men, at a colliery on the other side of the Tawe, in 1831. 'We understand,' ran a local report, 'that the workmen in this, as well as several other collieries... decline to use the Davy Lamp and to their obstinacy in this respect, no doubt, is to be attributed this fatal accident.' At the Mynydd Newydd colliery near Swansea ventilation was thought to be so effective that only firemen or deputies, who tested for gas before the men started their shifts, needed safety lamps. In 1844, a firedamp explosion killed five men and severely burned and injured several more. It is also possible that safety lamps were not issued in the otherwise near-perfect Hendreforgan colliery. Nicholas Wood, a well-known Gateshead engineer and associate of George Stephenson, reported to a Parliamentary Committee in 1835 that he had sent some lamps to Hendreforgan, but he felt it necessary to add that he did not know if they were still in use.

In the mining record, examples of careless practices are legion. In 1845, at the Charles pit in Llansamlet, nine-year-old Joseph Harris was asked to go into an empty, unworked stall to fetch an iron bar. The owners of the pit had recently installed a new 'blowing machine' or mechanical fan, but empty, unworked stalls were seldom reached by ventilation systems and were notorious harbours for gas. The boy went in with a lighted candle and, within seconds, there was an explosion. His clothes were nearly burned off his body and his hands and face were 'dreadfully lacerated'. He died that evening, his body swathed in oil. Joseph Harris's death, however, prompted no lasting changes at the pit. Twenty-five years later, in July 1870, the pit's reputation for gaslessness restored, an explosion caused the 'almost instantaneous death' of 19 men and boys. About three years before the explosion, colliers had driven through to the old workings of the Swansea Coal Company. They detected gas and, to prevent it filtering into the Charles pit, they built two brick 'stoppings' five yards apart and filled the space between them with rubbish. The wall, however, dammed up water in the Charles pit and, to get rid of it, two holes were drilled in the stoppings and three-inch pipes inserted that drained the water from the Charles pit into the old workings. As soon as the water level in the Charles pit fell below the level of the drain holes, the openings, to prevent an invasion of gas from the old workings, were plugged with wood. Two men, one during the day and the other at night, were assigned to the work of unplugging and plugging. Although the evidence was not regarded as conclusive, after the accident the plugs were found out of the boreholes. The *Mining Journal* acknowledged that gas escaping from the old workings had almost certainly caused the accident, but deplored the practice of allowing naked lights in mines supposed to be well ventilated, and pleaded for government regulations to prevent it. Paul Reynolds, the Swansea historian, when writing of the disaster, pointed to a tragic irony. It was in Llansamlet, and quite possibly in the Charles Pit, that safety lamps were first introduced in the Swansea district.

Farther up the valley, in the anthracite collieries, practices were even more lax. Most of the collieries were fairly shallow drifts and in them, because of anthracite's low volatility and slowness to oxidize, there was less danger from both firedamp and chokedamp. In general, gas was regarded as a problem only in mines where ventilation was inadequate, and there were, of course, many of these. Inevitably, the men were even less inclined to work with safety lamps, occasionally with fatal

*Open-flame peg and ball lamps, Resolfen 1910.*
*Curling box in the foreground. NMW.*

consequences. In August 1858, at the Cyfing Colliery, Ystalyfera, six men were killed and four seriously injured by a firedamp explosion. At the inquest, James Rogers, a surgeon from Ystalyfera, testified that David Jones, cutter, and the senior of the four men, had suffered a crushed skull ('the skull was smashed in and the brain torn out'), breaks in both legs, and severe burns and lacerations to his body. He could not say if the body had 'burst', because it was covered with coal dust and debris. Cyfing was a pit with a single brick-divided shaft that served as both the downcast and upcast for its ventilation system. Above the upcast side of the shaft was a furnace to encourage the flow of air. The men worked with naked candles and were in the habit of having a chat and a smoke in the pit bottom before going to their stalls. The spell, *mwcyn gweld*, also allowed their eyes to adjust to the darkness. There were no regular inspections for gas, even though a man had been burned, 'It was but a slight flash.' four months earlier, and on at least one occasion, the men had to come up because the air underground was 'dull'. At the inquest, it emerged that there was virtually no movement of air in the western section of the pit, except for a stirring effect caused by the movement of men and horses. The explosion occurred on a hot day, when there would have been little natural convection, and there was some doubt whether the furnace above the upcast had been lit the previous night. Lionel Brough, a government Inspector of Mines, and a witness at the inquest, recommended regular inspections for gas before the start of work and the building of a second shaft with a furnace at the bottom to encourage circulation.

In all coal-mining districts, certain disasters, either through the scale of the disaster, or by exposing gross failures in methods and management, became benchmarks. At the Eaglesbush mine, a mile and a half south of Neath, in 1848, twenty-three years after the introduction of the Davy lamp, a firedamp explosion killed twenty-one men and boys and an unspecified number of horses. As required by law, the inquest which followed focused on the death of one of the victims, a Cornishman named Thomas Christmas who, his wife testified, had worked in copper and tin mines but not previously in a coalmine. A notoriously fiery mine, the Eaglesbush produced so much firedamp that the coal was easy to work. Gas, stored in fissures in the coal, was under such pressure that, in a freshly exposed coal surface, it escaped through the joints with a hissing sound and with enough force to loosen the coal. The main seam, about four feet thick, was described as bituminous and 'very binding', and suitable for coking. Eaglesbush was a slant, entered by a roadway six feet high by five and a half wide that dipped with the coal for about 880 yards. Coal was drawn up the incline by a stationary steam engine. Extraction was by pillar and stall. Leading off the roadway were cross headings, driven at right angles to the main heading and rising only enough to drain water. The headings, two of which were worked-out, were one hundred yards apart. The stalls or rooms, six yards wide and fifty to eighty yards long, were driven at right angles to the cross headings. Referring only to the getting of coal, Joshua Richardson considered the colliery to be one of the most efficient in south Wales. A pupil of George Stephenson, the great civil and railway engineer, Richardson had come south to Neath in 1842.

Ventilation, however, by a down-cast and an up-cast shaft, was a different story. At the top of the upcast shaft was a furnace, with a chimney, to encourage updraught. In warm, windy or foggy weather, unaided ventilation was very sluggish, the air moving from side to side rather than along its designated mile-and-a-half course through the mine. The furnace, of very imperfect design according to Richardson, had rarely been used and at the time of the explosion it was dilapidated. To ventilate the stalls, 'bolt-holes', through which air could pass, had been drilled through the walls dividing them. As the face of the stalls moved forward, the older bolt-holes near the entrance to the stalls and the worked-out areas behind were 'gobbed up' with dry waste, without mortar. Nothing was done to direct the air beyond the open boltholes to the advancing work face. As a result, gas accumulated at the upper, working end of the stalls. In the worked out stalls and headings there was no ventilation at all, and because the gobbing was not tight and had been loosened and holed by rats and mice, fire damp – which could be heard hissing out of the abandoned stalls – leaked its way into the working stalls. Inspecting gob holes for rat damage was one of the daily duties of the overman David Griffiths. In those parts of the working stalls not reached by the ventilating currents, the men resorted to beating out the gas; that is, using 'fans' or wooden, canvas-covered frames about two feet square to drive the firedamp away from the face toward the bolt holes.

According to Neath writer Harry Green, both the abandoned and the working stalls were a bomb waiting for a detonator. At 2pm on Wednesday 29 March 1848, between the sixteenth and twenty-fourth stalls in number three heading, detonation duly occurred. The sound of the explosion carried to Neath. According to David Griffiths, the point of ignition was in one of the working areas and the explosion, by knocking down a partition, detonated the gas in an abandoned stall or stalls. At the inquest, he testified that on the morning of the day of the explosion he found several of the deceased smoking. He also noted that the cap of one lamp had been removed, and in answer to his inquiry about firedamp, he had been told by the men that there was none present. The assistant overman, Thomas Hill, testified that he heard two reports, one directly after the other. 'It was as loud as any thunder I ever heard.' He was then struck down by a 'kind of blow on his back.' Near the explosion, both men and horses had been terribly burned and mutilated, and drams hurled across the roadway, preventing easy escape.

On the insistence of H S Coke, a solicitor who served both as town clerk and clerk to the Magistrates, the inquest was adjourned to allow two independent surveyors, one of whom was Joshua Richardson, to inspect the mine. They were joined by W P Struve, a civil engineer and mineral surveyor, who represented the owners. In 1847 Richardson had been awarded the Telford Medal, the highest award of the Institute of Civil Engineers, for an essay on the ventilation of mines. Disturbed by the frequency of firedamp explosions, Coke had also written to the Secretary of State, Sir George Grey, requesting the presence at the inquest of a government inspector or scientist. Only the attendance of a qualified, impartial observer, he insisted, would satisfy the public mind. When questioned about his role in the proceedings by the attorney for Penrose and Evans, the operators of the mine, Coke replied that he appeared for the Crown, not to incriminate any person or persons, but to try to determine how Thomas Rose and his fellow miners had come to their deaths.

Although Coke was ostensibly neutral, his insistence on inspection and the attendance of a government scientist was designed to thwart any attempt by the owners and managers to lay the entire blame for the explosion on the miners. David Griffiths, the overman at Eaglesbush, testified – one could almost say predictably – that an hour and a half before the explosion he had found men smoking and that one of the miners had taken the cap off his lamp. On the Monday following the explosion, Rosser Thomas, one of the surviving miners and a leading witness, had gone with his mates to the colliery to collect their lamps which, blown out by the explosion, they had left in their stalls. At the time of the explosion, he and two of his workmates were cutting an airway after complaining about firedamp in their stall. Thomas feared, as did the other miners, that the lamps might be tampered with. At the entrance to the mine, however, they had been intercepted by George Penrose, one of the owners, and turned away. Penrose accused him and his mate, John Parker, of being 'bad fellows' who had been responsible for injury to one of their workmates, and intimated that the explosion had originated at or near their workplace. In his testimony Thomas declared that this was his second session at the mine. He had worked at Eaglesbush in 1845 but had left after an explosion had severely burned several of the men. He returned because the coal, pushed out by the gas, was easy to cut; a coal face that was as dry as bone had 'no work in it.' He vowed, however, that he would now be too afraid to work at Eaglesbush again. Thomas was twenty-eight and had worked in mines for twenty years.

The court-appointed surveyors examined the drift two weeks after the explosion, by which time the wreckage had been cleared. At the resumed inquest, they reported that gob holes had been rebuilt and refilled with mortared stone. Firedamp, however, continued to hiss out of the coal at rates the ventilation could not remove; the air flow through the workings, fifty-three cubic feet per second, was only about one third of the rate required. They also concluded that the overman should have operated the furnace above the upcast. A surgeon from Neath, W G Jones, testified that, during the previous four years, forty to fifty colliers had been burned at Eaglesbush, but none fatally. In 1845, Penrose and Evans, lessees of the Eaglesbush colliery, had applied to the magistrates for summonses against workmen who left without giving the required notice. But Eaglesbush's fiery nature was so well-known that the magistrates sided with the men and rejected the application. In the men's favour, too, had been Penrose and Evans's persistent refusal to have the mine surveyed, even though they had consulted W P Struve about means of improving ventilation and were considering adopting a mechanical fan of Struve's invention. Struve had advised the owners to build partitions or brattices at the entrance to each stall, to direct the air toward the face, and to replace the chimney above the upcast with a culvert running uphill to a furnace and a chimney. At the inquest, Struve, in support of the owners, expressed the opinion that the explosion had probably occurred not far from where the naked lamps had been found. A year later, however, in his testimony to a House of Lords Committee on Accidents in Mines, he declared that,

'If you were to allow this colliery [Eaglesbush] to stand idle for twenty-four hours, all these stalls would fill with the fire-damp.' The jury, like most at inquests of this kind, returned a verdict of accidental death. On the rare occasions when manslaughter had been the verdict, the problems of assessing responsibility proved so difficult that the decisions were overturned.

Cases of completely careless management still figured in the accident reports of the 1860s and 70s. At the Park Colliery, near Neath, in June 1863, six lives were lost to firedamp. The mine was inadequately ventilated by a small fan and, as at Eaglesbush, there was no provision for getting air to the working places and there was no regular inspection of these before the men went to work. The whole colliery, according to a subsequent mines inspector's report, was in an explosive state right up to within a few yards of the shaft. So 'gassy' was the mine that, again as at Eaglesbush, the men were in the habit of removing the gas by 'brushing it out with their coats.' At the coroner's inquest, the owner and manager were each fined twenty pounds, the maximum penalty (for an offence not specified in the newspaper report), but the verdict was accidental death.

Verdicts of accidental death attributable to smoking and the opening of safety lamps remained standard into the twentieth century. Commenting on the report of one accident he'd witnessed, one of B L Coombes' workmates remarked that, against the instructions of the manager, they had entered a stall where two men had been killed. The men had one lamp between them but, 'When the inspector came he found two lamps there, one opened, and they counted as most likely he'd been smoking. Dead men can't argue… and ever since when I hears of matches been found or opened lamps after an explosion I wonders how they did get there, aye I do.' The readiness with which owners, managers and, on occasion, the press attributed explosions to smoking had earlier enraged Will Abraham, the renowned miners' leader. After the deaths of six men, four by explosion and two would-be rescuers by asphyxiation, at the Genwen-Cwmfelin pit near Llanelli in 1907, rumours immediately began to circulate that at least three of the men had been smoking at the time of the explosion, and that two or three of the lamps had been found unlocked. When interviewed, one of the co-owners of the colliery offered that there was little doubt that the men had been smoking. The explosion had occurred shortly after the men's six o'clock meal break. Two headlines in an evening paper read: 'Inviting Death' and 'Six Lives for a Smoke'. The pit was known to be fiery, yet in the report book for the previous twelve months there had not been a single entry for gas inspection. The under-manager testified that he had not heard, nor had he ever known, of smoking in the pit. In any case, as J D Lewis, HM Inspector of Mines, asserted, pipes and tobacco may have ignited the firedamp, but they were the instrument not the root cause of the explosion. The mine was known to be gassy and precautions to prevent accumulations had been inadequate. Will Abraham attacked the owners for starting the rumours, and the press for spreading them. Such fabrications, he thundered, 'gave the impression to the man in the street that there was no blame attached to anybody except the workmen, but people who knew about colliery work would realise… that the workings must have been a kind of 'living gasometer' before an explosion could have occurred where the men were taking their food, even if they had a thousand pipes.'

The solution to the ravages of chokedamp and firedamp lay in adequate ventilation complemented by systematic inspection and the elimination of naked flames. Richardson advocated that all mines be equipped with an anemometer to gauge the velocity and volume of the airflow, and a barometer to measure changes in barometric pressure that would indicate rates at which gas might be escaping from the coal face. The lower the barometric pressure, the greater the rate of release. Until mid century there had been no advance on convectional systems of ventilation. A furnace at the bottom of the upcast shaft was found to be more effective than one at the top, and cold water poured into the downcast shaft, as in Hussey Vivian's mines near Swansea, improved circulation in muggy weather. After chokedamp had suffocated an engineer in the shaft of a Llansamlet pit in 1833, the agent ordered the miners to divert 'a stream of water and wind into the pit.' Steam jet ventilation, which was first used at Hendreforgan, had few takers. Tests revealed that, on balance, it was no more efficient than convectional systems and it used inordinate amounts of coal. The breakthrough came with W P Struve's invention of a steam-driven ventilator that consisted of two great bells or aerometers moving up and down in a masonry seal. The aereometers drew the air from the pit as they rose and expelled it through valves as they fell; creating a vacuum that once again was filled with air from the pit. Struve was born in Jersey and learned his engineering at the Neath Abbey Ironworks. In a report to the Swansea Scientific Society, he demonstrated the inadequacy of the ventilating powers of even the best furnace which, while consuming enough coal to power a fifty or sixty horsepower steam engine, could itself produce only 25 percent of a horse power. Struve's ventilator was driven by a five horsepower engine. In 1848, following the exposure of the woefully inadequate ventilation system at the Eaglesbush colliery, the lessees of the mine invited Struve to install his ventilator. Writing in 1851, three years after the installation, Joshua Richardson reported that it had worked satisfactorily for three years and increased the air flow at Eaglesbush from 3,000 to 13,500 cubic feet per minute. In July 1849, Struve, recently elected a member of the Institute of Civil Engineers, was invited to give evidence before a Parliamentary Select Committee on the Prevention of Accidents in Coalmines.

South Wales, too, was the setting for the introduction of the centrifugal fan. Brunton, an ex-employee of Boulton and Watt, conducted his first trial at Gelligaer in 1849. Although its action was continuous and its design less complex than the Struve fan, Brunton's prototype lacked power. Later fans, however, were both more powerful and more reliable and by 1870 they had consigned convectional systems to the mining margins. Among the more successful of the later fans was one by G Waddle of Llanelli, a member of the South Wales Institute of Engineers. In 1863, he installed a fan at the Bonvilles Court Colliery – known later as the Fan Pit – that remained in service until the colliery closed in 1930.

But offsetting any improvements in ventilation or the detection of gas, so owners invariably asserted in the case of an accident, was a countervailing complacency on the part of the men. On 8 March 1877, eighteen men were killed by a firedamp explosion at the Weigfach Colliery, just off the road between Llanelli and Swansea. The pit was ventilated by an air fan considered so efficient that safety lamps were not always thought to be necessary, except in recent extensions to the pit. In these, naked flames were expressly forbidden, except when sanctioned by a fireman or the overman and, at the first sign of gas, the men were to leave the area and inform the fireman. On the day of the explosion, according to testimony at the inquest, the overman, who was killed by the explosion, overruled the fireman and entered the new workings with an open flame. He and seventeen colliers were killed, either directly by the explosion, or the subsequent afterdamp; the overman's open lamp was found nearby. The dead colliers were also drawn into the circle of blame. March was the date of the Llangyfelach fair, and the men had failed to work their usual turns on the day before the explosion. As a result, a small auxiliary fan had not worked for eighteen hours or more, allowing gas to accumulate.

In other collieries, ventilation remained primitive. Hendreforgan in 1869 relied on convection aided by a furnace at the bottom of a chimney or stack above the upcast shaft. The colliery, for the most part, was worked by naked lights. In November 1869, a fall from the roof in one of three seams being worked appears to have released a large quantity of firedamp that directly, through explosion, or indirectly, as afterdamp, killed six men. At the inquest, Thomas E Wales, Government Inspector of Mines for the South Wales District, concluded that in all his experience he had never met a case where 'less knowledge of mining was brought to bear.' The ventilation system he dismissed 'as of the worst description.' Not only was the amount of air circulating through the workings inadequate for the purpose but the same current of air had to pass through the workings of all three veins being worked. At the very least, he asserted, each vein should have had its own supply of air. Despite contrary opinions delivered by technical witnesses for the mine owners, the jury returned a verdict of death by suffocation for the three deaths under investigation and recommended that the colliery be placed immediately under the control of a competent mining engineer.

# Accidents and Occupational Disease

Efficient fan ventilation that swept air through the roadways and headings greatly reduced accumulations of firedamp but, in one of the great ironies of mining history, explosions continued and took their most devastating form in some of the best-ventilated mines of the day. William Galloway, an inspector of mines and author in 1914 of a book on mine explosions, could not understand how firedamp explosions could reach 'into the remotest points of districts ventilated by separate currents of intake and return air.' His transfer from Scotland to south Wales in 1875 helped solve the problem. In south Wales, he noted that all the mines in which the greatest explosions had occurred were 'dry and dusty', and that some of the highest dust levels were found in mines in which the ventilating currents were strongest. As Anthony Thomas, Humphrey Mackworth's agent for his mines at Baglan, had done two hundred years earlier, Galloway posited a link between coal dust and the intensity of the firedamp explosions. Safety from firedamp, as authors Helen and Baron Duckham would point out, had been achieved – but at the expense of greater danger from dust. Galloway's ideas shocked contemporary orthodoxy, but through patient advocacy, most notably in a series of papers in the *Proceedings of the Royal Society* between 1876 and 1884, he managed to convince a sceptical mining community. He ended his 1884 paper with an uncompromising and startling assertion: 'Air containing too small a proportion of firedamp to render it inflammable at ordinary pressure and temperature becomes so when coal dust is added to it.'

Subsequent research and experimentation demonstrated that, in a dry atmosphere charged with coal dust, a firedamp content of as little as two percent was enough to cause an explosion. Galloway added the rider that, the more volatile the dust, or the coal from which it came, the greater the danger from explosion. There was practically no danger of explosion from anthracite dust. Some dusts, however, were so volatile that, given a sufficient source of heat, they were capable on their own of producing explosions of intense violence. They had no need of an accompanying gas. In a dry mine, an initial explosion of firedamp would raise the dust and, under certain conditions, produce an explosion of terrifying magnitude. It was eventually demonstrated that a pinch of coal dust, 0.09 oz of coal dust per cubic foot of air space, might be sufficient. The Royal Commission on Accidents in Mines, 1879-86, dismissed some of Galloway's views, but the 1887 Coalmines Act required that dust be watered within a twenty-yard radius of a gunpowder shot. Later commissions, however, were more attentive and in bituminous mines, watering or dusting procedures, i.e. mixing inert stone dust with coal dust, became obligatory.

In coalfields throughout the world, the most mystifying of all the gaseous phenomena were 'blowers', spontaneous outbursts of coal dust and methane gas under enormous pressure that could within minutes obliterate a coalface or fill a roadway. There was no ignition or explosion but the great clouds of dust and the gas could, and did, suffocate. The most violent of the recorded episodes in western Europe occurred during the sinking of a shaft at the Pas du Calais, in 1907, when dust, coal and gas erupted with volcanic force and from a fountain 120 feet high layered the countryside for miles around with a coating of fine dust. Gas poured out of the shaft for twelve hours. In Britain, blowers or outbursts were confined to the Gwendraeth Valley. In the Gwendraeth, the expulsions were usually preceded by a noise, not unlike that of a two-stroke motor-bike engine starting up and then accelerating, which appeared to come from the coal seam, and lasted from a few seconds to few minutes. 'Pouncing', as the sound was known locally, was accompanied by cracking noises from within the coal face. The ejections themselves were avalanche-like outpourings of pulverized coal, often as dust so fine that it could not be handled by the conveyor system and had to be shovelled into sacks or drams fitted with covers to prevent the dust from blowing away. Flat shovels were useless for the task and had to be replaced with shovels with sides. In most cases the outburst left a cavity in the coal face, but in no case did the size of the cavity bear any relation to the amount of coal ejected. In some cases there was no cavity at all, the pulverized coal being ejected from some invisible subterranean source through a small opening between the coal seam and the overlying strata. The dust was sometimes as fine as a snowdrift so that any miner close to the outburst would have been unable to see or breathe. The first recorded outburst in the Gwendraeth was at the Great Mountain Colliery, Tumble, in 1913, and it coincided with the expanding and deepening of the Gwendraeth drifts. Earlier drifts had been unaffected, but once they reached threshold depths of 800-900 feet, the problems began. The causes are still unclear but there was a consistent and helpful correlation. The outbursts occurred in areas of heavy normal and reverse folding, where the coal might have been broken up and where occlusions could have contained pockets of methane under enormous pressure. Mining, of course, would release the pressure.

Another early occurrence was at Ponthenry, 1919, in a colliery that became notorious for its outbursts. Two men working at the coal face filled a dram, which they took to the main roadway, and had just returned to the face when the pouncing began. The coal face ruptured and within seconds two hundred tons of fine coal dust had filled the heading. The pressure flung one man across the heading into a tram while the others were 'hurled like balls' in different directions. There were 147 men, with lamps, in the mine that morning and every lamp went out, throwing the mine into complete darkness. Men had to grope their way five hundred yards up the slant or inclined roadway to the entrance. Two hundred and eighty tons of coal dust and an estimated one and a quarter million cubic feet of gas were released. In March 1923, there was another fatal blow-out at Ponthenry. Two men were working in a heading of the Pumpquart vein, about eighty yards from the main slant, in an area of the mine where the coal had taken on a soft, powdery texture, an ominous sign ignored or dismissed by the men. About 7pm the pouncing, which was also heard in other parts of the mine, began, and the two men must have begun to run down the heading toward the main roadway or slant. They were found about twenty yards short of the slant, overcome by methane gas, and their lamps out. Two other men, working near the entrance of the heading, were knocked over by the force of the gas and their lamps also were blown out. More than a hundred tons of coal dust were ejected and the gas was under such pressure that it travelled 300 yards up the slant against an incoming current of air. The blast blew out several pairs of timbers, turned an empty tram up on end, and crushed flat a twelve-inch iron pipe.

Outbursts also plagued the giant new mine at Cynheidre. The mine, which worked coal at levels of 1680, 1980 and 2280 feet, began production in 1961 and from the outset was beset by accidents. Six men lost their lives by falling in the shafts and others were killed through roof falls and accidents with haulage trams and explosives at the coal face. Outbursts began in 1962/63, when more than thirty incidents forced the abandonment of an entire working area. There were a further sixteen outbursts in 1965, one of which filled a heading for a distance of seventy yards with eight hundred tons of fine coal. By 1971, the year of the most serious outburst, when the mine had been open for ten years, there had been no fewer than sixty-six outbursts. In April 1971, six men were killed and sixty-nine others affected by varying degrees of asphyxia from an outburst that gave little warning. On the night shift before the day of the outburst, shot firing had produced more dust and loose coal than usual and sprays had to be employed to keep the dust down. The deputy in charge also noticed that small coal was 'spalling' off the coal face and the sides of the heading, and there were signs that the roof immediately in front of the face was beginning to rise slightly. Tests for firedamp revealed no change and there was no pouncing. The colliers filled the loose coal into bags and packed them behind the arched steel pillars. The only warning of something amiss was a fizzing sound as if something was passing through the duct of a ventilation fan, at some distance from the face, and a cloud of dust that appeared to come from the fan. A collier working within sight of the fan saw the flame of his safety lamp rising and, with a number of repairmen who were nearby, he rushed toward the working area. The victims were found at some distance from the face and the outburst coal, suggesting that, like the victims of Ponthenry, forty years earlier, they had run for some distance before being overtaken by the gas.

Of all the ways of dying in a mine, none seems as horrifying as drowning. Falls of stone and rock might be removed but in a water-filled pit there were few escape hatches. One of the worst incidents of flooding in south

# Accidents and Occupational Disease

Wales occurred in the Garden Pit at Landshipping, Pembrokeshire, on a February afternoon in 1844. Workings had extended beneath the tidal waters of the Cleddau estuary where, in places, only a few feet of bedrock covered by tens of feet of estuarine sand and mud separated the colliers from the river. Accounts of the prelude to the disaster vary, but all point to the heedlessness of the management. According to one account, on the day of the disaster a runner was sent to the surface to report that water had seeped into the mine and, as a precaution, the mine was cleared. An hour later, however, the fifty-eight colliers were sent back to work. At the surface, the first intimation of the disaster was the sudden formation of eddies and whirlpools in the river as water poured into the mine. At the same time, workers near the mouth of the shaft felt the blast of a current of rising air so strong 'as to bear up a hand when held unresistingly over it.' Underground, the air rushed through the roadways with so much force and noise that colliers at first thought it was a firedamp explosion. The membrane of rock had been breached relatively close to the shore so that the thirty-three colliers working in distant stalls beneath the bed of the Cleddau were irretrievably trapped and drowned. The remainder ran towards the shaft, shouting for assistance. One survivor reported that a rushing wind, stronger than any he had ever experienced, carried him and his companion off their legs. The ensuing torrent dashed them against the sides of the roadway but they managed to reach the shaft. Alerted by the noise, the man at the whim gin put three horses into a gallop and was able to rescue four men and fourteen boys. Water in the shaft rose forty feet within a minute. The last man to be saved missed the bucket but managed to stay afloat in the rising waters until a bucket could be lowered to him. The sequel to the flooding was a violent explosion the following morning as air, compressed in the recesses of the pit, exploded into the river, throwing large pieces of timber to heights, according to witnesses, of thirty to forty feet. No bodies were ever ejected or recovered, and so there was no inquest and no public inquiry. Local newspaper editors admonished the mine agent. The pit was abandoned; mining continued in the area, but at some distance from the river.

In the zone of water-bearing rocks, abandoned pits tended to be

*The quay at Landshipping, and (below) the memorial to the drowned miners.*

| | | | | |
|---|---|---|---|---|
| THOMAS GRAY | | BENJAMIN PICTON | (16) | |
| BENJAMIN HART | | RICHARD COLE | (18) | |
| WILLIAM LLEWELLIN | (30) | JOHN COLE | (16) | |
| JOHN LLEWELLIN | (12) | WILLIAM HUGHES | (15) | |
| THOMAS LLEWELLIN | (45) | JAMES JENKINS | (14) | |
| WILLIAM LLEWELLIN | (58) | WILLIAM HITCHINGS | (13) | |
| BENJAMIN JONES | (25) | JOHN NOWFIELD | (18) | |
| JOSEPH PICTON | (40) | THOMAS DAY | (11) | |
| JAMES PICTON | (15) | JOHN COLE | (16) | |
| MARK PICTON | (13) | THOMAS COLE | (14) | |
| JOSEPH PICTON | (11) | RICHARD JONES | | |
| JOHN COLE | (25) | MINER WILKINS | | |
| JOHN HITCHINGS | | MINER HART | | |
| JOHN RICHARDS | | MINER LLEWELLIN | | |
| ISAAC OWEN | (23) | MINER JOHN | (CHILD) | |
| JOSUA DAVIES | (22) | MINER DAVIES | | |
| JOHN DAVIES | (18) | MINER BUTLER | | |
| THOMAS JOHN | (20) | MINER BUTLER | | |
| EDWARD JOHN | (13) | MINER THOMAS | | |
| JOSEPH PICTON | (11) | UNKNOWN MINER | | |

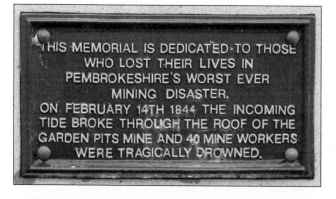

THIS MEMORIAL IS DEDICATED TO THOSE
WHO LOST THEIR LIVES IN
PEMBROKESHIRE'S WORST EVER
MINING DISASTER.
ON FEBRUARY 14TH 1844 THE INCOMING
TIDE BROKE THROUGH THE ROOF OF THE
GARDEN PITS MINE AND 40 MINE WORKERS
WERE TRAGICALLY DROWNED.

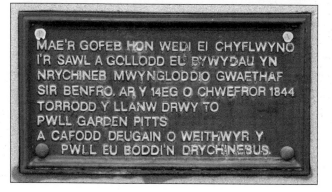

MAE'R GOFEB HON WEDI EI CHYFLWYNO
I'R SAWL A GOLLODD EU BYWYDAU YN
NRYCHINEB MWYNGLODDIO GWAETHAF
SIR BENFRO. AR Y 14EG O CHWEFROR 1844
TORRODD Y LLANW DRWY TO
PWLL GARDEN PITTS
A CAFODD DEUGAIN O WEITHWYR Y
PWLL EU BODDI'N DRYCHINEBUS.

reservoirs and miners broke into them at their peril. In May 1852, twenty-six men and boys – the entire night shift bar one – were drowned in the Gwendraeth Colliery near Pontyberem. Water had been 'gaining' in the pit for some time and, at ten in the evening, a trickle, thought to have come from old, flooded workings, not, as was originally reported, the nearby Gwendraeth Valley canal, became a torrent. The sole survivor, David Evans, was working with a few others around the cage at the bottom of the shaft when he heard a loud roar from the far end of the pit, accompanied by a blast of air which nearly overpowered him and his companions. They gave the signal for the cage to be lifted just as water pouring down the roadway dashed the cage from its guides. Evans, with a boy, hanging on to his coat, scrambled up the guides while another man attempted to climb the rope, but he and the boy clinging to Evans were plucked off by the turbulent water. Evans managed to stay clear of the water 'shooting up the centre of the shaft' and climb to the top. The water was so muddy that pumps were ineffective and no effort was made to recover the bodies. In the field above the mine were large sunken areas, ten to twelve feet deep, marking the place where the waters from the old workings invaded the new.

The striking of a water-filled vein worked by the 'old people' also destroyed the Cae Colliery at Marble Hall, Llanelli in November 1858. Waters poured into the headings and roadway with the force of a dam burst and rose to three fathoms in the shaft. A large pump was brought into service but it was unable to reduce the level by more than a few inches. Ten men and two boys working in the pit perished. The *Cambrian* was forgiving: 'The only consolation which can be derived from this melancholy catastrophe is, that it does not arise either from carelessness or recklessness on the part of any person connected with the management of the colliery but [in a hand-wringing conclusion] is one of those sad accidents which is liable to occur every day, and to which the lives of colliers are daily exposed.' The *Mining Journal*, 17 December 1858, was not as conciliatory, opening its account by quoting a government inspector of mines: 'It was a beastly hole for any human being to go into. That a colliery,' the *Journal* continued, 'should be permitted to be worked in such a state was disgraceful. The flooding,' it asserted, 'was the result of heedless and culpable carelessness.' The owner of the mine had plans of old workings but the lessee had not consulted them.

An obvious precaution in the effort to prevent the inadvertent rupture of abandoned, water-filled workings was the compulsory registration of colliery plans, but, despite the advocacy of experts like John Buddle, only slight attention was paid to the question. The Mines Act of 1850 obligated the mine owner to maintain an accurate plan of his workings that could be shown on demand to a mines inspector. The latter, however, was not allowed to copy the plan. Not until 1872 and 1887 would the depositing of plans of old workings with the Secretary of State be made compulsory within three months of their abandonment.

The ineffectiveness of existing legislation was demonstrated in April 1859, when water from old workings invaded the Main Colliery, Bryncoch, two miles from Neath. Borers in the Main Colliery were looking for an old shaft in an adjacent worked-out mine that might be used both as an upcast, to improve ventilation, and as a second avenue of escape in case of an accident. The pit, Pwll Mawr, had been sunk c.1806 by William Kirkhouse, the engineer and builder of the Tennant canal, and at nearly six hundred feet, it was one of the first deep pits in south Wales. A single shaft for both entering and coming out of the pit, however, had been declared inadequate by a Government inspector and, in the light of the recent flooding at Marble Hall, the overseers decided to break into the old Fire Engine Pit. The borers were not apprehensive, having been assured that the old mine, when abandoned, had been dry. On breaking into an old heading, water immediately began to pour into the Main colliery. The borers tried to plug the hole but the water, which was under great pressure, brushed them aside. There was a general rush to the mouth of the shaft, where the winders, alerted to the danger, sent down cage after cage. Fifty-five men and boys and two horses were rescued, but twenty-five others were left in the pit. Two hours after the accident, the water in the shaft had risen to sixty-three feet, rising ultimately to eighty feet. The two horses saved themselves by leaping into trams in the ascending cage, and a boy escaped by clinging to the tail of one of the horses. The drowning of the colliery traumatized the community. Decades later, when the historian D Rhys Phillips was a boy, elderly miners were still speaking of it with awe.

In spite of the hazards of operating with only a single shaft, it was another three years before two shafts would be compulsory. The pivotal disaster that prompted the legislation occurred at the Hartley Colliery, near Newcastle, in January 1862. A forty-tonne cast iron beam, supporting an engine that pumped sea water out of the mine, snapped and fell down the divided, bratticed mineshaft onto the ascending cage and its occupants. Two hundred and four men and boys, double the normal complement of the mine because the shifts were changing, were trapped. The wreckage lodged halfway down the shaft, preventing the escape of the miners below as well as blocking the flow of air into and out of the mine. Gases in the shaft slowed the work of sinkers and mining engineers and, on the fifth day of the rescue operation, clouds of gas from the workings rose up the shaft, signalling the fate of the 204 trapped men and boys. After the Hartley disaster, all new mines were required by Act of Parliament to have two shafts and all existing mines, except the very smallest, to have two by 1865.

Even if a collier managed to escape crippling or fatal injury, he seldom – at least until well into the nineteenth century – died of old age. James Brown, a surgeon at Narberth, who was interviewed by R H Franks of the Children's Employment Commission, 1842, estimated that the average lifespan of a collier was around forty years. Few reached forty-five. Among the entire population of Begelly and East Williamston, in 1863, only six miners had reached the age of sixty. David Morgan, manager of the Broadmoor Colliery, declared in 1841 that most men were unable to work by the age of fifty or fifty-five. These observations were endorsed by the 1842 commissioners, who noted that 'the seeds of painful and mortal diseases' were very often sown in childhood and youth. They assumed a 'formidable character between the ages of thirty and forty' and soon after the age of fifty 'each generation of this class of the population is commonly extinct.' There were no old miners.

# Accidents and Occupational Disease

Hannah Brown, a sixteen-year-old windlass girl from Begelly, reported to the commissioners that her father, who was 'not very old' (he was probably about forty) had been off for two years with 'bad breath' and was reduced to grazing a cow on the roadside. The cow and Hannah's wages were their sole sustenance.

Aside from the well-known respiratory diseases, 'bad breath', there were a number of minor ailments that were so much part and parcel of pit life that they went unrecorded and unclassified. If few miners, as John Benson remarked, died from rupture and rheumatism, many died with them. To aching joints, from working in water, many could add inflamed and infected limbs. 'Beat hand', 'beat knee' and 'beat elbow' were common to all mining regions. The constant chafing of knees, elbows, and hands when working in narrow seams and frequently foul, unsanitary conditions invited infection, blood poisoning and the inflammation and festering of the joints and limbs. Gas and fetid air, with barely enough oxygen to support the flame of a candle, and inhaled at temperatures of up to 90F, could produce throbbing headaches.

Most debilitating of all, however, were the various respiratory diseases that came from working in damp, wet or dusty conditions. It had long been known that the lungs of men working in rock containing quartz or silica could fill with immoveable, hard siliceous dust. Quarrymen were particularly susceptible as were miners who, in places where seams were narrow, cut into the overlying rock ('ripped the top') to make workspace, or cut through 'hard' headings to make new roadways and new airways or ventilation channels. Anthracite, 'sticking coal', could be so firmly attached to the rock above and below the seam that only blasting could remove it. Nobel's high-explosive powder, *pwdwr gwyn*, shattered both the coal and the embracing rock and filled the air with stone dust. Also at risk were colliers in the steam coal and bituminous mines, where fine stone dust, which is inert, was deliberately discharged in main roadways to settle on ledges and other horizontal surfaces. When disturbed by blasts or strong currents of air it disarmed the coal dust and reduced the risk of explosions. Argillaceous clays, which were found to be just as effective in neutralizing coal dust and were harmless to health, later, replaced stone dust.

In the lungs, stone dust hardened into a cement-like mass, inhibiting, and eventually preventing, breathing. Some sufferers, however, died from tuberculosis, not from the dust itself. Dust-coated lungs were particularly susceptible to the tubercle bacillus. Silicosis was the worst of the lung diseases and, with the victim having to fight for every breath, it could, as one doctor remarked, inflict 'a terrible death and one never to be forgotten'.

> I saw my own brother: rising, dying
> in panic, gasping
> worse than a hooked
> carp drowning in air.
> Every breath was his last
> till the last.
>
> I try not to think about it.
> (Duncan Bush)

By early middle age virtually all miners suffered from 'miner's asthma', a train of breathing and pulmonary ailments attributed to the inhalation of coal dust. In 1863 the *Miner and Workman's Advocate* reported that few young men above the age of twenty-five were quite free from some form of lung complaint and that above the age of thirty-five more than 90 percent suffered from asthma and chronic bronchitis. Above the age of forty there were no exceptions. Lungs were coated either with a black fluid, similar to printer's or common ink, or with a harder layering similar to lamp black or charcoal powder. But as mine ventilation improved toward the end of the century, the incidence of pulmonary ailments decreased. By the end of the century, as complacency set in, coal dust was thought to be relatively harmless. In 1919, J S Haldane went a step farther, declaring that certain kinds of dust, such as coal dust and some shale dusts, actually stimulated the cells of the lungs through the coughing and spitting required to get rid of them. He followed this, in 1923, with a declaration that, 'The inhalation of coal dust causes no danger to life but on the contrary gives protection even against the development of tuberculosis.' In certain mining populations, rates of tuberculosis were in fact relatively low. Asthma, chronic bronchitis, 'black spit', and near universal breathlessness were attributed to damp, wet working conditions and poor ventilation.

The hypothesis of the relative harmlessness of coal dust could not, however, survive the advent of radiography. X-rays showed that the lungs and bronchial passages of miners who drilled and cut coal were just as dust-coated as those who cut headings and airways through stone. The condition was named pneumoconiosis and because its identification happened to coincide with the introduction of machine cutting, more and more men were certified with the disease. At first, compensation was confined to miners who could demonstrate that they had worked in silica rock, but in 1934 it was extended to all men who worked in coal. The most seriously affected were colliers working in the hard, dry coals of the anthracite districts. The painter Josef Herman noted them on his arrival in Ystradgynlais in 1944:

> They are waiting for death.
> Victims of silica dust.
> You can pick them out with your finger
> They will say with a sad smile: 'A bit short of breath.'

To appreciate the effect of anthracite dust on delicate lung tissue, B L Coombes suggested sprinkling a silk handkerchief with hard-coal dust and rubbing it with the fingers. According to Coombes, a measure of the general weakness of the miners' lungs was the late start of the gardening season in the upper Nedd and Dulais valleys. In part this was due to a slightly later spring than nearer the coast, but the more telling reason, according to Coombes, was the miner's instinctive fear of working in chill winds and in cold, damp ground. Work underground may have strengthened muscle and bone but the constant heat, he asserted, left the miner's lungs tender and susceptible to colds, so in the spring he waited for the air and the ground to warm.

A cough and persistent breathlessness were the unmistakable badges of an ageing collier but another, just as infallible, if less common, was a condition of the eyes that made it difficult for him to focus and fix on an object. On coming up from the pit into daylight, many miners automatically tilted their caps over their eyes and stretched their necks. In some cases this might have been a reaction to release from the darkness and confinement of the mine, but in others it was an unconscious effort to find the angle at which their eyes converged and their vision focused. Accompanying physical symptoms were the oscillation of the eyeballs and an involuntary twitching of the eyelids. Other tell-tale signs included headaches, giddiness, night blindness and photophobia, a dread of light. The condition, labelled nystagmus, was first identified in Belgium in the middle of the nineteenth century and recognized generally about 1875. A list of possible causes included poor light and the miner's preoccupation with the stability of the roof and the coal face. His gaze was generally upward, frequently when kneeling or lying on his side. The light hypothesis eventually prevailed. In 1912, Dr T L Llewellyn found that the complaint was six times more common in pits worked with safety lamps than with naked lights, and that it had become more common as safety lamps replaced candles. In its most serious manifestations, the patient appeared to have suffered from shock, reminding one examining doctor of the condition of soldiers who had suffered the stresses and strains of war. Unlike damage to the lungs, however, nystagmus was curable, and would be largely eradicated by electric lighting, although the recovery could take months and, in some cases, years.

For the hewer with nystagmus life at the coalface became impossible, even if he could pick his way there without mishap. His livelihood depended on his ability to strike the same part of the coal face several times in succession, and his safety on his ability to notch timbers with great precision. At the end of the nineteenth century, a fifty-year-old collier delivered the following lament with the customary matter-of-factness of workers for whom the insupportable, by the standards of today, had become the norm: 'Up to the last two years before I failed I had no trouble with my eyes and earned good money. During the last two years my eyes got weak, but I struggled on, hoping things would mend. I lost days and days, and on times a week. At the time it was not safe for me to go to the face without the help of another man. I could not recognize anybody, and I had to walk with my lamp held behind my back. I could always tell by the sound if it was safe. My wages fell to a pound a week, and the manager stopped me at last and told me that it was not safe to work any longer. If I could only have known before, I might have saved my eyes.'

Joshua Richardson, the Neath engineer, ended his monograph on the prevention of accidents in mines with an appeal. He characterized miners as an uncomplaining, long-suffering race exposed, in performing work indispensable to the nation's well-being, to more danger and misery than any other group of Victorian workers. Removed from the world's gaze, however, they had received far less than their fair measure of attention from government. Yet if any worker had a claim to every possible protection from the legislature, then none, he concluded forcefully, was more eminently entitled to it than the British miner. Reading Richardson's monograph a century after its publication, B L Coombes remarked that had it not been for the faded covers he might have imagined, from its style and tone, and to some extent its content, that it had been written in his own time, perhaps twenty-five years earlier. Richardson wrote simply and directly. In the century since the book's publication there had been great improvements in mine safety but, as Coombes noted, schemes of ventilation appeared much the same and much of the work was still being done by hand. Implicit in his remarks is the affirmation that mines could never be safe places and that no book written on mine safety and the prevention of accidents and ailments could ever seem completely out of date.

# SETTLEMENT
# AND LANDSCAPE

A LONG THE COAST AND in the valleys, mining and metalworking, canal and railway construction, and the building of new settlements and the expansion of old ones, were transfiguring. Only Pembrokeshire, where coalmining had not bitten as deeply as in the counties to the east, escaped with minor changes. Until the industrial revolution, farming had been the dominant way of life everywhere. People were farmers, farm labourers, or farm servants, or else they worked at crafts closely associated with farming and common life. East of the valleys of the Gwendraeth Fawr and the Amman, both of which were suitable for some arable as well as dairying, farming predominantly was of the upland variety. Topography, climate and soils favoured pasture and the raising of animals over the growing of crops. Oats, used for cattle feed, was easily the chief grain crop. In 1782, of the 12,550 acres in the parish of Llangiwg in the upper Tawe valley, only 503 acres were in arable: 97 were in wheat, 138 in barley and 266 in oats. Cattle were kept chiefly for their milk, and sheep – on upland farms – for their wool. The latter were of the small, mountain variety whose short wool was used to make flannel, blankets and felt hats. A measure of the importance of pastoral farming was the prominence of the spring and autumn fairs at Llangyfelach, Llandeilo, Neath, Alltwen, and Gwter Fawr (Brynaman). At the autumn fairs, farmers sold stock for which they had no winter keep, and at the spring ones they stocked up for the summer with milk cows and steers.

Most of the farms were tenantries of large estates. People lived on the valley slopes and in the uplands, either in isolated cottages and farmhouses, or in hamlets and villages gathered around a crossroads, an inn, a church or a chapel. The valley bottoms tended to be poorly drained and in places they were covered with trees and a heavy undergrowth of shrubs; where broad and flat they were also subject to flooding. In the Nedd valley, summer and autumn floods were such a danger to hay and corn fields that a charge on landowners for river bank protection, according to D Rhys Phillips, was a fairly constant item of accounts. Like the farmsteads and the hamlets, roads also kept to the high ground and the valley sides. The farms in general were small, most within the range of thirty to one hundred acres, but with a sizeable proportion under thirty acres and only a few above two hundred. Farm workers, and wage labourers in general, usually had enough land for a vegetable patch and a pig.

By the standards of English high farming, Welsh farming was primitive. Most farms were held on long leases of three lives or ninety-nine years, a comfortable arrangement that, reformers argued, did not keep farmers on their toes. English visitors and sojourners found techniques to be primitive, farm implements antiquated, and farm organization rudimentary. The more elevated the farms, the worse the practices. A particularly severe critic of upland farming was the naturalist Alfred Russel Wallace, who, with his brother, in 1841/42, worked as a surveyor for the valuer who apportioned tithes in the parish of Cadoxton-juxta-Neath. Wallace had surveyed in Bedfordshire, where he had taken an interest in English high farming, and where he also read carefully Sir Humphry Davy's *Lectures on Agricultural Chemistry*. The Cadoxton parish encompassed the entire northern flank of the Nedd valley, from the village of Cadoxton, opposite the town of Neath, to Pont Nedd Fechan, a village fifteen miles upstream. While engaged on the survey, the Wallaces lived on the Bryncoch farm of David Rees, who was also the bailiff of the Duffryn estate. On the farm they lived very well, enjoying, as Alfred Russel Wallace put it, the luxuries of home-made bread, bacon, fresh butter and eggs, unlimited milk and cream, and cheese made from a mixture of cow's and sheep's milk. Another delicacy was the true Welsh flummery, *sucan blawd*, a dish made from the husks of oatmeal steeped in water until sour, and then strained and boiled until it was a pale brown, sub-gelatinous mass. It was

usually eaten mixed with new milk. Wallace revisited the Nedd valley
in old age and, in one of his last letters, written in 1913, he asked David
Rees's daughter for details of how to prepare it. She, in turn, provided
a recipe and promised a supply of oatmeal.

Although satisfied with lowland farm fare and, one assumes, lowland
farm practices, Wallace had little good to say of farming on the Pennant
uplands, even allowing for crippling, non-Bedfordlike conditions:
wretched soils, a cool, wet climate, distant markets and, in his phrase,
the entire absence of what the English farmer would consider capital.
Most upland farms had ten to fifty acres of improved land, and an
equal amount of rough, usually boggy pasture. Above the farms were
unenclosed, rough mountain pastures. Driven by habit and custom,
'carelessness, prejudice, and complete ignorance,' farming practices were
matched in poverty only by the land being cultivated. Green crops were
unknown and weeding was a desperate measure undertaken only when
crops were about to be engulfed. Against criticism from the twenty-one
year old Wallace, the hill farmer's defence was 'old custom' and the
adage that what was good enough for his forebears was good enough for
him. The farmyards, dung-filled and framed by tumbledown buildings
with broken, gaping doors and rough floors, were studies in disorder.
Yet, like Benjamin Malkin, Wallace noted that even tumbledown farm
buildings and houses were treated to an annual coat of lime, 'at the very
least.' The farmer's use of improved land Wallace found 'dreadfully
wasteful and injurious.' He was particularly perplexed by the use of the
'short hay' meadows. These were large, undulating tracts on the lower
slopes of the mountains that were covered with very short, brownish-
yellow turf of a kind he had not seen in England. At the end of the
summer, they were mown for short hay, so named because much of it,
too short to be picked up with a hayfork, had to be raked and gathered
by the armful.

Contemporary opinion was divided over the relative importance
of soil quality and farming practices in upland areas. In his survey
of south Wales, Walter Davies pointed out that regions of rich soil
seldom produced minerals, and that in places where minerals were
found the soils were generally poor: 'The elevation of a country favours

the discovery and working of mines, at the same time contributes, in conjunction with other causes, to the sterility of the soil.' The coal tract of south Wales was a case in point. At the surface was a poor and weepy topsoil underlain by a mixture of sand and peaty earth four to eight inches thick. This, in turn, rested on a base of yellowish, blueish, light brown clay. According to a successful Llangyfelach farmer, the soil of the upland tract required frequent tillage to be kept as light as possible, and when dry and well-limed to counteract soil acidity and to break down the heavy clay soils, it could produce fine grass and excellent crops of corn. Frequent liming, and sowing early, before the Autumn rains set in, were the keys, and if practiced widely they would dispel much of the unfounded prejudice against the soil of the 'coal tract'.

The improvement of upland farming had been one of the goals of the Glamorgan Agricultural Society, founded, in 1772, chiefly to introduce the methods of English high farming to lowland farms. At its annual meetings, often held at Neath and Swansea, it stressed the importance of liming and manuring, crop rotation and the adoption of new implements. Turnip husbandry, and its role in rotations, it described as 'the fountain head of all good cultivation,' and it distributed free to all bona fide applicants samples of Norfolk turnip seed. In 1772, upland farms fallowed annually as much as a quarter of their cultivable land. Two experienced turnip hoers were employed by the Society to instruct farmers in methods of planting and hoeing. Potato culture, for animal feed initially, was also encouraged, as well as the selective breeding and improvement of stock. William Vaughan's introduction of Cheviot sheep to his Rheola estate was said, in 1818, to have considerably improved the native mountain breed. Prizes and awards were an important part of the Society's programme. Long-serving farm labourers with large families received small monetary awards, while for farmers there were prizes for stock breeding and for the drainage and improvement of previously uncultivated land. In 1790 the Society's honorary medal was awarded to Sir Herbert Mackworth for reclaiming rough land on the Gnoll estate. By 1829 the Society could report great improvements in crop yields, and in the general quality of stock, but its expectations for marginal upland farms were thwarted by the expansion of mining and metalworking.

Wages in the mines and the copper and ironworks were considerably higher than those on the farms and greater than the returns from marginal upland farms. Farm labourers and subsistence farmers, who either gave up their tenantries or abandoned the struggle to improve their farms, gravitated to the mines and metal works. Unable to find tenants for all the farms on his estate, the squire of Ynyscedwyn complained in 1816: 'Such labouring poor as have employment are better off at 8s. a week than our small farmers, whose lands present the melancholy picture of neglect and abandonment.' Neglect of the countryside and country matters was also the gist of William Weston Young's complaint in the 1830s: 'Where works are extended into any part of the country, the character soon alters; their horses are employed in carrying iron ore, coals etc., and they drive them, becoming, in a great measure, day labourers; they are not improved by the change.' In Pembrokeshire, the shift from farm work to coal carting and habitual tippling seems to have been a well recognized progression. Horses were in such demand, both underground and at the surface, that in coal districts farm leases usually contained a clause that required the lessee to keep, at customary rates, a certain number of horses for use in their landlord's coal works. When horses were in short supply, or when farmers could not afford them, oxen were sometimes substituted and in south Wales they may well have been the earliest draft animals to haul coal. The needs of farming were paramount only during the harvest season, when few former farmers or farm workers could resist the siren call of the hayfields and cornfields. In coalmining, when the harvest season coincided with the season of damps, the interruption was usually not serious, but in the smelting industries wholesale absenteeism meant that untended furnace fires burned out. Managers of both the Vivian works in Swansea and the Nevill works in Llanelli complained bitterly of the harvest exodus as well as similar losses during the spring and autumn fairs. For a copper master, a cold or 'dead' fire was a calamity.

D Rhys Phillips noted that, in upland areas, rates of farm abandonment accelerated after 1840-45. Places where plough furrows had once reached almost to the hill tops reverted to rough pasture.

On lowland farms, the reversion had begun even earlier. Faced with plummeting prices and rents during the post 1815 depression, farmers and landowners readily leased lands to colliery proprietors and rented croplands for use as pasture for draft animals. They were also unable, as Walter Davies noted in 1814, to resist the demand for saplings used in mine timbering. A much greater profit and a 'much readier penny' was to be made by selling off juvenile trees than allowing them to grow to maturity. Unable to compete with American and other cheap foreign produce, Glamorgan farmers and landowners were so desperate that, in 1834, they petitioned the House of Commons to 'adopt such measures as would raise the price of agricultural products to meet the heavy burdens pressing thereon, or to lower the burdens to meet the low price of produce.'

Saddened by the substitution of 'fern-clad wastes' for once-happy habitations, D Rhys Phillips rose to the defence of landowners who were accused of want of public spirit, presumably for not lowering rents sufficiently: 'The landowners have been blamed for their want of public spirit, but the crux and cause of the depletion of the countryside was the depreciation in agricultural values and the growth of wage-earning industries, whose proprietors neglected corn lands at full value in order to pasture their draught animals, extend their works, build workmen's dwellings, and desecrate unwittingly what was once devoted to the growth of produce by tram roads, incline-planes, sidings, screens, and graceless rubbish-tips.' Yet in one case, in the Nedd valley, the neglect of farmland does seem to have been brought about by the parsimony of the landowner. On the Aberpergwm estate, the colliers, who were also occasional farm labourers, lived in rent-free tied cottages, and at the colliery were paid at just over one third of the rate at the nearby Resolfen colliery. The Aberpergwm colliers were understandably restless and, when the proprietor Morgan Willams refused their demands for higher rates and repairs to the cottages, they retaliated by leaving and by refusing, in the summer of 1873, to help with the harvest on the usual terms. Their demand of five shillings per day plus food and beer for themselves, and two shillings for their womenfolk, was turned down and much of the hay and corn were lost to rain.

As farms became fewer and mining and metalworking more widespread, country craftsmen had to serve new markets in order to survive. In his memoir of life in the anthracite coalfield, James Griffiths, the miners' leader and distinguished Parliamentarian, described how his father, a blacksmith and son of a blacksmith near Ammanford, found himself sharpening mandrils and making hobnails for the colliers' pit boots. The new clientele changed working hours at the smithy because the colliers would bring in their boots at the end of the shift, around five in the evening, expecting them to be ready by the next morning. On dark winter evenings, Griffiths and his brothers had to hold candles while their father sharpened the tools on his anvil and tempered them by plunging them into a bosh of water. On Saturdays, the boys went around the houses of Betws, gathering money for work done during the week.

With the steady drift to the mines and works, small farms in the uplands were neglected or abandoned and, in groups of four, five and six, according to D Rhys Phillips, they were consolidated into 'mere sheep walks' and attached to larger holdings. He cited one five-mile stretch of western upland in the Nedd valley, between the Hendregeledren brook and Aberpergwm, which early in the century had supported twenty families and by the end supported only three. Mary George, who worked as a servant at Rheola House, related that, when she was a girl, in the 1820s, her father, an upland farmer, had walked eight miles to work at Briton Ferry. He set out early in the morning and returned late in the evening. He had so few opportunities to cultivate his hilltop farm, which he rented from the squire of Ynysygerwn, that she could recall many late Autumn nights when he reaped his crops by candlelight.

While Mary George's father and other half-farmer, half-collier/ metalworker tenants were able, or willing, to walk to a mine or a works, and while mining and metal-making were in their pre-modern phase, there was often no need for separate housing. In Pembrokeshire, where coalmining never enjoyed a truly modern phase, the need hardly arose. The mines were small and most could be manned from the locality. In 1854, Herbert Mackworth noted how little the Pembrokeshire collier differed from the agricultural labourer, by which he meant that often they were one and the same. The coal was usually worked in shallow, temporary pits that afforded occasional or seasonal employment. The miners also worked on farms and many had a freehold interest in a cottage or a hovel to which some land was attached. The unusually close pattern of dispersed cottages and small, irregular fields surrounded by earth banks topped with hedges around Landshipping and Martletwy is attributed to the need of workers in the mines for a cottage and some land of their own. In Saundersfoot, in 1930, 55 percent of the local colliers had smallholdings. Cottages were sometimes built for Pembrokeshire miners, but never in long rows and never in sufficient numbers to seriously disturb existing rural patterns. George Edwards quotes the example of a colliery development at Reynalton during World War I, employing a hundred men, a large mine for the district. At the time, however, only six new houses were built in the village, the miners coming in daily from surrounding villages. Such cottages as were built were the subject of contemporary comment. In his *Guide to Tenby*, 1843, M A Bourne remarked that, at Saundersfoot, the hamlets that housed the colliers were of the most wretched description and the people existed in a state of poverty that would scarcely have been credited in some of the rural districts of England. Mackworth noted that the cottages, known as 'clom' cottages, were built of a mixture of mud, road scrapings and stones, and were thatched with straw. They had no ceilings and were divided into two rooms by earth or boards. The chimney, at one end of the building, was made of wattle and daub wrapped around with hay rope for greater strength. Except in summer, the windows were covered in sacking, and the only lighting was by tallow or rush candles.

Built with no thought to aspect, health or amenity, they could be found on waste or unwanted ground, or on roadsides where high bank hedges restricted air movement and allowed moisture to gather around the walls. In an effort to keep the mud walls dry, fires of 'stummin', a mixture of anthracite culm and clay, were burned continuously. When abandoned, the cottages crumbled and returned to the ground from which, literally, they had been made. 'Clom' is a Norwegian word for earth. George Edwards reported that, in the 1950s, elderly residents of the village of Stepaside could recall upwards of forty clom cottages, of which there was then no trace. Even less habitable than the clom cottages were the hovels built as temporary shelters near the coal works. At Hook, in 1790, a visitor, Mary Morgan, having declined to be lowered into the pit, accepted an invitation to enter a miner's hut. To do so she had to crawl on hands and knees through a narrow opening and, once inside, she could not stand up. The chimney was a hole in the roof and, although the miners ate and sometimes slept in the hut, there was no furniture and no utensils that she could see. 'The miners,' she noted in a telling observation, 'sit upon their hands, as the Indians do.'

To the east, in Carmarthenshire and Glamorgan, housing was more substantial. To accommodate his Shropshire miners, Humphrey Mackworth, presumably sensing local resistance, had found it prudent to house them separately, in a row of cottages, the Mera, then on the edge of Neath. There were also two early developments in the lower Tawe valley. To house Pembrokeshire colliers brought in, so it was said, to break a strike of local miners, John Morris, c. 1775, built a block of flats of, for the place and the circumstances, remarkable elaboration. Writing in 1812, Walter Davies described it as 'a kind of castellated mansion of a collegiate appearance with an interior quadrangle.' According to Davies, it housed forty families, all colliers, except for a tailor and a shoemaker, whom Davies described as 'useful appendages to the fraternity.' Nothing is known of the life of the community but Davies's use of 'fraternity' suggests that some degree of communal life was practised, or at least hoped for.

The castellated look came from four corner towers capped with battlements made from blocks of copper slag. Each tower had a basement and three storeys of apartments, and each of the ranges connecting the towers, two storeys. Except for a few string courses of copper slag blocks at the floor levels, the slag coping stones for the battlements, and a little brickwork, the building was made entirely of local sandstone. Diagonal chimney flues provided a form of central heating, each floor being heated from the floor below. Conventional heat came from fireplaces connected to a common flue. There was also a centralized system of rubbish disposal. Chutes placed alongside the windows of tenements in the upper storeys channelled refuse into a large collecting container.

In spite of features that seem decidedly modern, 'Morris Castle', as it was inevitably called, was not a success. Although they had gardens or potato patches, the miners, who were rural men, disliked living in apartments, and it is unlikely that they would have embraced the idea of communal life. But the really insurmountable difficulties appear to have been physical rather than social or psychological. The Castle was built high above the valley, on the crest of Craig Trewyddfa, ostensibly so that the workers might enjoy a view and breathe air free from copper smoke in the valley below. Its location on a rock far above the water table and the spring line meant that it never managed to obtain an adequate water supply, and to enjoy the view and the fresh air the colliers had to trudge up the side of the valley, after a twelve hour shift in the collieries below. John Morris may have thought he was serving his colliers but a Gothic Revival building in a romantic location suggests that it was built as much for his own pleasure, balancing Clasemont, his mansion house to the north, rather than as a haven for miners. Yet in spite of its failings, his Castle was probably the first example since Roman times of a purpose-built apartment building for industrial workers.

No one is quite sure for how long the building was occupied. It was put up for auction in 1811 and appears to have been abandoned in the 1850s. By 1880 it was in ruins. Quarrying around the base of the building had brought down the two southern towers, and a recent storm one of the two remaining northern towers. Sometime in the 1850s, a visitor to Swansea saw the castle from the train and left a description that seems to be as much an echo of local sentiment as his own assessment: 'Made imposing by distance and dim light, it [Morriston Castle] looks like an old Norman fortalice; but is in reality nothing more than an assemblage of labourer's dwellings, built by some benevolent gentleman, who, fondly imagining that workmen might live together like bees in a hive, erected this huge barrack for their accommodation, discovering his mistake only when it became desolate or was adopted by rats and rooks.'

The limited appeal of his tenement building and the scepticism of the locals may have been apparent from the outset, but they did nothing to suppress John Morris's appetite for good works. His next scheme was more ambitious and far more practical. He referred both to the scheme and his reasons for undertaking it in a letter, written in 1819, to the then prime minister, Lord Liverpool: 'About forty years ago I appropriated a farm for the purpose of inducing the artificers and labourers of the County to build thereon, giving them a long term of years, at a nominal acknowledgement with a sufficient plot laid on, for raising potatoes. The scheme at the time was thought a visionary one, by all around me; but I have lived to see about 300 stone cottages with tiled roofs built by this class of persons, and I need not add that such persons never become burthensome to the Parish but continue to hold out the best example of prudence to their neighbours.'

Although engagingly modest, Morris's description of the scheme is misleading. His design was for a model town, not just a collection of houses that would accommodate both miners, at his Trewyddfa, Pentre and Clyndu collieries, and copper workers at the Forest works. To lay out a plan for Morriston, he engaged William Edwards, a well-known engineer and bridge-builder, who is best known for a beautiful arched bridge he built in Pontypridd. Like most planners of new towns, Edwards decided on a grid, or rectangular pattern of streets and he laid them out on a sloping terrace of green fields near the Forest copper works, about three miles above Swansea. The plan's only distinguishing features were the spaciousness of the streets and the placement of a chapel of ease at the intersection of the two main streets. Instead of building the houses himself, the usual practice in philanthropic schemes of this kind, Morris leased plots on very favourable fifty-year terms to colliers and copper men.

The houses, built to a prescribed plan, had a central doorway, two storeys and a whitewashed front. Most faced the river and each had its own garden. His objective was to provide the men and their families with a link to the countryside, from which most of them had come, and a degree of independence. He encouraged the steadiest of them to keep a cow on Trewyddfa common. With free fuel, a potato and vegetable

*Cottages built by John Morris at Morriston, c. 1790, for his miners and copper workers. WGAS.*

patch and, possibly, a cow they would, *in extremis*, be able to sustain a family. Construction seems to have begun in the late 1780s and by the mid 1790s there were 141 houses up, accommodating 619 people, a modest ratio for the time. Built from local stone by local masons and by the workers themselves, the houses were detached, roomy, and had good gardens. Almost a century before any state-provided scheme, he introduced a form of workmen's compensation and set up funds to protect workers against sickness, injury and old age. Later, he built houses for the poor. But in the plan for Morriston there were failures of detail. In his report to the General Board of Health in 1849, George T Clarke noted that the streets and roads were poorly made, and that there had been no attempt to keep them clean. Lighting and ventilation were no better than average and none of the houses had drains. Some also backed into the side of the valley and, with no through ventilation, were damp as a result. Water was drawn from shallow wells, some of which were contaminated with sewage.

Although Morriston was the only planned settlement in south-west Wales, its quasi-rural character may be taken as a metaphor for the industrial settlement as a whole. With the exception of parishes in the lower Tawe, the coalfield west of and including the Nedd valley was spared the ranks of terraced houses fronting the streets which filled the eastern valleys. In the western valleys, mining and metalworking began early and developed slowly. Small collieries, spread over a wide area in a region of mostly marginal hill farming, made large urban settlements unlikely. Growth for the most part was slow and orderly, and mining settlement, while it disturbed the prevailing agricultural order, did not obliterate it. Whereas the Rhonddas, by the end of the nineteenth century, were home to 50,000 miners, and the Taff to more than 30,000, there were fewer than 9,000 in the Nedd valley. Slower population growth and gentler relief meant that there was far less pressure on larger amounts of building land. In the narrow eastern valleys, where streets had to be etched out of the steep valley sides, the costs of excavation and of building embankments and retaining walls were frequently higher than the costs of house construction. With building land at a premium, and with the builders intent on maximizing their returns, terrace housing on an unprecedented scale was the inevitable result.

In the western coalfield, house-building, for the most part, was able to keep up with demand. There were cases of overcrowding, but they were seldom permanent, and they were more a result of sudden growths in the tinplate industry than in mining. In the parish of Llangiwg, an industrialized parish in the upper Tawe valley, the average number of occupants per house in 1861 was only fractionally higher than it had been in 1801; and this after a decade in which the population had doubled. Most of the colliers were recruited from within the region and most clung to their rural roots. If the house had a sizeable garden, the collier and his family grew vegetables, kept chickens and, over the summer, one or two pigs, fed on bran and garden and kitchen waste. J H Howard wrote that, in Llansamlet in the 1880s and 90s, a pigsty was as necessary an adjunct to the house as a garage, or at least a parking space, is to a modern one. The pig, as important in Llansamlet as it was in Eire, was the 'gentleman who paid the rent, or interest on the

*High Street, Tumble. In the background, the farms and fields of the Gwendraeth valley. NMW.*

mortgage,' and on most days of the week, he furnished the table. For Howard as a child there were two stages in, as he put it, the drama of the sty. In the early autumn, he and his mother bought a piglet at the Neath fair, and in the spring, another at the Llangyfelach fair. The pig was driven home with a rope tied to its hind leg. The second stage of the drama was the killing of the pigs in November. The spare ribs were cut into pieces and usually shared among neighbours; the sides and hams were home-cured and wrapped in muslin, and then hung from hooks attached to kitchen beams.

Frustrated colliery owners and overseers sometimes accused the men of deliberately provoking work stoppages in the spring, so that they could spend whole days working in their gardens. Disputes and stoppages, that coincided with the spring and autumn fairs, raised similar suspicions. In 1919, at the Gelliceidrim colliery, a dispute with management over the miners' right to collect manure from the colliery stables led to court proceedings. So strong was the attachment to country ways that, in the Ammanford district, colliers without land of their own were allowed to plant a row of field potatoes in exchange for help with the harvest. Thus the neat and frequently quoted apothegm of the miners' agent,

John James: 'The anthracite collier has a pick in one hand and a garden spade in the other.'

B L Coombes, who lived on a farm in Herefordshire before becoming a miner in the Nedd Valley, was never free of the lure of the countryside and the fields: 'I carried the smell of the wood fire with me, and it has hung in my senses ever since. Little things like the thud of a falling apple, the crackle of corn being handled, and the smell of manure drying on a warm day… are still very sweet to me. Every year the smell of drying grass makes me crave for the hayfields.' In his memoir of life in the anthracite coalfield, Jim Griffiths tells how his mentor in the mine, Twm Penyrargoed, whom he described as 'a craftsman at the coalface', returned immediately to country ways once he finished at the pit. His metier was poaching hares and rabbits with a ferret, which he tucked in his shirt behind his back, and a brindle greyhound. Once the days began to shorten, he would poach salmon in the Cennen River, using his pit lamp as the lure. When not poaching, his favourite recreation was attending the spring and autumn fairs in Carmarthen,

*The Nant Melyn farm and engine house in the Dulais valley above Seven Sisters. The farm was the intended site for a new pit and the outbuilding housed a steam engine. In the background is Mynydd y Drum. Courtesy W T Davies.*

Llangyfelach and Llandeilo.

In 1903, Will Abraham, the south Wales miners' leader, commented on the leverage, in disputes with owners and managers, given to miners who kept one foot in the country and who were able with relative ease to acquire houses, gardens and smallholdings. Colliers with a vegetable garden, field potatoes, a couple of cows and a pig or two, did not have to 'follow the loaf' or go 'on the tramp' quite as assiduously as wholly wage-dependent colliers in more urbanized and industrialized coalfields: 'I don't know,' noted Abraham, 'that the anthracite workmen enjoy any more legal liberties than any other body of workmen in the coalfield. But this I do know, that they are much better equipped and able to maintain those that they have than almost any other body of workmen in the United Kingdom… houses and large gardens are as a rule easier to get at more reasonable terms than in other portions of this busy coalfield.' Colliery owners would have agreed, one from Llansamlet complaining that he could not hope to break a colliers' strike, 'because each family had three mounds of potatoes [stored in soil heaps] to fall back upon.' The collier's other lever was that, barring the collapse of coal prices, he need not fear unemployment. Until the arrival of the great combines, he could always, as J H Howard remarked, go from pit to pit, and was always sure of employment.

Even though collieries and works were probably the largest single group of house owners in the western coalfield, compared with other coalfields, the percentage of colliery or works-owned houses was small. Colliers who needed houses could buy or rent on the open market from speculators, who were frequently groups of local business and professional men who invested in new housing, or they could build their own through building clubs. The colliers' building club was a Yorkshire invention that south Welsh miners adopted wholesale during the second half of the nineteenth century. From their wages colliers would put aside money in a building club which, on the advice of a secretary (who was usually an accountant), would arrange for a number of houses to be built by contract. When about a quarter of each house had been paid for, the houses were then allotted by ballot, subject to a mortgage that could be paid off gradually. To ensure fairness in the allocation by ballot, all the houses, which usually had front and rear gardens, were built to a single design. By the end of the nineteenth century, roughly a quarter of all new houses built in the mining districts of south Wales were contracted by building clubs. Initially, however, renters would easily have outnumbered owners in all the mining settlements, but by 1913 the proportion of miners in south Wales living in their own houses was 19-20% against 7% for the UK as a whole. By 1948 in the south-west the proportion of owner-occupiers had ballooned: in Pontyberem 48 percent of the houses were owner-occupied, in Ammanford 75 percent, and in Brynaman 67 percent. In Glyncorrwg, on the other hand, where, as in the valleys immediately to the east, heavy immigration was accompanied by heavy speculation in house construction, the percentage of owner-occupiers was still only 29.5 percent.

As in the eastern section of the coalfield, the general effect of industrialisation and the associated housing was to fill in the valleys, although not as overwhelmingly. Canals, tram roads, railways and pits, as distinct from drifts, sought the low ground, and the result was the development of a tier of industrial settlement below the agricultural one on the valley slopes and the hills above. In his study of the anthracite coalfield, I L Griffiths identified two basic types of mining settlement: the valley villages and the *gwaun* or upland villages. The *gwaun* settlements occupy sites, often at road intersections, on high open land at the heads of the valleys or, in several cases, between the valleys. Cross Hands, Gorslas, Penygroes, Saron, and Capel Hendre are on the *gwaun* between the valleys of the Gwendraeth and the Llwchwr, while Tai'r Gwaith, Gwauncaegurwen, Onllwyn, Coelbren and Banwen occupy similar sites between the Tawe, the Dulais and the Nedd. The valley villages, which are the more numerous, are found in the trough along the northern edge of the coalfield as well as in the valleys themselves. In all cases, the villages lie on slopes and terraces above the flood-prone bottomlands, their alignment determined by relief and the direction of the main roads. In rejuvenated valleys, such as the Twrch and the lower Dulais, villages are confined to the narrow gorge cut by the

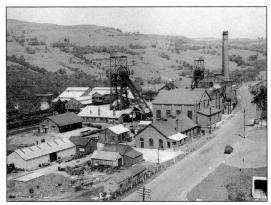

*Cefn Coed Colliery, 1955, below the village of Creunant in the Dulais valley. As a commuters' colliery drawing workers from Neath, Port Talbot and Swansea, it created no mining settlement. NMW.*

*Quasi-rural miners assembled at the Creunant Colliery, 1912. In the background is the valley village of Creunant.*

CRYNANT COLLIERY 1912

Source: Swansea Uni

re-energized stream or to the terrace-like remnants of the old valley floor above. Cwmtwrch Isaf and Cwmtwrch Uchaf are both squeezed into the gorge, whereas Creunant, in the lower Dulais, has been able to spread a little on the terrace between the gorge and the side of the valley. In the larger valleys, settlement is usually on drift or alluvial deposits just above the level of the valley floor. Ammanford lies on a broad river terrace between the Llwchr and the Amman rivers a short distance above their confluence. In the Tawe valley, Ystradgynlais was also built on a river terrace, whereas Ystalyfera, in the absence of either a river terrace or an alluvial fan, had to be built on the steep valley sides. Cyfyng, the old name for Ystalyfera, means narrow place.

In the Nedd valley, alluvial fans, deposited where the Clydach and the Gwrach join the main river, provided dry-point sites for Resolfen and Cwmgwrach. Downstream, villages such as Clyne, Melin Court, Tonna, Aberdulais and Cadoxton cling to steep valley sides that once were riddled with coal and iron workings. East of the Nedd, Glyncorrwg, the outlier village, occupies the side of a valley cut deeply into the Pennant upland. Other settlements were built at nodal points, where natural route ways converge. Ammanford lies at the point where the Llwchwr cuts across the east-west coalfield trough, while Clydach, Pontardawe and Ystalyfera are all located where tributaries join the Tawe and present transverse routes that cross the main longitudinal route up the valley.

The growth of hamlets into villages and towns, in a few cases, involved a change of name. A Guide of 1860 described Cross Inn as a pleasantly situated hamlet, surrounded by some fine trees, on a bank of the Amman. Across the river was the village of Betws. Within fifteen years, the opening of collieries and the building of tinworks had transformed Cross Inn, whose inhabitants, to avoid confusion with other communities of the same name in Cardiganshire and Pembrokeshire, and possibly to underline the settlement's greater importance, rejected the plain but functional 'Cross Inn' for the more stately 'Ammanford'. A precedent had been set sixteen years earlier, when the Swansea Vale railway completed its branch line to Brynaman. Until then, Brynaman had been Gwter Fawr (the Big Ditch), but 'Brynaman' appeared on the platform signs of the new station.

Except for Morriston, the coalfield settlements developed without benefit of planning. The usual pattern was growth by accretion around a hamlet or a cluster of buildings that happened to be close to a mine or a works. As these expanded, they frequently merged with adjacent centres to form villages. The configurations were usually ribbon-like, the houses, shops, chapels and pubs following the existing roads. Initially, Ammanford developed along three main roads whose centre, 'the square', is merely the junction of the three roads. At Gorslas, formerly Chwech Heol (six roads), the ribbon development followed each of the roads. In some places, the road followed was a tram road or wagon way. Neath is threaded by streets along which trams and wagons carried coal from the collieries to copper works and shipping places on the river and the canal. The most conspicuous are those that parallel the road that once carried Humphrey Mackworth's sailing wagons from his collieries to the river. One of them, Greenway Terrace, is named after the Greenway vein, which ran alongside the tram road. One street, just outside the town, was named simply Heol y Wagon but was subsequently changed to Dŵr y Felin, when a pond was built to supply motive power for a corn mill.

In housing, as in mining, investment was on a small scale. Prominent among the private investors in the Tawe and the Nedd valleys were farmers who slipped, according to Ieuan Gwynedd Jones, with astonishing ease into the role of urban rentier. Company houses were needed only where there were large pits and they were built as close as possible to the pithead. At Resolfen, the village grew around a block of four parallel streets built by the owners of the Glyncastle colliery. Glyncastle was the first pit to be sunk downdip from the northern outcrop. For the shaft sinkers at Seven Sisters, the Evans and Bevan Co. built three-room, single-storey, brick row-houses that were occupied later by colliers. They were known as the Seven Sisters row houses, the name that was eventually applied, but with no official adoption, to the village. To work the mine, men came from the Tawe valley on foot, crossing Mynydd y Drum, as well as by goods train from Creunant and Neath. The approach to the pit was a railway track made up of rails ten yards long. The sleepers were one yard apart, except for the last pair where the gap was only eighteen inches. It was said that you could always identify a Dulais Valley miner by his gait: nine long steps and one short. To meet the need for housing, in 1880 the company built a brickworks on a nearby farm and used the bricks to build row houses, a chapel vestry and an hotel. The village, in effect, was a company town, centred on the row houses.

Company houses were also built elsewhere, but usually only in single rows. By 1945, the giant Amalgamated Anthracite had built far fewer houses than the much smaller company of Evans and Bevan Ltd. At Gwter Fawr, in the 1820s, John Jones built a row of houses near the office of his colliery. The colliers were paid from one of the

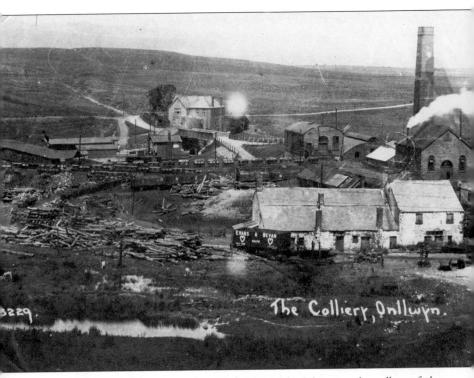

*Onllwyn Colliery on the gwaun or high ground between the valleys of the Tawe and the Dulais. In the background is the outsize Halfway Inn. SWCC, Swansea University.*

houses, so the row became *Tai yr Office*, Office Houses. In the 1870s, the colliery company at Gwauncaegurwen built twenty new houses on the common, partly in response to persistent complaints that pressure on housing was driving prices beyond the means of working people.

Whereas company houses were grouped around the pit or the works, private houses tended to be strung out along roads where services such as sewerage, water, gas and, later, electricity and buses were available. In the anthracite area, in particular, many miners lived in cottages and smallholdings scattered throughout the countryside, not in villages. Some of the smallholders had grazing rights on the surrounding hills. A quite common custom, according to the Ystradgynlais historian Len Ley, was for several siblings to lease a parcel of land and, as their families grew and children married, to build additional houses or cottages as they were needed. In the mining villages themselves, most houses had gardens and the villages were surrounded by fields and commons. A visitor to Ystradgynlais from the Rhondda, in 1909, was surprised by the bucolic atmosphere: 'Houses are extremely well-built in pleasant situations with a large garden at the back, in contradiction to my native valley with its straggling streets and rows of uniform size built with grey stone of a peculiarly depressive hue. The trees and flowers give one the agreeable impression of being in a rural village rather than a mining district.' The impression is reinforced by the survival of the original village square beside the river and the Ynysgedwyn Arms. The industrial town gravitated toward the main road, Commercial Street, but beside the river and the inn the village-like air remains.

In spite of the prevalence of owner occupancy and, the corollary of this, far fewer row or terrace houses than in the eastern valleys, most of the housing was still unmistakably utilitarian and industrial. This was particularly true of colliery and works housing, as the unflinching B L Coombes reminded us: 'The massed greyness of the average colliery street, when built by the colliery company, makes me shudder. It looks like a long stone wall with doors and windows set in at regular intervals. I know that most of the houses are cosy, chiefly because the wives have been working every minute to make them so. With ample building material at hand, ready to be quarried, with immense stretches of open land across which the fresh winds blow all around them, with cheap and plentiful electricity available and often distributed by themselves, and with an immense supply of water always ready, why did those old builders commit these crimes against generations of humanity?' Glynneath, a mining village a few miles up the valley, to which Bert Coombes moved later, was much more to his liking. Some of the houses had been built by a building club of local investors which, besides the usual shopkeepers and publicans, included a colliery manager, a physician and a watchmaker. The club bought a block of land from the Aberpergwm estate and, by 1907, it had built twenty-five out of a projected fifty houses. More brick than was usual had been used in their construction and many were semi-detached. In the 1940s, at the time of the Coombes family's move, they were freshly painted, with flowers in front and a well-tended vegetable garden behind. For Coombes, a neglected garden was a sure sign of a rented house.

Houses built by the collieries, works and speculative builders were usually built to the minimum standards required by the Victorian housing bylaws. The result, as Coombes recorded, was a depressing uniformity. In general, the quality of the housing was better than that provided for farm labourers, but there were many examples where it may well have been worse. Outside Pembrokeshire, some of the worst housing was on the sparsely settled *gwaun* of the upper Dulais valley. Company house-building in the Dulais dated from 1848, when John Williams, an iron master, built two rows of terraced cottages, Y Tai Melin (Yellow Houses), to accommodate migrant workers at his mines and iron works. The 1851 census listed 105 Irish immigrants, refugees from the famine, living in two-up, two-down cottages. One house had thirteen occupants, a family of eight and five lodgers. The houses, which survived until 1964, were described by an anthropologist a few years before their demolition: 'The walls are of stone quarried nearby, and roofs are of slates. The floors are of stone flags laid immediately on the ground. Each house has upstairs two bedrooms, and downstairs a small pantry, a very small room which is used mostly as a lumber room and for laying out corpses, and a large living room into which one steps

*Y Tai Melyn, the Yellow Houses, Onllwyn. The Front Row, to the right, was built into the rise of the slope. The gardens lay across a narrow path in front of the houses. SWCC, Swansea University.*

directly from the street. There is neither kitchen nor bathroom, and warm water is provided by a large iron boiler built into the fireplace to the side of the fire.' When they were built, and for many years afterwards, water had to be carried from a tap in the street; all bathing and washing had to be done in the living room. In Front Row, which had a road immediately in front and behind, the gardens, privies and coal sheds were across the street.

Also at Onllwyn were two rows of colliery houses made from corrugated metal sheeting, 'biscuit tins', built late in the nineteenth century. Lower down the valley, at Pantyffordd, was 'tin town', built in the 1890s by the Dulais Anthracite Colliery Co. Observers passing through the valley expressed disapproval but the houses, although unprepossessing on the outside, are said to have been quite comfortable inside. At Seven Sisters in 1878, David Bevan also donated land for a corrugated iron chapel, 'Capel Haearn', with seating for two hundred. He was possibly following the example of Mary Grenfell, the devout daughter of the copper master Pascoe Grenfell, who built a prefabricated

*Brick Row, Seven Sisters, used as a location for the film* The Silent Village, *1943.*

iron church at St Thomas in Swansea. Sheet metal buildings were cheap and quick to build. At Glyncorrwg there was also a row of three-room, single storey brick houses, similar to those built for the sinkers at Seven Sisters, looking across colliery sidings to a mountain wall several hundred feet high. With no front gardens and abutting the street, rows of one and two storey houses were exemplars of the new, pithead settlements that could be found all across Europe. The type was so generic that Brick Row in Seven Sisters, a street of two storey houses, was used as a setting for the film *The Silent Village* – a tribute to the dead of Lidice, a mining village in Czechoslovakia – filmed in Seven Sisters and Cwmgiedd in 1943. At Lidice, in May 1942, 199 men and boys were executed in reprisal for the assassination of Reinhard Heydrich, the Nazi governor of Bohemia and Moravia. The village itself was razed.

Some of the worst housing was in the beautifully-named and dramatically-sited Ystalyfera. Unlike most of the settlements in the anthracite belt, Ystalyfera grew exponentially. In 1838, James Palmer

Budd bought a small ironworks in the Cyfing, the 'narrows' between the Tawe and the Twrch, that a quarter of a century later would be described as one of the greatest iron and tinplate manufactories in the world. Collieries, iron patches, furnaces, foundries and, later, tinworks were all under the inventive management of James Palmer Budd. By 1853, he had eleven furnaces in blast, a new forge and forty puddling and balling furnaces. From a few scattered farmhouses and cottages Ystalyfera grew, on one of the least suitable sites in the valley, to be the largest town in Cwmtawe north of Morriston. In 1938, a medical officer of health described it as, 'A long straggling village situated half way up the steep western side of the valley [which] is much exposed to the prevailing winds and rain. The valley here is narrow, and the abounding hills on either side steep, and reach 900 feet above the level of the river bed.' The hills cast long shadows, depriving the village of morning and evening sunlight, a condition that the medical officer thought accounted for the high incidence of tuberculosis.

With no accommodating alluvial fan or terrace in the valley bottom, Ystalyfera was built on the steep valley slopes. Hundreds of cottages and several large tenement-like houses were either perched on, or built into, the side of the valley, with no thought to drainage, ventilation or water supply. In the case of the tenement-like buildings, the ground was so steep that the units on the lower side had basement rooms which were frequently used as separate dwellings. They were described in a 1908 report by the Garden City and Town Planning Committee: 'In Ystalyfera practically all the old houses have underground dwellings with two entrances at different levels. Walking along the road one sees apparently ordinary two storey houses, not beautiful, but substantial looking and quite suitable for the purpose they are intended for; but an approach from the main road leading under these houses at the back reveals that they are three or four storeys high, with another front entrance from the garden. The backs of these rooms are of course against the earth, and where there are two rooms on the same floor there is an almost entire lack of light and ventilation. The lower floor rooms were 6'6" high while the upper rooms were a good deal lower than 5'0". In some instances the approaches and staircases were in such a bad state of repair that it would seem positively dangerous for them to be in general use.'

In the middle of the nineteenth century, there was no municipal water supply, no regular collection of rubbish and waste, and whole streets were without drains. Water from privies, cesspools, pigsties and graveyards seeped into the subsoil, the groundwater, the wells and the canal. The conditions were an invitation to cholera. The first outbreak, which also affected Ystradgynlais, occurred in 1854 and the second, and more serious one, came in the late summer of 1866. During the latter, 119 people died and many more were made seriously ill. To it, and the observations of a remarkable physician, James Rogers, we owe a detailed description of sanitary conditions in a rapidly growing nineteenth century industrial town. James Rogers, whom the Revd Thomas Levi described as 'uncannily able,' combined the talents of medical practitioner with those of an acute observer of social and cultural life. Although he appears to have subscribed to the then current theory of infection by poison waves of miasma that, in this case, were wafted up the valley by the prevailing westerly winds, James Rogers knew, if he could not prove it, that the incidence of cholera had as much to do with conditions on the ground as those in the air. His report on the outbreak, which was based on house inspections made a few months previously, was strikingly pointed: 'All died of local conditions – the effect of avarice or ignorance or neglect of sanitary precautions, in short given a case of cholera in a foul dwelling – death; in a healthy dwelling – recovery.' He described an underground tenement: 'The living room had a bed in one corner, a second bedroom opening into it, having a borrowed light from a small parlour built out into the front... This place was occupied by the man, his wife and five or six children.' And of a two room cottage: 'A man and his wife, a married daughter and her husband in delicate health, and one child, with two or three younger daughters.' In the cottages, bedrooms were in the unventilated and, in summer, stifling attics.

More serious, however, than overcrowding were the condition of the houses and squalid nature of the surroundings. Whatever James Rogers' assessment of the poison wave, or epidemic atmosphere theory of infection, he was in no doubt that in Ystalyfera the supposed wandering, airborne miasma had found a home. In his report he pointed out that cholera had been most rampant, 'where the individuals affected have been prepared for the reception of the poison by living in close, damp, overcrowded, badly ventilated, and undrained dwellings.' He referred frequently to poor ventilation and the dampness of the back walls of the houses and tenements, particularly those built into the valley side below the surface of the road. With no drains, no running water and no through ventilation, the smells were 'villainous', evoking a 'horrible loathing' that only the vigorous smoking of Franklen's tobacco made tolerable.

Just as dangerous as the conditions indoors were those in the backyards and the general neighbourhood. Rogers referred to pigsties adjacent to the houses, casks filled with 'festering and putrid' pig swill within a few yards of open windows, ash heaps of mountainous proportions, which were catch-alls for all manner of domestic filth. On one occasion, between six and seven hundred cartloads of what he described as 'very valuable manure' were removed from the back gardens of a row of thirty houses owned by the Ystalyfera ironworks. To add to the mayhem, animals were slaughtered in cellars and outhouses. Supplementing the filth that seeped into the soil from the backyard was that contributed by cesspools and graveyards. Houses were erected, wrote Rogers, wherever the fancy of each proprietor directed, many in places where 'loathsome nuisances' could percolate into the soil beneath and around them.

Local authorities were not indifferent to public health but few were prepared to contemplate major reforms. In 1840, the Neath Poor Law Union – until 1870 the Tawe valley was united uncomfortably in local government with Neath – commissioned Dr William Price of Ynyscedwyn to conduct smallpox vaccination sessions at Cwmtwrch (in the Lamb Inn), Gwter Fawr, Pontardawe and Alltwen. After the cholera outbreak of 1854, it appointed an Inspector of Nuisances for Ystalyfera, and, the following year, James Rogers read a report to the Union on sanitary conditions in the village. In 1855 the Neath district

Highways Board, acting as the local sanitary authority, instructed its surveyor, the acting Sanitary Inspector, to issue handbills cautioning the public interest against depositing filth and rubbish on the highways. He, in turn, reported on accumulations of foul deposits, offensive privies, filthy backyard pigsties and whole streets without drains. Proceedings were taken against some owners for failing to build privies, but the Board, which had few coercive powers, had to rely on the good sense of the public and property owners. But without compulsion, little progress was possible.

To the disastrous mix of official impotence or timidity, no planning, and no certain knowledge of the transmission of disease, must be added country people's ignorance of urban conditions. The transfer of rural habits to a village or a town could, through contiguity, have fearful consequences. The wastes from an isolated country cottage might be relatively harmless, but those from a village street could be deadly. James Rogers cited a particular case: 'In one house – an Inn, the landlady fell a victim to the disease, and it will not appear surprising when I state the fact, that in a yard at the back of the house, less than 30 feet square, were two pig-sties, two privies or cesspools, fowl houses, *and a well*; the said yard being wholly undrained, and it could have been effectively done for a sum less than five pounds – the poor woman had been warned of the dangerous condition of her premises – she had ample means, being a wealthy woman of her class, and one of the most cleanly women in her house I had ever met with.'

As a group, colliery owners were indifferent to the poor quality of much of the housing and to the lack of amenities in the colliery villages. With uncharacteristic severity, Ieuan Gwynedd Jones concluded that they were 'curiously unaffected by any philanthropic motive of a public kind,' and in an essay on coalfield communities, he quoted a passage from a submission to *Gardd y Gweithiwr*, the published proceedings of the 1860 Ystalyfera eisteddfod. 'Where, given the legendary riches of the coal owners,' asked the collier essayist, 'are the convenient dwellings and gardens... for the workmen? Where are the hospitals and alms-houses for the sick and needy? Where are the savings banks and libraries? Where are the means provided by the masters for their workmen during their leisure hours? Very little, and literally nothing in some localities.' Colliers in these matters, he concluded, were thrown entirely onto their own resources.

# LANGUAGE AND CULTURE

W HEN WILLIAM LOGAN, THE Canadian-born geologist and copper
works manager, moved inland from Swansea to examine outcrops
and interview miners and quarrymen, he found English to be of such
limited use that he bought a Welsh grammar. He admitted later that he
found Welsh to be as opaque as Cree or Algonquian, and for any detailed
questioning he would have had to rely on an interpreter, but he was
one of the few members of the incoming managerial and entrepreneurial
class to make any effort to learn the language. There was, in any case,
little need to do so. Swansea in the 1830s and 40s was one of the most
anglicized towns in Wales and, on those grounds, considered the most
progressive. In 1804, the town launched the weekly *Cambrian,* Wales'
first English-language newspaper, whose aim, declared in its inaugural
editorial, was to bring Wales into the modern world; English was the
language of science, industry and commerce. Most of the copper workers
would have spoken Welsh, but the language of the owners, the agents
and, increasingly, of the workers themselves, was English. Except for
southern Pembrokeshire, however, the language of the coalfield remained
adamantly Welsh, much to the dismay of Swansea's Dr Thomas Williams,
for whom the persistence of, as he regarded it, a peasant culture a few
miles inland, producing a commodity on which the copper works were
utterly dependent, was a jarring incongruity.

Spared the explosive growth of the steam coal valleys, the western
coalfield developed quietly, recruiting its colliers locally, or from the
neighbouring rural counties. Many of the very early colliers were
English, and for some of the more technical work in the larger mines
experienced men continued to be brought in from outside Wales, but
in the main the workforce was overwhelmingly Welsh and Welsh-
speaking. In the industrialised parish of Llangiwg, in the upper Tawe
valley, in 1861, only five miners were from England and, if they stayed

in Llangiwg, they and their children would undoubtedly have picked up village Welsh. A celebrated case was the son of Yorkshireman Joseph Hargreaves, the general manager of Gwauncaegurwen collieries, who is said to have spoken Welsh with 'clearness of articulation.' In his address to the Labour Congress, at Westminster Hall, London, in 1891, Enoch Rees, secretary to the Federation of Anthracite Miners, noted that 95 percent of his members, who lived 'in hilly, country districts scattered through three counties,' were Welsh-speaking and that he conducted the business of the Federation entirely in Welsh, even when in London. With the permission of the accommodating chairman of the Congress, he delivered his report in the language of the people he represented. One London reporter thought it was the first time Welsh had ever been spoken in Westminster Hall and he generously offered that it, presumably in translation, 'gave light to the underground darkness before the high gentry of London.'

Among the small percentage of non Welsh-speaking colliers in the anthracite district were a group of northern Spanish ironworkers, who came to Abercraf via Merthyr/Dowlais early in the twentieth century. They arrived in Dowlais in 1907 and, shortly afterwards, a number left to work at a colliery in Abercraf, then an almost entirely Welsh-speaking community. They lived in a single row of houses that became known, predictably, as Spanish Row, or Espaniardos Row. Colourful, Catholic, lively and, one assumes, a little noisy, they were welcomed by the young. But the older members looked askance, even though the Spaniards were good workers and strong supporters of the union. A strike to dislodge, or at least discomfit them, was narrowly averted in the summer of 1914, and thereafter animosity and distrust seem to have abated quickly. The younger Spaniards learned Welsh and the younger Welsh colliers added a few Spanish phrases to their vocabulary. According to David Williams and Hywel Francis, comprehensive chroniclers of labour relations in the coalfield, it would not have been uncommon to hear a Welsh hewer shout from the coalface: 'Caballista! Uno caballo.' (Haulier! One horse.)

Percentages of Welsh-speakers in the western coalfield remained high into the twentieth century. In 1911, 80 percent of the people in the Ammanford and Cwmaman Urban Districts, and the Ystradgynlais and Pontardawe Rural Districts, were counted as Welsh-speaking. At the end of the nineteenth century, only Neath and Swansea had suffered serious invasion from English. In his reminiscence of Llansamlet in the 1880s, J H Howard wrote that the village, though barely three miles from Swansea, was a world on its own, essentially Welsh in tongue and sentiment. His guardian, Thomas Davies, and many of Thomas Davies's contemporaries were monoglot Welsh-speakers.

In Llansamlet, as in all the colliery villages, distinctiveness of language went hand in hand with distinctiveness of religion. Colliery settlements were overwhelmingly Nonconformist. Dissent had taken root after the Civil War, when the Roundheads chose Swansea as a centre from which to disseminate Puritan belief and practice. In country districts, meetings at first were held in houses and barns and later in remote hilltop chapels, safe, following the Restoration in 1662, from persecution. But what had begun as sporadic guerrilla-like resistance from outside the established Church was overtaken, in the eighteenth century, by an organized revolt from within. The evangelizing missions of the Calvinistic Methodists, led in Wales by Howell Harris, William Williams (Pantycelyn) and Daniel Rowland, found a society thirsting for change. John Wesley himself had preached in or near coalfield villages in Pembrokeshire in the 1770s, and in 1781 he addressed 'a large congregation of honest colliers' at Jeffreyston. Earlier, Howell Harris and William Edwards, the bridge-builder and planner of Morriston, preached at several places in the Tawe valley, making a particular mark among the miners of Llansamlet who, like all miners, needed no convincing of the uncertainty of life. An explosion in 1787 that killed nineteen colliers is said to have delivered many converts to the Methodists. By Methodist standards, Edwards was cerebral, but the Methodists' stock-in-trade were feeling and enthusiasm. Instead of ritual and restrained sermons and prayers, they offered dramatic, uplifting sermons, congregational singing, and – peculiar to Wales – a kind of rhythmical stamping akin to dancing. By the end of the eighteenth century, Nonconformity, the refusal to conform to the restrained practices and measured tones of the Church of

England, was no longer an underground movement. On the shoulders of the valleys and on the moorlands between the rivers, a network of Nonconformist chapels had emerged to serve the then largely upland rural population.

Anglicans and Nonconformists both responded to the growing industrial population, but at different rates and in different ways. In the pyramid organization of the Anglican Church, authority and initiative filtered down through the bishops and the clergy to the more influential parishioners – the landowners and the professional and managerial class. Free of structures and hierarchies, Nonconformist groups, by contrast, were able to do as they pleased. Each, as Canon E T Davies described them, was a little democracy, an autonomous ecclesiastical republic, able to respond at will to local needs. To perform a service, or make plans for a new chapel, all that was needed was a friendly house or barn and a willing preacher. Around 1750, the Independents at the head of the Tawe valley began worshipping at a house in, or near, a wood, Ty'n y Coed, and applied the name to their first chapel, built later in the century. As the valleys filled with mining and manufacturing populations, the chapels, which also were not tied to a parochial system, simply moved downslope. To quote Ieuan Gwynedd Jones: 'With astonishing speed the pre-industrial congregations of the old ridgeways... established daughter churches in the valleys sometimes almost as if in advance of urbanisation.' Ty'n y Coed, for example, spawned new chapels in Ystradgynlais, Ystradfellte, Glynneath and Onllwyn. These daughter chapels multiplied in turn and gathered in, sometimes with little effort, new members for their congregations. Newcomers from districts where dissent was already well established often arrived with a letter of recommendation, *llythyr canmoliaeth*, which handed them over to the care and supervision of a sister chapel in the district in which they were settling. So wide and accommodating was the Nonconformist net that by 1851, in Llangiwg, Nonconformists outnumbered Anglicans by ten to one.

The most successful dissidents were the Methodists, whose appeal to mining communities, dating from John Wesley's and George Whitefield's successes in colliery villages around Bristol and Newcastle was particularly strong. The social historians Lawrence and Barbara Hammond attributed Methodism's appeal to its anodyne qualities: '[It] spread more quickly and in its extreme form among workers living in the darkest gloom... the Methodists told the miner that the sovereign happiness of all, the happiness of faith and resignation was not the prize of wealth or power or conquest but a state of mind that the poor could obtain as readily as the rich.' Offered peace of mind and happiness to the same degree as their betters, the poor responded with a will. Methodist societies were founded, meeting at first in private houses but later in chapels; by 1782 the Llansamlet Society had built a new chapel, which it enlarged in 1823 and again in 1831. Two of its four local trustees were colliers. The enthusiasm of the Methodists was infectious, spreading to the older dissenting groups in and around the village, who, to save themselves journeys to Neath and Swansea, built their own chapels. The Independents built Bethel in 1818 and the Baptists Tabernacle in 1830.

Not until the 1830s and 40s did the Anglicans begin to counter what they regarded as the neglect and spiritual destitution of the industrial population. But strategically their position was weak. The parish system worked best where, as in lowland England, the parishes were small and where settlement was nucleated – concentrated in one, or at most a few, villages. In much of south-west Wales, however, the population was scattered throughout hilly and upland areas, and to serve it the churches, like the early chapels, were located on the shoulders of the valleys. The parishes, too, like the diocese of St David's itself, tended to be larger than the average English parish and, as the population grew and filled the valleys, contact between the incumbents and their parishioners became more and more infrequent. When questioned by the bishop about the state of the large Llangyfelach parish, in 1828, the curate replied that he himself lived a mile and a half from the parish church, while the incumbent, Evan Lloyd, lived in Tilbury, Essex. The same curate also served the Llansamlet parish, on the other side of the Tawe, until 1841. His replacement at Llansamlet was also expected to serve the parish of St John's. In 1851 the rector of Ystradgynlais told the Census Commissioners that the parish church, situated in the extreme

*Above: Gellionnen Chapel, built in 1692 on the high moorland or gwaun above the Tawe valley. The hollow of the valley is just discernible on the horizon. Below: the chapel and graveyard.*

*Plaque on the wall of Gellionnen Chapel.*

corner of the parish, lay beyond the reach of a large proportion of the population. Like Evan Lloyd, several of the incumbents were absentees and some remained monoglot English, even though, in Welsh-speaking districts, the churches provided at least a morning or an evening service in the vernacular. In some parishes, too, services were infrequent and irregular; the church buildings in poor repair and, in winter especially, unaccommodating and cold.

Until the appointment of a reforming bishop, Connop Thirlwall, in 1840, the Church languished. The Swansea district's only new church in the first half of the century, consecrated at Gorseinon in 1839, was a product of private rather than ecclesiastical initiative. The builder, J D Llewellyn of Penllergaer, was a wealthy landowner. Under Bishop Thirlwall, some of the large, populous parishes were divided and new

*Llangiwg Church, built on a flat shoulder of the Tawe valley above Pontardawe. The tower is Norman, built in the 13th century, and aisle, built in the 16th century, Tudor.*

churches were built but these too were financed in whole or in part by contributions from local gentry. They were not only Anglican but, as Ieuan Gwynedd Jones remarked, anglicized, and regarded by the common folk as little more than monuments to the fame of local industrialists and places to lay their bones. In the new churches there were few concessions to Welsh, in spite of Bishop Ollivant's counsel that the Welsh, whether Church or Sectarian, attach themselves 'to that place of worship... in which their language alone is used.' St Peter's, Pontardawe, with its 200 feet high tower and tapered spire, was built by the industrialist William Parsons entirely out of his own pocket on land provided by a local squire. Most of the enlargement costs for Trinity Church, Ystalyfera, in 1864, were met by J P Budd, owner of the Ystalyfera Iron Works. He and his wife had also supported the building of the original church in the 1840s. In 1887, Howel Gwyn, who had been a major contributor to a fund for a new church at Clydach, paid for the building of a new church at

Alltwen. If donations fell short of needs, or were slow in coming, Anglican congregations could always fall back on the Ecclesiastical Commissioners, who distributed the Parliamentary grant, or tap the considerable resources of the Church itself.

Without the patronage of local squires and industrialists, chapel congregations had to scrimp and save, getting by on money raised from teas and from subscriptions eked out of the wages of colliers, iron and tinplate workers. There were occasional wealthy benefactors but most chapels were classic products of workers' self help. At Morriston in the 1840s, a congregation of copper workers and colliers built their chapel, Horeb, in stages. They conducted their first meetings and ordained their first ministers when only the walls were up. Roof, windows and doors were added as they could be afforded. Seats they made from planks resting on slags from the works, and a pulpit they fashioned from a large piece of timber fished out of the floodwaters of the Tawe. Not surprisingly, hard-pressed Nonconformists, who had their own chapels to support, resented the parish rate, a tax levied on property owners by the established church and, in the Nedd valley, reluctantly assessed by Alfred Russel Wallace. At Ystradgynlais, resistance organized and led by the Revd Thomas Levi and Squire Morgan of Ystradfawr, who broke ranks with his fellow landowners, prevented the building of a new church in the parish.

For the collier, the tinplate and the ironworker and their families, the attraction of the chapel was that they were among equals. There were no pews reserved for the well-to-do and no differences of dress, accent and manner to remind them of their inferior status. In answer to a *Methodist Times* question, 'Why the Working Classes do NOT go to Church?, J Davies responded: '[They] give as a reason... that they cannot dress as respectably as they should like, for they feel there is a marked distinction made between those who dress well and those who wear meaner clothing.' For the men also, the chapel offered a role and a voice. Aside from the parish vestry and the two churchwardens, the laity in the established church had no function and little influence on the affairs of the church or the parish. But in the chapel, the working man was an engaged and, if he so wished, active participant: he could join a committee, teach in the Sunday school and, by becoming a deacon, even participate in chapel government. He could also, if he had the aptitude, serve as a lay preacher and, if he was ambitious, aspire to the ministry. The leading light of the 1904 Revival, Evan Roberts of Loughor, worked as a miner and blacksmith until he was twenty-five. Roberts attracted columnists and journalists from England and overseas, among them Constance L Maynard, Principal of Westfield College of the University of London, who heard him preach at Llansamlet in 1905, and left this vignette: 'He is a strange offshoot from rough mining districts. I looked at the men around me, mostly of short stature, some with broad shoulders, cropped heads, thick skins, and hard-set, bull-dog faces, and among them rises this slender stem, this shoot from another world... Yet he belongs here... He is their own, their very own. From this race he springs, in the miner's cottage he was born, and the coal-pit has nurtured him; he is their making, their property.' Evan Roberts also preached at a chapel in Betws, where a very young James Griffiths and his parents sat in the packed pews. In his seventies, Griffiths couldn't recall a word of Roberts' address but his memory of the curious spell he cast remained vivid: 'I can still see him standing up in the pulpit, tall, with dark hair falling over his face, and the quiet voice reaching the gallery as if he were singing.'

To dispel the 'darkest gloom', particularly in times of religious fervour, it was inevitable that the miners would take their religion underground into, in Constance Maynard's phrase, 'the most sordid earthliness of human conditions that it is possible to think of.' In the Mynydd Newydd Pit at Fforest Fach, near Swansea, the miners built two chapels not unlike those described by the Swansea copper master John Henry Vivian, on his visit to salt mines in Austria in 1814/15. Mynydd Newydd opened in 1844, at first working the Five Foot seam at 348 feet and, a few years later, the Six Foot seam at 750 feet. After an explosion in 1844 that killed five men and seriously burned several others, there were impromptu gatherings for prayers at the beginning of every week. In August 1846, the *Cambrian* reported, these were formalized after a meeting of the men with the colliery manager, Thomas Jones. A religious man, Jones encouraged the holding of 6 am, Monday, underground

*Underground Chapel, Mynydd Newydd, 1899. NMW.*

*Bible, Mynydd Newydd Chapel. NMW.*

services, at which the men would pray for divine protection during the week. Some time afterward, chapels were built in both the Five Foot and the Six Foot seams, where the men conducted half-hour services of readings, hymns and prayers. The chapel in the Six Foot seam was eighteen feet wide by forty-eight feet long. Overhead pressure and creep forced the closure of the Five Foot chapel in 1908/1910 but another was built, using the same furniture, after the re-opening of an old airway. This second chapel functioned until the closing of the pit in June 1933. The Six Foot chapel, which had to be abandoned when water flowed in from workings at a higher level, had whitewashed walls and was lit by candles; Mynydd Newydd suffered very little from gas. Smoking was permitted underground and only in the 1920s was the regular use of safety lamps introduced. There was also a chapel in the Tyrcenol pit, Morriston, which is said to have been larger than the ones at Mynydd Newydd. It was used until flooding closed the pit in the 1870s. There were also underground prayer meetings at pits without chapels, especially during the revivals and after serious accidents. In the 1860s, prayers were read every morning at three headings in the Bonvilles Court colliery, Pembrokeshire, followed once a month by a united prayer meeting. 'Awstin', the special correspondent for the *Western Mail* during the 1904/5 Revival, described an underground service at the Nantymelyn colliery, near Pontardawe:

'Seventy yards from the bottom of the shaft, in the stable, we came to a prayer meeting. One of the workmen was reading the 6th chapter of Matthew to about eighty comrades. He stood erect amongst the group reading in a dim, fantastic light that danced with the swinging lamps and vanished softly into the surrounding darkness. A number of lamps were attached to a heavy post closely wedged to support the roof, and around the impressive figure the colliers grouped themselves. Some were in the characteristic stooping posture, others half reclined against the road with their lamps fastened to their pockets; others, again, stood in the middle of the passage. Earnest men, all of them; faces that bore the scars of the underground toiler; downcast eyes that seemed to be 'the homes of silent prayer'; strong frames that quivered with a new emotion.'

Except for the underground chapels, the coalfield chapels were not exclusively or even, as Ieuan Gwynedd Jones has emphasised, primarily religious institutions. They succeeded precisely because, unlike the established churches, they were not centres of liturgy and thanks to the translation of the Bible into Welsh in 1588, they were able to operate entirely in the vernacular. The buildings themselves were unconsecrated, therefore, with no sacredness to protect, they could, within limits, be used for other purposes. For Alfred Russel Wallace it was the social function of the chapels that impressed, and even amused. Doctrines that emphasized salvation through faith rather than deeds were unlikely, he thought, to promote morality among the 'lower orders'. Attendance at two or three services on a Sunday, and perhaps one or two others during the week encouraged rather than suppressed what he saw as the natural hedonism of the Welsh. As John Steinbeck's Jim Casy would discover, half a century later, in the American Midwest, the more evangelical the sect, and the more fervent the sermon, the greater the animal excitement generated. Any lessons the service might have intended to convey were nullified. For the young, upland chapels serving both collier families and the dispersed farming population were natural trysting places. Evening prayer meetings, the twenty-one year old Wallace noted, were particularly well-attended. In this context, the established church, with its set, restrained services could hardly compete. It offered, he concluded, 'not enough of an exciting character… to allure them,' and even though the English among the clergy might have spoken Welsh, they did so as foreigners.

Of the official, secular functions of the chapels, the most highly regarded, and even revered, was education. As well as giving working men a voice, the chapels and their associated Sunday schools also gave them their first contact, however slight, with the world of letters and learning. In them working men and women, possibly for the first time ever in Wales, were invited, even if at an unsophisticated level, to engage in enlightened argument and debate. Until the advent of the Sunday schools, *yr ysgolion Sul*, the only schooling available to the working poor had been through private venture and charity schools, and the circulating schools of Griffith Jones of Llanddowror. In the circulating schools, instruction lasted only a few months before the teacher moved on, while other schools were scattered haphazardly, available only to the few. Illiteracy was endemic and, as the population grew, it was regarded as one of the crucial social problems of the day. With their genius for improvisation, the chapels filled the educational void by providing schooling. In the early days, they served the upland population by holding Sunday classes in farmhouses, moving them according to a fixed rota so that each family would know where the school was to be held on a particular Sunday. When the chapels moved downslope into the industrial communities, they built schoolrooms, the usual method of propagation being to build the schoolroom first, and then the chapel. So successful was the Sunday school experiment, that it is now widely regarded as the most progressive educational movement of the nineteenth century, reducing illiteracy and even spawning a publishing industry to satisfy the need for texts.

As well as appealing directly to the industrial population, the schools operated on the one day when colliers, tinplate workers and their wives and children had at least a half day holiday. By not interfering with daily work and the capacity to earn, they were tailor-made for a society that used child labour. Eight-year-old James Davies of Saundersfoot, who worked as trammer with his eleven-year-old brother, told R H Franks, the employment commissioner, that he had been to Sunday school, but never to day school. Unlike some of the later government schools, the Sunday schools also functioned entirely in Welsh; there was no 'Welsh not' and no compulsory use of English. Like the chapels themselves, they were autonomous, democratic units with a simple but efficient organization: a minister in overall control and below him a lay superintendent of the school, teachers and scholars. The latter were divided into classes according to age: adults, youths, children and infants. The emphasis in all the schools was on literacy, on teaching men and women, as well as children, how to read through the scriptures. There were no technical or teaching appliances and, except perhaps for a map of Palestine, no visual aids. The Bible or biblical extracts, were the standard texts and the lessons consisted of reading, reciting, and interpreting passages of scripture. Classes were conducted by working men: colliers, tinplate workers, and farmers, who acknowledged that their instruction did not extend far beyond teaching their pupils to read: 'We can read, and we can teach others; but for the understanding, we do come far short.' From time to time, however, teachers would get together 'to expound the Scriptures... so far as we do understand them,' and this understanding they passed on to their charges.

In their responses to the 1842 commissioners, on children's work in the mines, many of the collier boys mentioned that they were learning their letters at Sunday school. But despite the efforts of the schools, rates of illiteracy remained high. An official at a Llansamlet colliery estimated, in 1841, that only about a third of the colliers could read. 'They go to work so young.' A survey of five leading collieries in the Swansea Valley, conducted by the Children's Employment Commission in 1842, confirmed his estimate. Out of 351 children and young people, 99 could read, 18 could write, and 118 were attending Sunday school. But for those willing to attend regularly, the chapels and the Sunday schools provided more than just basic literacy. In the adult classes, the dialectic methods encouraged discussion and debate of religious and ethical issues. And in the absence of community halls, the schools and the chapels were also the venue for lectures, penny readings and adult education classes. A contributor to the Calvinistic Methodist *Treasury* in 1881 noted that, 'The chapel... is the social centre around which its adherents gather; it is school, lyceum, club, church, all in one.' He added that the chapels were also gathering grounds, not just for people of faith, but also for those committed to the use of 'a peculiar and ancestral tongue.'

Run entirely by the laity and with a high proportion of teachers to students, the Sunday schools were conducted to almost universal approval. R R W Lingen, who conducted the 1847 inquiry into the state of education in Carmarthenshire, Glamorgan and Pembrokeshire, emphasized both the value of the instruction given and its social importance: 'The universality of these schools and the large proportion of persons attending them who take part in their government have generally familiarized the people with some of the more ordinary terms and methods of organization. They satisfy,' he continued, 'the gregarious sociability which animates the Welsh... [and] present the charms of office to those... who have no other chance of distinguishing themselves... every man, woman, and child feels comfortably at home in them. It is all among neighbours and equals. Whatever ignorance is shown here, whatever mistakes are made, whatever speculations are started, there are no superiors to smile and open their eyes... Whatever Sunday schools may be as places of instruction, they are real fields of mental activity. The Welsh working man rouses himself for them. It is his best chance all the week through of showing himself in his own character.' In a report on popular education in Neath and Merthyr in the half century up to 1861, John Jenkins, a voice of nervous authority, was just as enthusiastic. Not only did the Sunday schools dispel illiteracy but, he added – possibly with the risings of 1848 in mind – by promoting 'peacefulness, order and sobriety,' they assuaged a potentially unruly industrial population 'more effectively than any other institution in history.'

In spite of the efforts of the Sunday schools to dispel illiteracy and promote discussion of moral and ethical – if not political – issues, the collier's world remained a narrow one. Towards the end of the nineteenth century, miners' institutes with reading rooms and libraries, built and maintained by weekly deductions from the collier's wages, extended horizons; but for most of the century, home, work, the chapel and the pub were the inescapable parameters of the collier's life. Thomas Davies, J H Howard's revered Llansamlet guardian, may have been typical of at least the more self-denying members of his generation. He read no newspapers, neither English nor Welsh; the only magazine that came into the house was Thomas Levi's *Trysorfa'r Plant* (Children's Magazine), while the entire library consisted of the Big Bible, a hymn book, *Barnes' Commentary,* and an illustrated *Pilgrim's Progress,* all in Welsh. His farthest railway journey from home was to Swansea, three miles away.

Doctrines of austerity and restraint could issue, without the taint of hypocrisy, only from buildings that were themselves simple and unadorned. In keeping with their Puritan origins, the dissenters clung stubbornly to plain, classical forms. Ornament and perpendicular, Gothic styles had no effect upon chapel architecture until the last few

*Bethel Chapel, Tumble. NMW.*

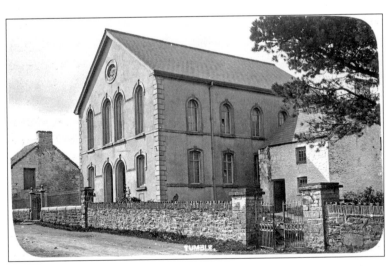

*Bethania Chapel, Tumble. NMW.*

decades of the nineteenth century, and then only among the better-off congregations. Early chapels had simple, box-like shapes and easily constructed, gable-ended roofs. Designed for preaching rather than devotions and prayer, their interiors were open, amphitheatre-like and well-lit, so that the preacher could be seen and heard by every member of the congregation. Some have compared the box-like structures to the angular colliery winding houses, fan rooms and lamp-rooms which, more often than not, were built by the same builders and of the same stone taken from the same quarries. They fitted easily into residential streets and, unlike some churches, they did not intimidate.

Their most eloquent champion was John Betjeman, a connoisseur of the apposite in landscape and architecture: 'Not since medieval days had the people clubbed together to adorn a place of worship, and this time it was not a shrine but a preaching house… They were anxious not to look like the Church, which held them in contempt; nor like a house, for they were places of worship; nor like the theatre for they were sacred piles. They succeeded in looking like what they are – chapels, so that the most unobservant traveller can tell a chapel from any other building in the street.' If their form somehow failed to identify them, then their names would. Anglican churches were given Saints' names but chapel names, Horeb, Tabernacle, Calfaria, Bethania, Nebo, were strictly Biblical.

By the last third of the nineteenth century, however, chapel builders, like Victorian builders in general, chafed under what they had come to regard as the restraints of classical form. In chapels built by the richer, and particularly English-language, congregations, the plain, box-like structure of the early chapels retreated behind elaborate facades, pilasters, Doric capitals and mouldings. The basic form remained because chapels were still halls or theatres for preaching but they had lost the austere, pared-down look of the Puritan meeting house. The exemplar of the new style was Morriston's palatial Tabernacle, the 'Cathedral of Welsh Nonconformity', according to one recent historian. On the sides are tall, arched Renaissance windows and in front a pediment supported by capitals and long Corinthian pillars. Crowning the whole is a tall, pointed tower.

Aside from the Sunday school, the most distinctive and elevating product of coalfield/chapel culture was the eisteddfod. Originally a guild-like meeting of poets under the patronage of a medieval aristocracy, the eisteddfod had been revived at end of the eighteenth century by London Welsh societies keen to perpetuate traditional Celtic arts. By the middle of the nineteenth century, it had been adopted by a chapel-oriented, working-class culture and transformed into a democratic and popular institution. Every sizeable community on the coalfield, and many of the larger chapels, organized an annual eisteddfod. Colliery and works owners might have defrayed some of the costs, but the local eisteddfodau were essentially folk festivals paid for by the communities themselves. To guarantee an inaugural eisteddfod for their village, in 1873 a hundred working men from Brynaman contributed a guinea each.

At first, the emphasis was on literature, prizes being awarded for both poetry and prose. Singing developed later and, although extremely popular, it never displaced the literary competitions in public esteem. Adjudications and results of the competitions were reported in local newspapers as well as in denominational and other magazines. After 1860, volumes of transactions, containing prize poems, essays and detailed adjudications, followed. The entrants were working men, for the most part: colliers, metalworkers and clerks who mastered archaic and structurally difficult verse forms. D L Moses, a native of Cribyn, Cardiganshire, who in the 1850s came to work as a clerk in Amman Valley ironworks, taught interested colliers and ironworkers the rules of the classical bardic metres and encouraged them to compete in local eisteddfodau. A master of the difficult *cynghanedd* form, Moses was dubbed the 'literary father' of the district. He nurtured a group of poets who were so 'drunk on poetry' that, according to Penar Griffiths, they 'hit each other with *cynghaneddion* like children throwing snowballs.' Among them was the well-known poet Watcyn Wyn, who began work as a child carter at the Tri Gloyn level in Brynaman. Wyn liked to relate that, during breaks from cutting and hauling, he and other aspiring poets worked on their compositions. His first prize was a box of matches for a verse on a set subject quickly composed and chalked on a flat stone. Much of the writing and versifying may have been unpolished but Ben Davies, minister of Panteg Chapel, Ystradgynlais from 1891 to 1926, and himself a former miner, could still write of the 'literary atmosphere' at Brynhenllys colliery. With the help of a tattered copy of a bardic grammar, which his brother had bought second-hand in Ystalyfera, Ben Davies learned the rules of composition and practised entirely on his own.

As vehicles for working class aspirations, the eisteddfod literary competitions were a great success, complementing the educational work of the chapels and the Sunday schools. In the published transactions of the larger competitions, collier poets and essayists saw their work in print for the first time. Ieuan Gwynedd Jones cites, as a classic of the genre, the transactions of the 1860 Ystalyfera eisteddfod, appropriately entitled *Gardd y Gweithiwr* or Workingman's Garden. The papers in both Welsh and English reveal preoccupations, which today seem remarkable, of colliers and ironworkers with art, philosophy, religion and current affairs. The first prize in the essay competition at the Easter eisteddfod at Ystradgynlais in 1857 went to Roger Thomas (Adolphus), a collier at a pit in Cwmtwrch, who became a notable local essayist and novelist. Dozens of miners also sent verses to the two radical weeklies, *Tarian y Gweithiwr* (the Workers' Shield) and, later, *Llais Llafur* (Labour's Voice).

Although poetry and prose never lost their primacy in eisteddfod competitions, after 1850 they had to share the eisteddfod stage with choral singing, yet another product of chapel culture. Set to traditional folk airs and even popular tunes, hymns were a vital element of Methodist strategy. At first, there were few Welsh hymns, and few tunes to which to set them, but in William Williams, Pantycelyn, the Methodist movement in Wales would produce its own mesmeric hymn-writer. By mixing literary language and dialect, and borrowing freely metres and images from contemporary as well as earlier poets and writers, he produced compelling free verse. Impassioned congregational singing, in contrast to the austere chanting of the established church, electrified the chapel services. Often, these ended with a protracted round of singing, the same tune, when the blood was up, being sung over and over. At her second Revival meeting, in a chapel several miles west of Swansea, Constance Maynard found that the singing was 'even more extraordinary' than it had been in the village of Llansamlet, 'the base and tenor voices closing in flood over the powerful sopranos, and making a thunderous body of sound that thrilled the very walls of the building... Think of the congregations of our Sussex villages singing like that...' The meetings opened with spontaneous hymn singing as the congregation assembled and, punctuated by a short reading, prayers, and exhortations from the congregation, continued for two hours and more. The hymns were so familiar that no one used a hymn book, and Roberts was so insistent that the 'spirit', not he, should control the meeting, that there was no order of service and no posting of hymns. At the second meeting were fourteen miners who had walked fifteen miles from Carmarthen.

At first, congregational singing was more enthusiastic than organized. There seem to have been early attempts at harmony but until the arrival in 1850 of William Griffiths ('Ivander'), a clerk/accountant and then manager of a tinplate works near Pontardawe, the singing was instinctive and unstructured. Griffiths became secretary of the Sunday school in the small Methodist chapel at Trebanos and opened a singing school in which he gave lessons in reading music using painted staff lines and moveable octave notes on a twelve inches by six wooden board. At about the same time, the copper master John Henry Vivian invited to Swansea John Hullah, the author of a system of sight-reading or sight-singing for choristers unable to decipher staff notations. Over several months, hymn-singing leaders from chapels in the valley and the Swansea district attended Hullah's evening classes and returned to teach the method to their congregations. Hullah's fixed sol-fa system improved the quality of singing, but it restricted the choristers to singing in one key only. To give every voice something that it could manage, what was needed was an easily-learned form of musical notation that would allow singing in different keys. The solution was the tonic sol-fa, a method of sight reading using letter symbols (doh, re, me, fa, sol, la, te, doh) that gave the singer a sense of relative pitch and accurate time. Invented by Sarah

Ann Glover, and modified and popularised by John Curwen, a London Congregational minister, it made possible singing in two, three and four parts. After a lecture in Liverpool attended by two Welsh Sunday school superintendents, Welsh versions of Curwen's handbook and sol-fa hymnbook were soon circulating in Wales. A book of Welsh hymns with sol-fa notations, John Roberts' (Ieuan Gwyllt) *Llyfr Tonau*, was published in 1863. Chapels and Sunday schools offered sol-fa classes and to lead them Welsh ministers and conductors descended on the Sol-fa College in London, taking the lion's share of advanced certificates. In 1892, the name D Evans from Resolfen appeared five times in the honour rolls. D Evans was then a coalminer who went on to a doctorate in music at Oxford and a professorship of music in Cardiff.

Mastery of the tonic sol-fa made possible good four-part singing that led to a seasonal choral festival, the cymanfa ganu, initiated and made popular by the composer Ieuan Gwyllt, that was held in the chapels on Christian holidays. At the same time, choral competitions became a regular feature of the eisteddfodau. As a universal system of notation, the sol-fa could be applied to any choral work and by the 1860s congregations and choral societies in south Wales were able to perform choruses from the works of Bach, Handel, Haydn and Mendelssohn. So popular were they that Haydn and Handel were added to the repertoire of commonly used Christian names in south Wales.

One of the largest choral societies was the two-hundred strong United Temperance Choir, or Temperance Choral Union, assembled by Ivander Griffiths. It began as a small choral society that met on Sunday evenings to sing oratorio choruses in the Reading Room, a small local library in Pontardawe. In 1855 the choir competed for the first time in an eisteddfod at Cwmafan, the choristers walking six miles to Neath and completing the journey by 'Tent Wagon'. When it competed at the Cwmaman eisteddfod, 1858, there were six other choral entrants: from Ystalyfera, Cwmllynfell, Carmel, Furnace, Dryslwyn and Llandeilo. In an eisteddfod at Alltwen in 1861, Ivander conducted choirs, in the same competition, from Pontardawe and Cwmgiedd. At Ystradgynlais, on Easter Monday 1862, he conducted another choir, from Onllwyn. Between competitions, Ivander organized temperance singing festivals, the first at or near Capel Gellionnen, Pontardawe, in September 1860, as a counter attraction to the revels at the Neath Fair.

His most ambitious undertaking, however, was a choir that drew members from all the villages in the Tawe valley. With the announcement of a great eisteddfod at Carmarthen in 1862, plans were laid in Ystalyfera for the formation of a choir that might compete with the great battalions from the eastern valleys. Within a week 150 choristers had enrolled, ranging from the very uppermost villages in the valley and beyond – from Brynaman, Onllwyn and Ystradgynlais, down to Clydach, Glais and Ynystawe. Ivander's energy and enthusiasm aside, the choir was a child of the just-completed railway between Swansea and Brynaman. Practice sessions for small groups were held at five or six centres, the choristers either taking the train, or walking several miles in each direction. At Carmarthen, where the United Valley Choir shared the honours with the Great Choir from Aberdare, there were thirteen choirs of the same dimension, all from south Wales. They sang before an unprecedented audience of 3000, whose enthusiasm for battle was so strong that they prevailed upon the rector of Neath to cut short his opening address.

After the eisteddfod, the United Valley Choir, eager for more work and attracting even more members, began rehearsing Handel's *Messiah*. To coach the separate sections of the choir, now 300-400 strong, Ivander travelled up and down the valley by train. At Panteg Chapel, Ystalyfera, in January 1863, the choir, for the first time in Wales, performed the *Messiah* in its entirety. The soloists came from London and the instrumentalists from Bristol and Swansea. To take home choristers, instrumentalists, and concert-goers from Swansea and the lower valley, a special train left Ystalyfera at 11 pm. There were subsequent performances at Clydach, Swansea and Neath. Some music critics complained of a lack of finesse, but at the Swansea concert, a 'gentleman' in the audience was heard to remark that gathering and keeping together that many choristers, 'especially of the working class', was achievement enough, but that they should combine to perform 'such a magnificent work' was truly remarkable. If one adds to gala performances such as this concerts, cymanfas (hymn-singing festivals), eisteddfod competitions and regular Sunday congregational singing, 'It would be safe to say', wrote Swansea's Professor T J Morgan, 'that a greater quantity of melodious decibels ascended to high heaven from the Swansea area during those forty years [1870-1910] than from any other part of the world and period of history.' For miners and other industrial workers, Professor Morgan concluded, choral singing offered not just relief from an often tedious and grim daily round, but transcendence: release for spirits too long pent in mines and works.

By the end of the century, choral singing was so much part of the coalfield culture that it was said of Will Abraham, the charismatic miners' leader who was both a conductor and the custodian of a fine tenor voice, that when he wanted to bring an unruly crowd to order, all he had to do was to raise both arms and hum or sing the opening bars of a well-known hymn. Like tracker dogs picking up a scent, the miners would lift their heads and, instead of barking dissonantly, begin to bay in concert. 'Hardly had he reached the second line,' noted a bemused Scottish observer after one such Abraham performance, 'than he had the vast audience dropping into their respective parts, and accompanying him like a great trained choir.' Known universally as 'Mabon', a contraction of his bardic name Gwilym Mabon, Abraham conducted the 1904 annual eisteddfod at Saundersfoot and in his opening address he spoke of the contribution made by the eisteddfod to education in general and to his own development in particular. He allowed that whatever he had become he owed to the eisteddfod, the Band of Hope, and the Sunday school. Mabon was born in Cwmafan and worked as a collier (he was a door boy at ten) both there and at Waunarlwydd, near Gowerton. As a miners' agent, Mabon consolidated the loose associations of anthracite miners into a single trade union that in 1898 joined the 'Fed', the South Wales Miners' Federation.

But not all miners, of course, subscribed to the chapel-based culture of temperance and self-improvement. Census Sunday, March 1851, revealed that at least two-fifths of the population in Wales attended neither church, chapel nor Sunday school, and in the industrial areas the proportion may well have been higher than this. The census finding

*Cwmfelinfach miners, rat catching. SWCC, Swansea University.*

would not have surprised any alert observer. Drinking, gambling, fist-fighting and sports, some of them cruel, were as integral to the mining culture as chapel-going and choral singing. In a 1983 lecture prompted by his daily bus journeys down the Tawe valley, Ieuan Gwynedd Jones noted, perhaps mischievously, that matching the parade of chapels fronting the road to Swansea was an equally dense parade of pubs. In what may have been only a throwback to the old coaching days, it was the pubs, Professor Jones noted, not the chapels, which were the official stopping places for the bus. In south Wales, the dichotomy between piety and pleasure was cast in stone. But, as Professor Jones and others have been quick to point out, the divide between chapel and pub, although real, may have been exaggerated and may not have been blatant until the Revival of 1904/5. Aside from the free libraries with their newspaper reading rooms, which were not built until early in the twentieth century, the chapels and the pubs were virtually the only

*Onllwyn miners ferreting. SWCC, Swansea University.*

public places in the colliery villages where people could meet or, just as important, where colliers could escape from the house. Where families were large and the keeping of lodgers universal, privacy was a chimera and there was, of course, no entertainment within reach of a switch. Home for many, and especially for lodgers, most of whom were single men, was a place to eat and sleep; relaxation, recreation and amusement had to be looked for elsewhere.

Pubs, too, were often the only public spaces where colliers could rest. The inn or pub at Ysticlau-Gwynion, open from six in the morning until ten at night, is said to have been a haven for colliers waiting for the call to work at the Seven Sisters pit. On occasions when the railway wagons, that carried the coal down the valley, had not arrived at the colliery, the men could either sit around the pit head or gather at the pub where, with their beer, they would be served cawl from a large boiler provided by the landlady. As soon as the wagons arrived, the men would go to work and remain until they were filled. There were no regular hours of work, the men working when they could and for as long as they were allowed. (Supplies of beer were brought from Swansea by canal barge to Ystradgynlais, then carried across Mynydd y Drum on the tram road that connected the canal with the Seven Sisters pit, and from there carried down the mountainside to the inn.)

To suggest that pubs and beer were critical to physical as well as social health might be to stretch a point, but in his study of drink in Victorian Wales, W R Lambert made the point that beer had a role in hygiene. In mid-nineteenth century Britain, the most dangerous drink of all was tap or well water. Untreated water, especially in industrial settlements, was often a stew of lethal bacteria, whereas the water used in making beer was pumped from safe, deep wells and, an additional if inadvertent safeguard, it was boiled in the brewing process. Until it could be pasteurized, milk was almost as dangerous as water and there were no soft drinks to speak of until the 1870s. Beer was also cheaper than any of its social substitutes, chiefly tea and coffee, and a proposal by a Commons' committee, in 1833/34, for a reduction of the duty on tea as an 'immediate remedy' for drunkenness among the working classes was never taken up. Whatever its virtues, tea could hardly compete with beer as a stimulant and thirst quencher and no one believed, as was generally thought of beer, that it could impart physical strength and stamina. Converts to tea and to teetotalism expressed surprise that abstention had not weakened them. As the quintessentially British drink, beer also aroused patriotic, John Bullish sentiments, in Wales as well as in England. In the early years of the nineteenth century, portraits of Napoleon decorated the bottoms of the spittoons in the Lamb and Flag at Glynneath.

Crowded houses, exhausting and perennially dangerous work, lack of entertainment and, compared with those of agricultural labourers, relatively high wages, were a recipe not just for steady drinking but for drinking that was heavy and destructive. The practice of paying colliers in pubs, and the injections of cash provided by the two-weekly, long-pay system, exacerbated the problem. Men and their families could be ruined by drink. A reaction was inevitable. The temperance (in effect, abstention) movement originated in the 1820s, in that well of religious zealotry, nineteenth century America, and gradually, against the then prevailing cultural traffic, worked its way back across the Atlantic to England and Wales. It began as an anti-spirits movement, founded by a group of Connecticut farmers who swore off distilled alcohol, but by the mid 1830s it embraced all alcohol and, in fanatic hands, virtually all forms of pleasure. In the Tawe valley, the founder of the movement was Thomas Watkin of Ty'n y Coed whose sermons frightened Thomas Levi, himself a supporter of the movement but only, one senses, as a means of eliminating destructive drinking. The old Tafarn y Garreg, near the head of the valley, and a favourite resting place for the drivers of the coal and limestone carts, he described as one of the most welcoming taverns in Breconshire, even if its beer was execrable.

Backed by the chapels and the owners of the mines and metal works, who naturally favoured a sober workforce, the temperance movement threatened to further divide the sacred and profane elements of working class society. But on one issue, the vulnerability of the workers in a society that offered few safety nets, the two sides were united. *In extremis*, the poor had always been able to turn for help to the Poor Law, but the 1834 Amendment Act placed many categories of the poor or distressed outside the pale of assistance. The solution, in yet another expression of

*Remains of the Maendy Inn located just outside the grounds of Llangiwg Church. The inn was the meeting place of the Pontardawe Club, a friendly or benefit society for mechanics and labourers established in 1823. In 1836 the society moved downslope to the more conveniently located Dynevor Arms in Pontardawe.*

working-class self help, was the friendly or the benefit society. One of the earliest was the Friendly Society of Colliers established at Hanham, near Bristol, in 1756. In south-west Wales, the Clydach Society and the Society of Loving Brothers in Llansamlet, both founded in1794, led the way. Their aim was to encourage members to save against the proverbial rainy day. Early in the nineteenth century, local societies were replaced by regional or national ones that provided a broad range of social services that were subsequently taken over by building societies, insurance companies and trade unions. Miners, who were particularly susceptible to injury and sickness could, for a small weekly subscription, get accident and sickness benefits for short periods. By 1820 there was hardly a mining community in south Wales without a society. Clydach, a small village on the Tawe, had four in 1813, and by 1840, according to one colliery owner in the Nedd and the Tawe valleys, there was scarcely a man who did not belong to at least one society.

By 1850, mergers had produced national orders such as the Foresters and Hearts of Oak and, dominant in Wales, Oddfellows and Ivorites. Founded in Wrexham in 1836, the Ivorites quickly established a lodge in Carmarthen and from there the order spread rapidly through Carmarthenshire and into west Glamorgan. The central office and the principal lodges in south Wales were in Swansea but there were dozens of other lodges in villages and towns throughout the coalfield. Named after Ifor Hael (Ifor the Generous), who was the patron of the celebrated fourteenth century poet Dafydd ap Gwilym, it was the only working men's society that was exclusively Welsh. As well as providing accident, sickness and burial benefits, it encouraged both the speaking and writing of Welsh and, during the golden years of the order, between 1840 and 1870, there was hardly a year without an Ivorite eisteddfod. At Ammanford, home of one of the largest societies, the Ivorites built a large hall on Chapel Road, which was subsequently renamed Hall Street. With seating for 1500, the Ivorite hall became a venue for concerts, public meetings and eisteddfodau.

With so few public facilities available in most mining settlements, pubs were the natural meeting places for friendly and benefit societies as well as union lodges. Pub design was fairly standard: a long public

*Oddfellows Arms, Glynneath.*

bar on the ground floor, with adjoining rooms, equipped with chairs and tables, which were ideal for small gatherings and committee meetings. For larger meetings there was a 'long room' upstairs that ran the length of the building. Organizations using it were expected to pay the landlord a 'wet rent'. Occasionally, too, friendly societies, which often had ministers and deacons on their boards, would choose to meet at a chapel rather than a pub. But whatever the venue, the friendly society was the one organization where topers and teetotallers, the two extremes of the cultural divide, could meet. Social and religious differences were no barrier to a shared social philosophy; both groups, in the Revd Ben Davies's emotive phrase, wanted to lift the peasant class. At their meetings the societies maintained a strict code of conduct. Swearing and offensive language were forbidden as was turning up at meetings the worse for drink; for offenders the fines were punitive.

Later in the century, however, as chapel teaching leaned toward personal salvation and away from social and political reform, and as the friendly societies declared their trade union sympathies, the two institutions moved apart. A religion, as one collier noted, that denied recreation on the one day of rest, and justified the trials of this life in terms of prospective rewards in the next, had limited appeal. The laws against combination had been repealed in 1824/25, but there was no accompanying official sanction of workers' associations and assemblies. Perceived as proto trade unions, friendly and benefit societies developed in a climate of secrecy in which passwords, secret handshakes, oaths of secrecy and rites of initiation – all of which were contrary to Biblical teaching – were seen to afford protection from enemies without and betrayal within. Ivorites were given a booklet illustrating fifteen signs and handshakes, or 'grips', with explanations in both English and Welsh. Even as late as the 1920s, the password that gave entry to the lodges changed every six months. As a conservative order, the Ivorites were tolerated, but societies with ostensible political agendas were quickly broken up. Members of the Friendly Society of Coalmining, set up in 1831 as an affiliate of the National Association for the Protection of Labour, had to take an oath never – among other things – to instruct anyone but a brother in the arts of hewing, tunnelling, boring or engineering, and never to work where a brother had been forced off for standing up for his price, or in defence of his trade. Iron and coal masters in Merthyr and Dowlais were incensed and, by locking-out all the members, were able to suppress the association in the autumn/winter of 1831. An obvious reason for the society's sudden collapse, according to the miners' historian E W Evans, was the lack of support from Nonconformist religious groups, 'Which,' as he wrote, 'generally declined to interfere in industrial matters despite the vast influence they possessed.'

By the beginning of the twentieth century, the divide between the chapels and the friendly societies and trade unions was a chasm. At the time of World War I, the Ivorites' Hall in Ammanford was a major venue for political meetings, while the Socialist Labour Party of Gwauncaegurwen incensed local deacons by holding its meetings on Sundays. At Garnant, revolt was even more explicit, young miners announcing that they would attend chapel only if it was raining and then only to run a sweepstake on the first hymn. During the anthracite strike of 1925, which the chapels did not support, the Ivorites' Hall was put to many kinds of strike-supporting uses and, on the release of men imprisoned after the strike, the Hall was the venue for a mass rally that drew charabancs from all over the valley.

The chapels also lost ground as primary social and educational institutions. By granting free education to all up to the age of twelve, government-financed elementary schools supplanted them after 1891. Pennies that had been set aside weekly for children's education were channelled into the new welfare halls and miners' institutes that, in the two decades before World War I, were built in virtually every large mining village in the coalfield. Built and supported by the colliers themselves, the welfare halls and institutes, like the Nonconformist chapels, were yet another manifestation of workers' self help. After the Miners' Welfare Act of 1920, mining communities were able to draw on funds created by a levy on the mine owners of a penny for each ton of coal extracted, a concession that allowed smaller villages, in the anthracite coalfield in particular, to replace temporary and often shack-like buildings. Libraries and reading rooms were standard and in the larger institutes there were lecture halls, auditoria, games rooms, and meeting rooms where lodges and societies could conduct their business. As in most general libraries, fiction dominated, but it was not always of the light, escapist kind and, however buoyant, it was always anchored by weightier and usually radical volumes on politics, economics and social policy. For the historian Dai Smith the institutes were the miners' university, Prifysgol y Glowyr.

Even though loosely divided into chapel and non chapel-going camps well into the twentieth century, as small isolated settlements with one, or at most two industries, colliery villages were remarkably cohesive. Ammanford, the largest of the inland settlements, had a population in 1914 of only seven thousand. In the villages, every man, woman and child was attuned to the rhythms of the mine and the metal works: to the early morning exodus and the joint return in the evening, and to the collective rise or fall in their fortunes dictated by the vagaries of the trade cycle and the state of overseas markets. These were strong unifying forces. But an even stronger bond, as Ieuan Gwynedd Jones has argued, was the nature of the work itself. At his work-place a collier could survive only with the cooperation of his fellow workers; his butty was someone whom he could trust and rely on in a crisis, not just a helper or a workmate. In Professor Jones's phrase, there could be no such thing as an individual collier, only communities of colliers. In every mine there were different levels of skill, and different scales of pay, but there was no craft hierarchy that set workers apart. In the course of a lifetime, a collier, as he matured and then aged and weakened, would have undertaken most of the main jobs in a pit. There were no covert skills or processes. Everyone had a working knowledge of the various operations in a mine and understood how getting the coal to the pithead depended on the coordinated effort of several hundred colliers. The hewers, the kingpins of the mine, could do nothing without the carters, hauliers and winders and, in emergencies, survival depended on the help of everyone else. The expression of this mutual dependency was a single union, a 'great comradeship of craft', as B L Coombes described it, that embraced all colliers, whatever their station. Every attempt to form a rival organization failed. Tinplate workers had as many as four unions but for colliers there was only one, the 'Fed' – the South Wales Miners' Federation. As in the mine, so in the wider community: the chapels, the Sunday schools, the friendly societies and the pubs, despite differences in goals and attitudes, were democratic, community institutions promoting the common good. Although community bonds sometimes slackened, they were immediately tightened by the accidents that befell every mine and mining village. 'People,' James Griffiths wrote, 'clung together fiercely, sharing a 'fellowship of common danger.' A shared sense of vulnerability, of the precariousness of life, is humanizing. This was never expressed more eloquently than by W H Davies in his moving and stately poem, 'The Collier's Wife'. An explosion that killed a husband and four sons

> Had [left] five dead bodies in her house –
> All in a row they lay –
> To bury in one day:
> Such sorrow in the valley has
> Made kindness grow like grass.

# 'A WONDERFUL BREED
OF MEN'

ASIDE FROM EXPOSING THE urgent need for enforceable mine-safety regulations, the only consolation to be wrung from the nineteenth century disasters was the change in the perception of the miner. The scale and frequency of the catastrophes, and the horrifying circumstances in which miners were killed, injured or trapped commanded attention. At the same time, the disasters provided the drama that seems to have been even more necessary to Victorian sensibilities than our own. The speed with which miners gathered after an accident, and the readiness, even recklessness, with which they rushed into damaged and often gas-filled mines in search of the trapped and the injured provided rich copy for newspaper and magazine editors, reporters and illustrators. The two organs of Victorian journalism which gave the greatest coverage to the disasters, and did most to fashion the image of the miner and the mining communities, were the illustrated weeklies, the *Illustrated London News* and the *Graphic*. The other leading weeklies, the *Observer*, the *Sunday Times* and the *Weekly Chronicle*, also used illustrations, but only sparingly. Within a few years of its founding in 1842, the year of the publication of the Commissioner's Report on the employment of children in mines, the *ILN* was the most avidly read magazine in Victorian society. Unlike the Commissioners' Report, it did not at first show actual working conditions in the mines, but it presented its middle class readers, many of them for the first time, with images of mining communities and the workings around the pit-head. By 1853 the *ILN* had covered seven of seventeen major mining disasters, illustrating its reports with engravings of drawings made on the spot, either by its own artist/reporters, or competent local ones. For the 1862 Hartley Colliery disaster, it published ten engravings.

Even greater coverage of the mining communities followed the publication of the *Graphic*, in 1869. Its owner, William Luson Thomas, was a liberal reformer who used the journal to confront his readers with details of the lives of the working poor. He insisted on accurate reporting and – he was a master engraver – drawings and sketches of the highest quality. Within these broad guidelines, he gave his reporter/illustrators full freedom of style and subject matter.

Both the *Graphic* and the *ILN* covered the 1877 flooding and the subsequent rescue of miners at the Tynewydd pit in the Rhondda. To escape floodwaters that burst into the mine from old workings, the miners rushed to the shaft ahead of the surging water. All but fourteen, four of whom were drowned, managed to get to the surface, but the remaining ten, in two groups, took refuge at the head of inclined stalls, where only the great compression of the air kept the rising water at bay. Rescuers reached the first group after digging for twelve hours, but when they broke into the stall, a violent, cannon-like explosion, caused by the release of compressed air, lacerated the face of one of the diggers and crushed the skull of one of the trapped men, who was blown into the escape hole. His four companions were rescued unharmed. The second group of trapped men could be approached only from an upper level of the mine – which the floodwaters had not reached – by cutting downward along the inclined seam of coal for a distance of about forty yards. Teams of four men worked around the clock and after eight days had cut a narrow tunnel to within yards of the wall of the heading. The trapped men, with only candle grease and filthy water for sustenance, were still alive. In the darkness, they were unable to catch the rats trapped with them. To prevent the explosive release of air from the heading, the rescuers closed off the narrow tunnel behind them with an airtight door and compressed the air within their working area. When they were within a yard of the heading, an enormous rush of gas snuffed out their safety lamps and forced them back along the tunnel to the shaft. The retreat and the need to disperse the gas delayed the final stage of the rescue by two days. When the rescuers finally drilled into the heading, the compressed air escaped in great blasts that echoed throughout the mine. Unrestrained by air pressure, the water in the heading began to rise, threatening not only the trapped men but the rescuers in their narrow tunnel. The last of the trapped men was hauled out when the water had reached his chin. Queen Victoria sent messages of concern and congratulation, and awarded four of the rescuers the first-class Albert medal and twenty-one others the second-class medal.

In the seven pages it devoted to the rescue, the *Graphic* outlined briefly the technology of mining, gave details of previous disasters, and lionized the miners. Affected by the high drama of the rescue, its reporter presented them as heroic, quasi-romantic figures, never far from danger and sudden death: 'The colliers are a hardy race of simple, brave-hearted men, who daily carry their lives in their hands, for... their occupation is one of continual danger. When the swarthy workman leaves his humble cottage after kissing his wife and children, and shoulders his pick and shovel for his spell of labour in the gloomy bowels of the earth, he knows not whether he shall ever again see their loved faces and the glorious golden sunlight, or whether his mangled and blackened corpse may not, in a few hours be drawn up the shaft, and borne home to his bereaved widow and weeping babes.'

The collier would not have seen himself as a romantic or an heroic figure but panegyrics such as this could only have reinforced his growing confidence. By the end of nineteenth century, as Ieuan Gwynedd Jones has remarked, he had a fair measure of his own worth. Whether he worked in a level or a pit, he knew that his work demanded skill, sound judgement and self assurance as well as physical strength. Contemporary articles in the Nonconformist *Y Gwerinwr* emphasised the dignity of every honest calling, and early in the following century, Jay Gee, a Calvinistic Methodist writer, had his hero, 'Collier Jack', reprimand his Bible class: 'Don't look askance at the miner as he passes by and say, "He's only a collier," for underneath his grim exterior he has a generous heart. He is as brave as the most heroic soldier on the battlefield.'

The Tynewydd disaster brought the south Wales miner to the attention of most parts of the English-speaking world, but the recasting of his image had begun a few years earlier. The Tynewydd inundation followed two serious labour disputes in Dowlais, a strike in 1873 and a lockout in1875. Both the *Graphic* and the *Illustrated London News* covered the disputes and praised the restrained and dignified behaviour of the miners. While regretting the circumstances of the 1873 strike, the *Graphic* acknowledged that the conduct of the men had been exemplary. 'A great deal has been written about the ignorance and barbarism of the British miner, how in his obstinacy he refuses to work except for a very high wage, and how he spends his increased earnings upon legs of mutton for his dog and champagne for himself, while his wife and children have hardly the necessaries of life. The picture, however, is grossly exaggerated, and we may take it that the collier is very much like any other British working–man, somewhat rough-mannered and plain-spoken, perhaps, and a trifle overbearing when under the direction of Union leaders… Still for all this he is by no means destitute of the nobler instincts of humanity, and we can readily forgive much to men who, when their fellows' lives are imperilled, are so eager to strain nerve and muscle, and to brave the greatest dangers to rescue them.'

While covering the disputes, Herbert Johnson of the *Graphic* went underground, the first artist–illustrator in Wales to do so. In the Vochrin pit, he saw timbers, a foot in diameter, that had snapped like bent twigs and, through squeeze and pooking, roadways that had been reduced in height and width to no more than a few feet. In the earth's efforts to

*Rescue at Troedyrhiw, 1877. NMW.*

close its wounds, he discerned, as he phrased it, an awesome 'healing power' that could destroy the mine and the miner: 'Not only does the roof descend and the sides close in, but even the floor rises and cockles in an endeavour to reach the roof.' Ystalyfera's Dai Dan Evans would put it much more roughly, a century later: 'Men do not with impunity tear the guts out of the earth.'

The reassessment of the miner and manual workers in general also occurred in the fine arts as well as in the illustrative or graphic ones. In 1880, Van Gogh sketched a group of miners in the Borinage district of southern Belgium, impassively making their way to work on a wintry dawn. They were complemented by Constantin Meunier's paintings of a miner and a haulier, also of the Borinage. Both Van Gogh and Meunier were building on groundwork laid in France by Courbet and Millet, whose peasants, on the roadsides and in the woods and fields, unlike the decorative peasants in earlier classical and neo-classical paintings, actually work. Labour had been accorded worth and the labourer dignity, no matter how toilsome and disfiguring the work. In non-labouring eyes, such as Thomas Carlyle's, hard physical work was seen as redemptive, the antidote to base desires and the road, if not to saintliness, then to a more unsullied state. In Britain, exponents of the Carlyle school of thought were Ford Madox Brown and William Bell Scott. In Madox Brown's *Work* and Bell Scott's *Iron and Coal on Tyneside*, the workers, a young London navvy surrounded by fashionable men and women and sardonic idlers in one case, and sturdy metal workers enshrouded in smoke and flame in the other, are icons of a new age of industry.

Not all viewers, however, were captivated by the world of work. At the 1874 summer exhibition of the Royal Academy, the critic for the *Athenaeum* pounced upon Eyre Crowe's painting of a group of factory women taking their dinner break outside a Wigan cotton mill. The women are cheerful and frolicsome in the happy-peasant mould and there is no hint of exploitation or misery, yet the critic attacked Crowe on grounds that subjects such as *The Dinner Hour, Wigan*, and his even more unsavoury *Spoil Bank*, ought to be left to photography, a baser art. Painting was meant to embellish. Mine and factory officials, too, were often just as displeased with images of the workplace. William

Thomas, the Camborne Superintendent of Mines, accused book and magazine illustrators of sensationalizing both the nature of the work and its dangers for no other reason than 'to promote a transaction.'

About the time of the Great War, images of work began to emerge from the coalfield itself. At fifteen, William Edmund Jones of Pontypool, born in 1890, had begun to photograph his surroundings and by 1910 he had been underground, photographing in a gas-free pit; the open magnesium flash used at the time kept the camera out of gassy mines. Jones's photographs began to be shown at roughly the same time as the emergence of three painters of mines and miners from working-class backgrounds in south Wales: Evan Walters, Vincent Evans, and Archie Rhys Griffiths. All were from the western coalfield and from rural/industrial backgrounds. Evan Walters, the oldest, born in 1893, was from Llangyfelach, and Vincent Evans from Ystalyfera. Rhys Griffiths was born in Aberdare but grew up in Gorseinon. Two of them had also worked in mines. Vincent Evans started in the pit at thirteen, while Rhys Griffiths began his working life in a tinplate works and then spent four years at the coalface in the Mountain Colliery at Gorseinon. All were Welsh speaking and all three studied at the Swansea School of Art.

They painted against the background of deepening post-war economic depression and the general strike, but none was overtly political. For the 1926 National Eisteddfod at Swansea, Walters painted the prize-winning *Welsh Collier*, and for an exhibition at a London gallery, paintings with titles such as *The Miner's Bath* and *The Convalescent Collier*. Archie Rhys Griffiths clearly appreciated his years at the coalface, at least in retrospect: 'I was until a short time ago a miner myself, and, let me say that, so far from the iron having entered my soul, as it were, I am genuinely glad of the time I spent underground. There, in spite of all mental and physical disadvantages, I was caught up in that idealistic spirit which permeates all our little communities down there.' Two of his paintings, *Testing a Collier's Lamp* and *Miners Returning from Work,* suggested to the painter and critic Sir William Rothenstein that Rhys Griffiths 'had a moving sympathy with toiling and sweating

*'Miners Returning from Work', Archie Rhys Griffiths. NMW.*

workers underground.' In 1918, Vincent Evans was commissioned by Alfred Nobel to illustrate a calendar and he did so with a painting of a collier standing underground, clean-faced and at the beginning of his shift, with his lamp in one hand and his tommy box in the other. Of the three, Evans was probably the closest to the labour movement. He became a friend of James Griffiths, then president of the Miners' Federation of Great Britain, and among his subjects painted at the time was *A Miners' Federation Meeting Underground.* Suffering and hardship figure in many of the paintings but their miners are serious, solemn figures, not radical ones. Rhys Griffiths painted *A Fatal Accident* in 1922, and *Tro yn yr Yrfa,* which shows a procession of colliers taking home by night the body of a fellow workmen killed in the colliery, in 1928. Evan Walters' *Dead Miner* appeared in 1935. In 1933, Vincent Evans organized an exhibition of his own works at Gwauncaegurwen, the proceeds of which he donated towards the relief of poverty in the area. Yet his best-known painting, and the one which he regarded as his most important, *A Welsh Family Idyll,* is a dream of contentment: an Adonis-like young anthracite miner, surrounded by family and neighbours,

'A Welsh Family Idyll', Vincent Evans, Glynn Vivian Gallery. The setting for the painting is Ystalyfera.

tends his garden in an idealized semi-rural landscape.

In spite of the appeal of paintings of mines and miners, in art establishment circles the prejudice against paintings of workers and industrial life was slow to subside. Augustus John and Clough Williams-Ellis, leading exponents of the art-as-embellishment school, regarded paintings of colliers and industrial landscapes as beyond any acceptable artistic pale. After seeing a 1926 London exhibition by Evan Walters, whose talent he admired, Augustus John advised him to paint in Provence and develop a colour sense. Walters ignored the advice and returned to south Wales, where, in John's phrase, 'colour is apparently taboo or non-existent.' In 1951, John recalled adjudicating at an eisteddfod, 'Where I noticed a painting of a collier: At least, I took it to be a collier from the general blackness of the colour.' The painter was Evan Walters. In an exhibition of contemporary Welsh art, in 1935, only two paintings by Evan Walters were shown, *The Miner* and *The Welsh Collier*. Vincent Evans and Rhys Griffiths were both excluded, although both were well-known to the selectors. Among the latter was the painter Cedric Morris, grandson of Sir John Morris, the copper master and builder of Morriston, who, though raised near Swansea, was based in England. Morris was outraged by the effects of the Depression upon communities in the Tawe valley, and, while he painted, he boarded briefly with the family of an out-of-work miner. He also painted industrial landscapes in Merthyr and Dowlais, yet, in

*'The Welsh Collier', Evan Walters, 1926. Glynn Vivian Gallery.*

as much as he was responsible for the selection of paintings in the 1935 exhibition, he kept industrial paintings and paintings that might be interpreted as socially or politically provocative out of the exhibition.

For a painter who would embrace the miner unreservedly and exclusively, south Wales had to wait until the end of World War II. In 1944, Josef Herman, an émigré Polish painter whose pen was almost as evocative as his pencil and brush, settled for more than a decade in Ystradgynlais. He was born in Warsaw in 1911, the son of a Jewish cobbler, and came to Ystradgynlais via Brussels and Glasgow. After his arrival, he spent weeks walking in the hills above the village, studying the landscape, sketching, and looking at and talking to miners both on the surface and underground. It was a year before he began producing paintings. He found miners at first sight to be like other workers but, as he remarked, in some ways more impressive and singular. He took to heart the observation of a fellow Jewish émigré from eastern Europe, Moishe, or Moshe, as he was known in the village, who had worked for thirty-six years in Tawe valley mines before the dust began to trouble him. 'I'll tell you,' Moshe remarked, 'heredity never typifies a man to the extent his job does.' Herman would have heard similar sentiments expressed by his friend Will Roberts, an accomplished painter of labour from Neath, who believed, like Moshe, that a man's work could shape his body, mind and habits.

In Ystradgynlais, as in the other valley villages, the miners stood out: 'The miner,' Herman noted, 'is the man of Ystradgynlais... By this singularity of appearance, amid the clean figures of the shop-keepers, the tall and thin figures of the town councillors, the robust figures of the insurance agents, the respectable figures of the ministers, and the fatigued figures of the schoolmasters, the miners form, like trees among vegetables, a solid group. But what makes the group so singular outside is but the strong similarity within the group.' He cited their shared characteristics: the mauve scarf and their way of wearing it, their manner of nodding their heads sideways in greeting, their upright, square-shouldered walk and the feeling of liberation they express as they saunter down an open road, their custom of carrying sawn-off pit props (to be cut for kindling) under their arms, and their way of sitting near a wall and supporting their bodies with the heel of the foot. In short, coalmining had produced a new type of working man. The moment of epiphany for Herman occurred on a June or July day in 1944, when a group of miners stepped onto the bridge at Ystradgynlais, their heads silhouetted and framed by the sun. 'There was hardly a soul to be seen. In the distance low hills like sleeping dogs and above the hills a copper-coloured sky... Under the bridge out of a cool shadow trickled a pool of water... Then, unexpectedly, as though from nowhere, a group of miners stepped onto a bridge. For a split second their heads appeared against the full body of the sun, as against a yellow disc... With the light around them the silhouettes of the miners were almost black... The magnificence of the scene overwhelmed me...It became the source of my work for years to come.'

Like Will Roberts' paintings of farmers and tinplate workers, Herman's paintings of miners are symbols, not portraits. Faces, Will Roberts used to say of the farmers and tinplate workers he painted, did not matter to him. His interest was in the body and what it expressed of the work it had performed. So with Herman: 'I want my studies of miners to be more than real portraits. I am... trying to convey... a synthesis of the pride of human labour and of the fortitude, the calm force that promise[s] to guard its dignity... I like the miners and I like living

*'Pit Pony', Josef Herman. Tate Gallery.*

among them. In their warm humanity and their expressive occupational poses, the way they squat, the way they walk and hold themselves, I find the embodiment of labour.' The impact of Herman's paintings was immediate and not, in all cases, welcomed. In response to murals (*South Wales* and *Miners Crouching*) that Herman had been asked to paint for the Festival of Britain, Elizabeth Coombe-Tennant expostulated in a letter to Augustus John: 'A Pole now living at Ystradgynlais... Herman or some such name! And [there were two other painters from Wales] these cranks are now to go out into the world as representatives of art in Wales!!!' Nor on the political left was the response always favourable. John Berger took issue with what he regarded as misrepresentation:

*'Miners Singing', Josef Herman. NMGW.*

Herman's portrayal of miners 'as if they were peasants instead of one of the most militant sections of the proletariat.' There was also some local discontent. In response to a 1948 exhibition, 'Miners at Ystradgynlais', a local newspaper carried the comment: 'The miners and their womenfolk look like blotted, misshapen, prehistoric beings emerging from the primeval swamps of the Carboniferous age... ghastly travesties of the present-day miner and his womenfolk.' It was an assessment that might not altogether have displeased Herman, his friend Moshe, or Will Roberts. All believed in the convergence of the workman and his materials. Just as Roberts' farmers are impossible to imagine removed from the earth they work, so Herman's miners seem part of the fabric of the mine. Moshe put it well: 'Man's heart is really big; it can take communion with any material... People don't know how much art there is in mining! You sit, sit and think in front of that black mystery. And then you hit and nature gives way! It's no daydream, believe me. Yes, it was not easy to leave the mine. Once you get used to an art you don't just leave it for a caprice.'

Moshe's view is held by probably a majority of former miners. The prolonged and, for the miners, disastrous strike of 1984/85 combined with large reserves of gas and oil lying conveniently offshore in the North Sea, brought a swift end to an already ailing industry. The last deep mine in the western coalfield, Betws, survived until 2003 but all the others had closed much earlier. Coal is still taken from the northern outcrop, but with giant diggers from opencast workings, not, as two centuries earlier, with pick, shovel and cart from shallow scrapings. Today, apart from a few museum pieces, there is little ostensible evidence that coal was ever mined. The pithead gear has been taken down, the waste tips levelled and grassed over, the tram roads and railways torn up and the canals, for the most part, filled in. The industrial housing, most of it now much improved, is the only evidence that heavy, physical work was done here.

Among the older men, there is a sense of loss. Question a former miner and you risk plumbing a well of nostalgia, much of it deeply felt. For non-miners, this presents a fundamental paradox. How could work that was clearly so dangerous, and remains so in places where coal is still

*'Hanging On', 1981, a privately-owned mine high on the side of the Tawe valley near Ystalyfera.*

mined, be missed? As recently as the 1970s, when British mines were safer than they had ever been, a miner was seven times more likely to be seriously injured or killed than any other industrial worker. Some miners, having felt 'the sun on their backs,' vowed they would never return to the pits, but many would have, and would still, given the opportunity. Part of the answer lies in the freedom allowed the collier, especially under the old stall system. Output and safety depended on acquired skills, vigilance and judgement. When payment was by the piece, or by output, and when safety depended on the collier's assessment of the roof and the need for supports, close supervision was unnecessary. Freedom to exercise judgement and initiative gave the miner a feeling of independence. Under machine cutting much of the old autonomy was lost but it was never eliminated entirely. Cutting the coal and moving the conveyor forward may have been routine, but constant monitoring of the roof and the supports was still necessary and conditions were never the same in two places.

As well as honouring hard, physical labour, Josef Herman, Will Roberts and, more recently, the Swansea-born painter Valerie Ganz, were also recording its end, however unwittingly. Work of that hard, unremitting kind would never, in Britain at least, be done again. Coalmining called for a steady nerve, strength, and powers of endurance as well as intelligence and sound judgement. A big hewer or a renowned ripper who could drive hard headings through solid bedrock was the equivalent of a champion boxer. To have been a miner in a region so long identified with coalmining was a badge of distinction. The blue scars on hands and face, from cuts impregnated with coal dust, were campaign medals and, in the final days of coalmining, practically everyone, metaphorically speaking, wanted to wear them. Time after time in his 1978 survey of miners in the Amman valley, Stephen J Town discovered that men would describe themselves as having been miners for most of their lives when systematic questioning revealed that they had left mining ten or fifteen years earlier, to work in some other industry. His most telling example was of a man who had left mining through ill health at the age of thirty-six, and then held a series of semi-skilled jobs, including ten years working in a bakery before retiring early. At sixty-six, thirty years later, he still described himself as a miner. Even men who had never worked as miners often showed a close knowledge of the industry. A sixty-year-old factory store hand, who had worked in a tinplate works, not the mines ('let's be honest, I was too scared,' he told Town) gave a long and detailed account of the technical problems of mining in different collieries, and the reasons for their closure.

But the one allure of mining, against which no one was proof, even those who subsequently revelled in the sun on their backs, was the fellowship of the mine. Former miners speak of comradeship, camaraderie, in the same warm tones as soldiers home from the front, or shipmates from a rough sea. In the older pits especially, and under the old methods, miners were bands of brothers. Danger may not have been immediate, but it was always immanent and the knowledge that in an emergency fellow colliers would, without thinking, risk, and even sacrifice, life and limb to save you was a powerful and heady

*A mining renaissance? Rising prices for coal and uncertainty about the ability of renewable resources to meet future energy demands have, it is thought, made mines that formerly were uneconomic commercially viable again. The photograph is of the coalyard and mine surface of the recently re-opened Pentreclwydau South drift mine, owned by Unity Power, near Cwmgwrach in the Nedd Valley.*

*The Unity six feet (anthracite) seam. Reserves are large, sufficient to sustain an annual production of one million tonnes for the next twenty-five years. Industrial production is scheduled to begin early in 2008. For the sixty jobs that will be available there have been four hundred applicants.*

bond. 'There is no closer community than in mining,' remarked one of Town's respondents, and closeness and trust produced what seems to have been an inimitable atmosphere: 'There's nothing like the atmosphere you get in a pit, there's the cursing, there's the comradeship – you can be cursing a man one moment, but if there's a fall you are in there getting the rocks off him. You can tell a man off, but the next moment you are working together and it's forgotten. You don't get that in a factory – everybody is more selfish and you're always looking over your shoulder at some little Hitler of a foreman.' The last word should go to a thoughtful retiree who missed the fellowship but not the mine: 'Yes, I do miss it, if it's only the friendship. They are a wonderful breed of men. I suppose it's foolish to say you miss going underground – nobody wants to do that.'

# ENDNOTES

[1] Technically, coal is a sedimentary rock (of a somewhat unusual type), but for trade purposes it is spoken of as a mineral.

[2] Roughly translated, this reads:

> She lives in a house without a roof
> The old witch, Pegi the coal.
> Black her face, short her cloak,
> Her teeth look as if they are made of coal,
> She lives in a house without a roof
> And scares the neighbourhood children.

[3] Some of the Polish saltmines were 600 fathoms, 3,600 feet, deep.

[4] For readers familiar with Neath, the Mera was on the west side of present day Victoria Gardens, near the junction with Water Street.

[5] The custom was revived after the introduction of electric cap lamps. To test for methane, officials and selected workmen were issued with flame safety lamps.

# BIBLIOGRAPHY

## Manuscript and Unpublished Sources

Davies, D.J., 'The South Wales Anthracite Industry' (Univ. of Wales MA thesis, 1930).

Davies, Donald, 'The Llwchwr and Amman Valleys to 1939: a study in industrial development' (Univ. of Wales MA thesis, 1959).

Davies, H.W.E., The development of the industrial landscape of western South Wales during the nineteenth and twentieth centuries (Univ. of Wales M.Sc. thesis, 1955)

Davies, J.M., 'The growth of settlement in the Swansea valley (Univ. of Wales MA thesis, 1942).

Edwards G.A. 'A study of the Daucleddau coalfield, Pembrokeshire' (Birmingham Univ. MA thesis, 1950).

Evans, David Gareth, 'The growth and development of organized religion in the Swansea Valley' (Univ. of Wales Ph.D. thesis, 1977).

Evans, R.M., 'The Welsh coal trade during the Stuart period', 1603-1709 (Univ. of Wales MA thesis, 1928).

Griffiths, I.L., 'The anthracite coalfield of south Wales' (London Univ. Ph.D. thesis, 1959).

Harding, W.J., 'Llanguicke Parish 1660-1862, the change from agriculture to industry', Diploma in Local History, Univ. of Wales, Swansea, 1993.

Hughes, J.E.T.'Outbursts of Coal and Gas of the Anthracite Area of South Wales' (Univ. of Wales M.Sc. thesis, 1973).

Cotes, C.C., letter to Pleydell Courteen, 9 August 1736, Neath Antiquarian Society, GAT 1/1/B.

Ley, W.L. 'The Story of Ystradgynlais', Ystradgynlais Public Library.

Matthews, Ioan, 'The world of the anthracite miner' (Univ. of Wales Ph.D. thesis, 1996).

Morris, John, Commonplace Book 1780–1818, Univ. of Wales, Swansea.

Morris, Robert Jr., 'History of the copper concern, 1717–1730', Univ. of Wales, Swansea.

Price, M.R.C., 'Pembrokeshire – the Forgotten Coalfield' (Univ. of Wales Ph.D. thesis, 2002).

Boulton, Matthew and Watt, James, letters to John Morris, Royal Institute of South Wales, letter files, 23.

Roberts, Redvers P., 'The history of coal mining in Gower from 1700–1832' (Univ. of Wales MA thesis, 1953).

Royal Institution of South Wales, 'The Morris Family and Sir John Morris', Letter files, 23.

Sewel, J. B., 'The Upper Dulais valley, a sociological study' (Univ. of Wales M.A. thesis, 1970).

Taylor, Glen A., 'Early History of the Neath Coal Industry', Lecture, Neath Antiquarian Soc. Jan 1931.

Taylor, Glen A., 'Notes on Early Coalmining in the Neath Area', Neath Antiquarian Society, c. 1930.

Thomas, J.D.H., 'Social and Economic Developments in the Upper Swansea Valley with particular reference to the parish of Llangiwg, 1770–1880', (Univ. of Wales M.A. thesis, 1974).

## Newspapers

Cambrian
Swansea and Glamorgan Herald
Pembrokeshire Herald
Carmarthenshire Journal
Graphic
Illustrated London News

## Other Works

Anon., 'Impressions of a Rhonddaite', *Llais Llafur*, 18 Sept. 1909.

Belcham, Elizabeth, *About Aberpergwm* (Glynneath, 1992).

Benson, John, *British Coalminers in the Nineteenth Century* (London, 1980).

Briggs, Professor Henty, 'The Anthracite Problem', *Proc. South Wales Inst. of Engineers*, 39, 1923-24, 403-527.

Charles, B.G., *George Owen of Henllys* (Aberystwyth, 1973).

Coombes, B.L., *I am a Miner* (London, 1939).

Coombes, B.L., *Miners Day* (London, 1945).

Coombes, B.L., *These Poor Hands* (London, 1939)

Cooper, R.N., *A Dark and Pagan Place* ( Swansea, 1986).

Cowley, F.G., 'Pentre Colliery: a Short History, *Bull. South West Wales Ind. Arch. Soc.*, 79, 2000.

Cullen, Phil., *Curse below the Gwendraeth Valley* (Carmarthen, 2001).

Cunnington, Phyllis and Lucas, Catherine, *Occupational Costume in England* (London, 1967).

Davies, E.T., *Religion in the Industrial Revolution in South Wales* (Cardiff, 1965).

Davies, J.H., *History of Pontardawe and District* (Swansea, 1967).

Davies, W.H., *Complete Poems* (London, 1963).

Davies, Walter, *General View of the Agricultural and Domestic Economy of South Wales* (London, 1814).

Duckham, Helen and Baron, *Great Pit Disasters: Great Britain, 1700 to the Present Day* (Newton Abbot, 1973).

Edwards, George, 'The Coal Industry in Pembrokeshire', *Field Sudies*, 1, 1963, 33-64.

Egan, David, *Coal Society: History of the South Wales Mining Valleys 1840-1898* (Llandysul, 1987).

Evans, Chris., *Blaencwmdulais: a short history of the social and industrial development of Onllwyn and Banwen-Pyrddin* (Cardiff, 1977).

Evans, Chris., *Industrial and Social History of Seven Sisters* (Cardiff, 1964).

Evans, D.A. and Walters, Huw, *The Amman Valley Long Ago* (Llandysul, 1987).

Evans, E.W., *The Miners of South Wales* (Cardiff, 1961).

Evans, George Ewart, *Coalfield Study* (audio recording), Univ. of Wales, Swansea, 1960-1979.

Evans, Rev. J., *Letters written during a Tour through South Wales in 1803* (London, 1804).

Fletcher, C.M. 'Pneumoconiosis of Coal-Miners', *British Medical Journal*, 1, 1948.

Fletcher, Charles, 'Fighting the Modern Black Death', *The Listener*, 28 Sept.1950.

Francis, Hywel, 'Language, Culture and Learning: the Experience of a Valley Community', *Llafur*, 6,3, 1944, 85-96.

Francis, Hywel, 'Survey of Miners' Institutes and Welfare Hall Libraries', *Llafur*, 1, 2, 1973, 54-64.

Francis, Hywel, 'The Anthracite Strike and Disturbances of 1925', *Llafur*, 1,2, 1972, 15-28.

Franks, R.H., *Royal Commission Reports, 1842, on the Employment of Children and Young Persons in the Mines*, Vol. 15, 1842.

Freese, Barbara, *Coal: A Human History*, (New York, 2003).

Gabb, Gerald, *Coalmining in the Swansea Area (1) before 1700 (2) East of the Tawe*, Lower Swansea Valley Factsheets (Swansea Museums Service).

Gabb, Gerald, *Llansamlet Coal Owners and Miners*, Lower Swansea Valley Fact sheets (Swansea Museums Service).

Gabb, Gerald, *Tramroads and Industrial Railways*, Lower Swansea Valley Fact sheets (Swansea Museums Service)

Galloway, Robert L., *Annals of Coalmining and the Coal Trade* (London, 1898).

Galloway, Robert L., *History of Coalmining in Great Britain* (London, 1882).

Galloway, William, *Great Colliery Explosions and their means of prevention* (London, 1914).

George, T.N., *The Geology and Physical Features of the Swansea District* (Swansea, 1939).

Gray, Douglas, *Coal, British Mining in Art 1680-1980* (London, 1982).

Green, Harry, 'The Eaglesbush Colliery Explosion 1848', *Trans. Neath Antiquarian. Society*, 1979, 91-102.

Griffin, A.R., *Coalmining* (London, 1971).

Griffin, A.R., *The British Coalmining Industry* (London, 1977).

Griffiths, James, 'Glo Carreg: Memories of the Anthracite Coalfield', *Carmarthenshire Historian*, 12, 1968, 7-16.

Hadfield, Charles, *The Canals of South Wales and the Border* (Newton Abbot, 1967).

Hare, A.E.C., *The Anthracite Coal Industry of the Swansea District* (Cardiff, 1940). Edwards G.A., 'The Coal Industry in Pembrokeshire', *Field Studies*, 1, 1963, 33-64.

Harris, J.R.,'Skills, Coal and British Industry', *History*, 61, 1976, 167-182.

Herman, Josef, *Related Twilights, Notes from an Artist's Diary* (London, 1975).

Herman, Nini, *Josef Herman: a Working Life* (London, 1996)

Howard, J.H., *Winding Lanes* (Swansea, 1938).

Howells, Brian E. ed., *Early Modern Pembrokeshire 1536-1815*, Vol 3, *Pembrokeshire County History*, 1987.

Inglis, K.S., *The Church and the Working Classes in Victorian England* (London, 1963).

Innes, John, *Old Llanelly* (Cardiff, 1902).

J.C., *The Compleat Collier* (1708).

Jevons, J. Stanley, *The British Coal Trade* (London, 1915).

Jones, Bill and Williams, Chris, *B.L. Coombes*, (Cardiff, 1999).

Jones, Ieuan Gwynedd, 'The South Wales Collier in Mid-Nineteenth Century', *Communities, Essays in the Social History of Victorian Wales* (Llandysul, 1987).

Jones, Ieuan Gwynedd, 'The Swansea Valley: Life and Labour in the

Nineteenth Century', *Communities: the observers and the observed* (Cardiff, 1985).

Jones, Ieuan Gwynedd, *Explorations and Explanations: essays in the social history of Victorian Wales* (Llandysul, 1981).

Jones, Philip N, *Colliery Settlement in the South Wales Coalfield 1850 to 1926* (Hull, 1969).

Jones, Rhys William, *Royal Commission Reports, 1842, on the Employment of Children and Young Persons in the Mines, Western Glamorganshire and Carmarthenshire,* Vol. 17, 1842.

Jones, W.H., *History of the Port of Swansea* (Swansea, 1925).

Lambert, W.R., 'Drink and Work Discipline in Industrial South Wales', *Welsh History Review* 7, 3 (1975).

Lambert, W.R., 'Some Working-Class Attitudes towards Organized Religion in Nineteenth Century Wales'. *Llafur* 2,1, 1976.

Leifchild, J.R., *Our Coal and our Coalpits* (London, 1856).

Levi, Rev. Thomas, 'Cwm Tawy', *Y Traethodydd*, 1865, 237-249, 467-477.

Lewis, Brian, *Coalmining in the Eighteenth and Nineteenth Centuries* (London, 1971).

Lingen, R.R.W., *Reports of the Commissioners of Inquiry into the State of Education in Wales*, 1847.

Matthews, Ioan, 'The World of the Anthracite Miner', *Llafur* 6, 1, 1992, 95-104.

Matthews, Ioan, 'The Welsh Language in the Anthracite Coalfield c. 1870-1914', *Language and Community in the Nineteenth Century*, Geraint Jenkins ed., (Cardiff, 1998)

Morgan, Prys and Thomas, David, *Wales: the Shaping of a Nation* (Newton Abbot, 1984).

Morgan, T.J., 'Peasant Culture in the Swansea Valley', *Glamorgan Historian*, 9, 105-122.

Morgan, W.R., *A Pembrokeshire Countryman Looks Back* (Tenby, 1988).

Morris, J.H. and Williams, L.J., *The South Wales Coal Industry* (Cardiff, 1958).

Nef, J.U., *The Rise of the British Coal Industry* (London, 1932).

North, F.J., *Coal and the Coalfields in Wales* (Cardiff, 1931).

Owen, George (of Henllys), *Description of Pembrokeshire* (c. 1550).

Perkins, C.H. 'Anthracite Coal', Paper read at British Assoc. Adv. Science meeting, Swansea 1880 , Royal Institution of South Wales, Box, 84/7.

Phillips, D. Rhys, *History of the Vale of Neath* (Neath, 1925).

Phillips, Elizabeth, *Pioneers of the Welsh Coalfield* (Cardiff, 1925).

Price, M.R.C., *Industrial Saundersfoot* (Llandysul, 1982).

Raynes, J.R., *Coal and its Conflicts* (London, 1928).

Rees, D.Ben, *Wales, the Cultural Heritage* (1981).

Rees, William, *Industry before the Industrial Revolution* (Cardiff, 1968).

Reynolds, P.R., 'A High State of Perfection: Cox's Hendreforgan Colliery 1814-1833', *Morgannwg*, 30, 1986, 42-64.

Reynolds, P.R., 'Chauncy Townsend's Waggonway', *Morgannwg*, 21, 1977, 42-67.

Reynolds, P.R., 'Pentre Pit and Pentre Colliery 1785-1865', *Bull. South West Wales Ind. Arch. Soc.,* 1976.

Reynolds, P.R., 'Robert Mills, Viewer of Llansamlet Colliery, c. 1820-1853', *Bull. Southwest Wales Ind. Arch. Soc.* 75, 1999.

Reynolds, P.R., 'William Price Struve, 1809-1878, *Bull. South West Wales Ind. Arch. Soc.,* 1978.

Richardson, Joshua, *Journal 1841-48*, West Glam. Archives Service.

Richardson, Joshua, *The Prevention of Accidents in Mines* (Neath, 1848}.

Ridd, Tom, 'Pit and Pit Boys in the Swansea Area, *Gower,* 17, 1966, 44-47.

Roberts, R.O. and Hall, Elizabeth J., *The Building Industry in the Upper Swansea Valley and its Economic and Social Ramifications c.1870-1975*, Welsh Studies 16 (Lampeter, 2000).

Robson, Frederick, 'Coalminers' Nystagmus', *Proc. S. Wales Inst. Eng.*, 39, 1923.

Strahan, A., 'Origin of Anthracite', *The Coals of South Wales* (HMSO 1915).

Struve, W.P., 'On the Ventilation of Mines', *Swansea Scientific Soc. Reports*, 1846.

Symons, Malcolm V., *Coalmining in the Llanelli Area* (Llanelli, 1979).

Taylor, Glen A. 'A Dramatic Chapter in the Industrial History of Neath', *Trans. Neath Antiquarian Society.*, 1933-34.

Taylor, Glen A., 'The Streets of Old Neath', *Trans. Neath Antiquarian. Society*, 7, 1937, 75-76.

Thomas, Hugh, 'The Industrialization of a Glamorgan Parish', *National Library of Wales Journal,* 3 parts: 19, 2,1975; 19,3, 1976; 19, 4, 1977.

Till, R.D., 'Proprietary Politics in Glamorgan: The Mackworth Family and the Borough of Neath, 1696-1794, *Morgannwg* 16, 1972, 37-52.

Timbrell, W.E., *Reminiscences of Tumble from 1896* (Llanelli, 1974).

Town, Stephen W., *After the Mines: changing employment opportunities in a south Wales valley* (Cardiff, 1978).

Trott, C.D.G., 'Coalmining in the Borough of Neath in the Seventeenth and Early Eighteenth Centuries, *Morgannwg* 13 (1969), 47-74.

Tucker, Keith, *Chronicle of Cadoxton* (Neath, 1970)

Vivian, H. Hussey, *Notes on a Tour of North America* (London, 1877, repr. 1974).

Wallace, Alfred Russel, *My Life: a record of events and opinions,* (London, 1905).

Wilkins, Charles, *The South Wales Coal Trade* (Cardiff, 1888).

Williams Chris and James, Bill, *B.L. Coombes* (Cardiff, 1999).

Williams, D.T. The *economic development of Swansea and of the Swansea district to 1921* ( Cardiff, 1940).

Williams, Peter N., *From Wales to Pennsylvania: The David Thomas Story* (Cardiff, 2002).

# INDEX

Cardiff 76, 106

Carlyle, Thomas 263

Carmarthen, Carmarthenshire
24; coal as fuel 19–20;
culture 246, 248, 254;
early workings 35; miners'
working conditions 118,
136–7, 139, 153–4;
settlement and landscape
204; *see also* Amman valley;
Gwendraeth valley; *and
individual places*

cast iron 110

Castell Nedd *see* Neath

Cefn Coed colliery 115, 116,
146, 213illus

Channel Islands 25, 77

chapels 219–20, 229–49, 251,
253, 256–7, 258

charcoal 19, 20, 27–8, 29

Chaucer, Geoffrey 18

Child, J M 102

child labour 135–43

Children's Employment
Commission reports (1842)
135–40, 155–6, 159, 239,
240

chokedamp 47, 155, 157, 164–
5, 167, 171

cholera 222–4

choral singing 245–9

Christmas, Thomas 173

circulating schools 42, 239

Clarke, E D 61–3, 129

Clarke, George T 207

*Clawdd y Saeson* 78

Cleeves, Fred 111, 112

Clough, Arthur Hugh 114

Clydach 9, 214, 234, 248, 254

Clydach Society 254

Clyndu colliery 61, 206

Clyne 31, 214

coal: as domestic fuel 17–23,
93–4, 109–10, 114; geology
11–17; industrial use 23–
5, 27–9, 43, 59–60, 61,
66–7, 69, 72, 93, 94–108;
transportation 30, 31, 51–
2, 58, 61, 62illus, 63, 66–7,
69, 89, 91–2 (*see also* canals,
railways, roads); variations in
nature of 16–17, 19–21

coal trade 25–7, 28, 30, 33–4,
35, 43, 55, 56, 58–9, 61,
72, 73, 77, 84, 85, 93, 108,
110–14

Coalmines Act (1842) 159

Coalmines Act (1887) 182

coalmining: decline and future
prospects 270–3illus; early
workings 30–73; later
development 84–116;
nationalization 115–16; *see
also* miners; mining methods
and techniques

Cobbett, William 120

Coelbren 7, 107, 212

Coffin, Walter 93

Coke, H S 175

coke 29, 94, 96

*Compleat Collier* (1708) 37, 44

continental drift theory 15-16

Coombe-Tennant, Elizabeth 269-70

Coombes, B L 10, 128, 129, 133-4, 140, 144-5, 156, 162-3, 177, 193, 195, 210, 217-18, 258

copper industry 27-8, 29, 43, 59-60, 61, 66-7, 69, 72-3, 77, 200; workers in 123-5, 206, 226

Cornwall 24, 28, 29, 51, 59, 89, 93; miners from 67, 173

Cottan, George 97

Courbet, Gustave 263

Courteen, Pleydell 46, 51

Cox, James 90-2

Craig Trewyddfa 60, 61, 158, 205

Crane, George 96-7, 99, 100

Cresselly 27

Cross Hands 153, 212

Cross Inn *see* Ammanford

Crowe, Eyre 263-4

Creunant 7, 114, 151-2, 213illus, 214, 216

culm 20-1, 23, 24, 25, 26, 93

culture: religious 228-49; secular 249-58; Welsh

language 125, 226-8, 232, 233, 238, 239, 241, 247, 254

curling box 132-3illus, 172illus

Curwen, John 247

Cwm Llech 11-15

Cwmafan 28, 99, 249

Cwmaman 151, 228, 247

Cwmdu colliery 120

Cwmdulais 108

Cwmfelinfach 250illus

Cwmgiedd 220, 248

Cwmgors 114, 127, 161illus

Cwmgwili 160illus

Cwmgwrach 7, 9, 214, 273illus

Cwmmawr 83-4, 122illus

Cwmtwrch Isaf and Uchaf 89, 214, 223, 245

Cydweli 33, 76, 83, 84

Cyfing colliery, Ystalyfera 172-3

Cynheidre 115, 116, 184

Dalziel, Alexander 135

damps 32, 47-50; accidents 164-78; *see also* blowers

Darby, Abraham 29, 63, 94

Davies, Ben 137, 245, 255

Davies, E T 229

Davies, Elizabeth 80-1

Davies, J 234

Davies, James 239

Davies, Thomas 228, 241

Davies, W H 155, 258

# Also from *y Lolfa* ...

## Symphonies in Black

*Nicholas Evans*

The paintings of Nicholas Evans. A unique view of one of the hardest ways of life imaginable – the early days of coal mining in Wales.

**£9.95**
ISBN 0 86243 135 2

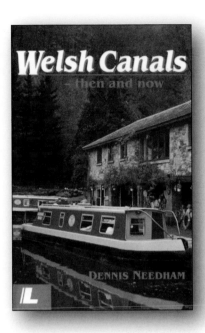

### Welsh Canals

*Dennis Needham*

The history and development
of the main Welsh canals.

**£6.95**
ISBN 0 86243 421 1

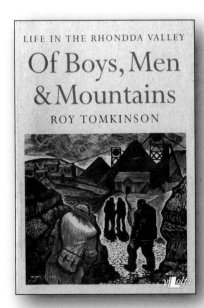

### Of Boys, Men & Mountains

*Roy Tomkinson*

An autobiographical look at
life in the Rhondda Valley.
Brought up in the tightly-knit
coal-mining community, the
author reflects on the vivid
personalities who shaped his
character and influenced his
life.
**£9.95**
ISBN 0 86243 135 2

This book is just one of a whole range of
Welsh-interest publications from Y Lolfa.
For a full list of books currently in print,
send now for your free copy of our new,
full colour catalogue. Or simply surf into
our website

**www.ylolfa.com**

for secure on-line ordering.

Talybont Ceredigion Cymru SY24 5AP
e-bost ylolfa@ylolfa.com
gwefan www.ylolfa.com
ffôn (01970) 832 304
ffacs 832 782